RIVER RUNNING

Verne Huser

Henry Regnery Company · Chicago

Library of Congress Cataloging in Publication Data

Huser, Verne
    River running.

    Bibliography: p.
    Includes index.
    1. Boats and boating — United States.   2. Inflatable
boats.   3. White-water canoeing.   I. Title.
GV776.A2H87 1975   797.1'0973   74-32123
ISBN 0-8092-8337-9
ISBN 0-8092-8336-0 pbk.

Published by Henry Regnery Company
            180 North Michigan Avenue
            Chicago, Illinois 60601
Manufactured in the United States of America
Library of Congress Catalog Card Number: 74-32123

International Standard Book Number: 0-8092-8337-9 (cloth)
                                   0-8092-8336-0 (paper)

Published simultaneously in Canada by
Fitzhenry & Whiteside Limited
150 Lesmill Road
Don Mills, Ontario M3B 2T5
Canada

Contents

Preface		v
Acknowledgments		viii
1	Introduction	1
2	Regulations and Information	7
3	Equipment	23
4	Inflatable Boats and Accessories	55
5	Planning	93
6	River Routine	103
7	How to Do It	127
8	Natural Information	151
9	Safety and Health	175
10	Regulating the River Resource	193
11	Rivers to Float with an Inflatable Craft	207
Appendixes		
A	Sources of Information	254
B	Sample Gear List	266
C	International Scale of River Difficulty	271
D	National Park Service River Running Policy Statement	273
E	Selected Bibliography	277
Index		290

To Heidi, Paul, and David,
in hopes that there will still be wild rivers to run
when they have children.

Preface

River running began with the beginnings of
America. The Saint Lawrence, the Hudson, and the James
were highways for native peoples and routes to the interior
for the first European explorers and settlers. Later explorers
followed the Missouri and the Columbia river systems for
thousands of miles. When John Wesley Powell eliminated the
last large *terra incognita* from the national map with his 1869
expedition, a river, the Colorado, was still the thoroughfare.

In Powell's time, of course, few thought about running
rivers for fun. Rivers were a source of transportation, hydro-
power, irrigation, sanitation, and water for morning coffee.
Rapids, in particular, were dreaded and, if possible, avoided.
Evidence for this attitude exists in the historic portage trails
around major stretches of white water—such as Muscle
Shoals on the Tennessee and the Great Falls of the
Potomac—and in the experience of SCUBA-equipped his-
torians. For years these men dove in vain at the foot of the big
rapids along the Quetico-Superior canoe routes of northern
Minnesota, used to transport furs and trading goods, but no
artifacts were recovered.

Finally, someone, probably a river runner, suggested that the divers were looking in the wrong places. Like their modern counterparts, the old-time rivermen respected the big drops and invariably portaged them. It was the smaller rapids, the ones where safety was marginal, that tempted a brigade of tired voyageurs to try a run. When they failed, trade goods and personal effects went to the bottom. And that is where they are being found today—at the ends of smallish rapids.

Today, a revolution in river equipment and know-how, described in detail in the following pages, has transformed pioneer terror into family fun. Far from being dreaded, rapids are anticipated with enthusiasm. Today's river runner lives for white water. When he can't run it, he talks about it—endlessly. Veterans dissect the big rapids wave by wave and rock by rock. Each change in water level starts the discussion anew. The simple fact is that running a rapid is a superlative, many would say incomparable, outdoor experience. As proof, we find river running full of the graduates of sailing, skiing, surfing, climbing, and sports-car driving. Running big water combines many of the skills and joys of all these activities, but it adds a unique dimension of finality, of ultimate commitment.

But there is an obvious lesson for the modern river runner in the voyageur's experiences, and Verne Huser underscores it time and again in the pages that follow. Rivers are very strong. All rapids should be respected. Lowering one's guard is an invitation to trouble. As Martin Litton told me once after an unmarked and unnoticed riffle in the Grand Canyon had nearly flipped his dory, "It's the little ones that get you."

So why run rivers? The awesome beauty is a factor. So is the marvelous camping and the chance to meet fellow members of the life community on their own terms. But, illogically in a sense, I think a key force drawing men to white water is fear. There are few occasions in any life in which your future is on the line the way it is at the head of a big drop. For some people, pressure like this paralyzes. But for those who are energized by fear, rapids are compulsive. Perhaps the basic reason is that our kind evolved in an atmosphere of almost constant fear. Civilization has changed this, but it hasn't obviated deeply rooted human needs for ultimate challenge. Rapids help us reenter the grooves of ancient experience.

No one should come away from this book without a commitment to go beyond the enjoyment of wild rivers and on to their preservation. The clear fact is that without such a commitment on the part of a significant number of Americans, rivers and river running will be on the road to extinction. There are fewer undeveloped, navigable rivers of meaningful length left in continental United States than there are condors or whooping cranes. The pressure for development, understandable in a pioneer context, is a liability in today's quest for quality of environment and quality of life. The new frontier is preservation; the new challenge involves restraining, not unleashing, technological power. River-management policy should reflect an awareness of both the alarmingly small inventory of wild rivers and the staggering growth in the national need and desire for wilderness experience. In my view, *all* of the nation's rivers that might *possibly* qualify for the National Wild and Scenic River System should be placed in that protected category *now*. The National Wild and Scenic River system, in other words, should act as a bank account for every American; "withdrawals" from the account for development should only be made after careful study and only with the authorized signature of an American people aware of the needs of an increasingly civilized future.

Roderick Nash
Chairman, Environmental Studies
University of California, Santa Barbara

Acknowledgments

My thanks to the following for helping me gather information for this book: Maurice "Red" Arnold (BOR), Dick Barker and Frank Ewing (Barker-Ewing Float Trips, Inc.), Jim Barrett and Jim Culp (USFS), Bill Belknap (Fastwater Expeditions), Jerry Bentley (Orange Torpedo Trips), Bob Burleson (Texas), Bob Burrell (West Virginia), Jim Campbell (Wild Rivers Idaho/Wilderness Encounters), Mac Carnes (*Oar & Paddle*), David G. Cowart (Commodore, ACA), Maggie Dewey (*Wisconsin Trails*), Jon Dragan (Wildwater Expeditions Unlimited, Inc.), Richard Estes (USFS), Fred Feindel (White Water Sports, Ltd.), Mike Ferguson (Rocky Mountain River Expeditions), J. H. "Stretch" Fretwell (New Mexico), William G. Freimuth (Stearns), Cal Giddings (AWA), John Ginsburg (Alaska Wilderness River Trips, Inc.), Dave and Joan Helfrich (Prince Helfrich and Sons), Dee Holladay (Holiday River Expeditions, Inc.), David A. Kay (ARTA), Bill Kenyon (BLM—Alaska), Vladimir Kovalik (Wilderness World, Inc.), George Larsen (AWA), Joan Mason (ACA), Ralph McCarty (Mountain Streams & Trails Outfitters), Hank and Sharon Miller (Idaho Adventures), Stan Miller (Idaho Primitive Area Float Trips), Bill Painter (American Rivers Conservation Council), Bill Parks (Northwest River Supplies), Rick Petrillo, LeRoy Pruitt (Oregon), Jerry Sehi (Seagull Marine), John Simms and Charlie Sands (Flagg Float Trips), Ron Smith (Grand Canyon Expeditions), Dave Sumner (*Colorado* magazine), Bob Volpert (Outdoor Adventures), Sam Warren (USFS), Bob Yearout (NPS), and numerous others representing various state and federal agencies; commercial outfitters; river-running equipment producers and salesmen; local, state and federal organizations.

My *special* thanks to Dr. Roderick Nash, with whom I've floated a few rivers, for writing the preface; to George Bettridge for photographic work; to Donna King for artistic assistance; to Dawn Boss for typing the final draft; and to my wife Willa for her support and encouragement (and for the loan of her typewriter).

Rafting on the Salmon in the Idaho Primitive Area. (Photo courtesy ARTA)

1

Introduction

From birchbark canoes and bullboats, to log rafts and dugouts, to the modern aluminum canoe and fiberglass kayak and inflatable craft that grew out of World War II, river running has underscored the historical development of America. Indian guides and French voyageurs led the westward movement by canoe. Lewis and Clark in the first decade of the last century bridged the continent with their classic float trip to the Pacific. And soon after their historic journey, mountainmen began to ferry furs out of the wilderness and opened up trade with Indians in the Rocky Mountain West, largely by river routes. When the bottom dropped out of the fur market, many of the white Indians, as the mountainmen were called, began leading pioneers further west to settle along the rivers. In 1869—the same year the Transcontinental Railroad was completed—John Wesley Powell first explored the unknown canyons of the Green and the Colorado rivers.

Lewis and Clark and Powell were true pioneers. Their followers—Captain Gulicke on the Salmon; Nathaniel Gal-

1

LEWIS AND CLARK

HOPING FOR AN EASY RIVER TRIP TO THE PACIFIC,
CLARK EXPLORED THE FIRST FEW MILES OF THE
RUGGED CANYON OF THE SALMON BELOW HERE
LATE IN AUGUST 1805.

His small advance party camped near here with
poor but friendly Indians. Clark reported that
the Salmon "is almost one continued rapid," and
that passage "with Canoes is entirely impossible,"
so the expedition had to buy packhorses and go
110 miles north to an Indian trail across the
mountains.

Idaho highways are well marked with historic flags like this one that speaks for itself. Several float trips in Idaho and Montana follow the Lewis and Clark route; other historic routes can be followed in several parts of the nation. (Verne Huser photo)

loway on the Green and the Yampa; the Kolb brothers and Norman Nevills in the Grand Canyon; Amos Burg, who pioneered inflatable boats on numerous rivers—were less explorers than adventurers. And in the 1930s and 1940s people began guiding trips down wild rivers, and commercial river running was basically born.

GROWTH OF RIVER RUNNING

World War II, with its improved technology in aluminum and fiberglass and rubberlike products, gave a tremendous boost to the river-running game, both for pleasure and profit, but the result was not immediate. By 1940, only 44 people had ever followed the route Powell had pioneered down the Colorado; even by 1949, the year Ed Hudson and Dock Marston drove the first motorboat through Grand Canyon, the number had increased only to 100.

If commercial river running had its birth and infancy in the 1930s and 1940s, it came to adolescence in the 1950s and reached its maturity in the 1960s when such well-known celebrities as the Kennedys and Ladybird Johnson began running rivers. By now it was relatively safe, had been tried enough so that guides knew the rivers and were relatively sure of their equipment. Throughout the 1960s, commercial float-trip business grew, and private parties increased, as knowledge and equipment improved, leisure time increased, and prosperity flourished.

The power of the Colorado shows itself as it twists this triple rig unmercifully on the Cataract Canyon run through Canyonlands National Park in Utah. Can you see three boats in this shot? (Photo by Eric Grohe, courtesy Holiday River Expeditions, Inc.)

Through publicity and word-of-mouth, a National Geographic Society article and movie on wild rivers, federal and state wild- and-scenic rivers legislation, and the Powell Centennial (also covered by *National Geographic* magazine), river running was popularized.

Ironically, the movie *Deliverance* also contributed in a manner I'm not sure I understand; it might well have discouraged people from running rivers. When *Deliverance* reached the public in the early 1970s, with Burt Reynolds showing his buddies how to run a river, people all over the nation began rushing to the nearest river with the first craft they could lay their hands on. With little or no experience, they began running some pretty healthy rivers. The result: 18 drownings on the Chattooga (where *Deliverance* was filmed) in less than three years, plus an increase in river traffic throughout the country, with a similar increase in fatalities, injuries, and accidents related to river running on many of the nation's waterways. Certainly the movie isn't totally responsible, but it does seem to have helped accelerate a trend.

REASONS FOR WRITING BOOK

It is in part to combat the *"Deliverance* Complex" that I decided to write this book. Another part of that decision is based upon my concern about the impact increased use is having on the river resource and the related problems precipitated by the great numbers of people running rivers. I want to help save the river resource from the people who use it just as I want to help save the people who use it from the river.

The foreword to the "Eleven Point National Scenic River Unit Plan," published by the U.S. Forest Service, says it: "The scenic river values must be protected for and from the people." In recognizing the truth of Pogo's observation, "We have met the enemy and he is us," the Forest Service plan for the Eleven Point River "is not so much a plan of management for the river and the land—nature will take care of these—as

Eastern Rivers have their share of crowded conditions, too. Some 60,000 floaters run the Youghiogheny commercially every season, and weekend crowds may look like this. (Photo courtesy Mountain Streams and Trails Outfitters)

it is a plan for management of the people who will come to the river to enjoy the river values."

Those values can readily be destroyed by man. Overuse can kill a river as surely as any other form of abuse: damming, channelizing, overcutting the watershed, using archaic mining practices, building roads.

While I recognize that this book may have a tendency to increase interest in river running, I hope it will also increase public awareness of problems related to river use. I have three rationales for writing this book:

1. I hope to discourage people who lack the experience and equipment from running rivers on their own;
2. I hope to help those who do run rivers to do so with greater respect for the river and better understanding of safety practices;
3. I hope to encourage people who run rivers to take better care of the river resource, to use it with love and respect.

River running in its broadest sense refers to all kinds of boating activities on a flowing stream—from jet boat to inner tube and air mattress. It includes the motorized craft as well as the hand- and foot-powered toys, but this book will direct itself largely to inflatable craft powered by people with paddle or oar or sweep, for whom there has been little literature in the past. However, as inflatable floaters find information of value in books addressed to the canoeist or kayaker, it is assumed that hard-hull paddlers will find useful information in this book, too.

No one book can tell it all, nor does this one attempt to, but hopefully you can—armed with this book—discover for yourself all you need to know about running a river on your own. This book suggests a natural progression: learn all you can about river running from the literature, written and oral; run a river with someone who knows what he's doing, and run several under different conditions; try it on your own on mild stretches, perhaps with rented or borrowed equipment. As your knowledge increases and your river experience grows, you may—if you are skilled and careful and lucky—become a river runner. But remember, no book can tell you how to read water until you have studied a river. No dozen books can tell you how to react to an emergency situation until you've had one. There's a lot more to river running than buying a $29.95 inflatable boat and heading for the nearest river.

2

Regulations and Information

F loat trips, especially in some of our western national parks, have become so popular in recent years that they threaten to destroy the very resources that make them unique. In Grand Teton National park more than 75,000 people floated various stretches of the upper Snake, during 1973, on river trips ranging from an hour to five days.* More people have floated the wild rapids of the Colorado through Grand Canyon National Park during the 1970s than during its entire previous history, and traffic in Westwater Canyon, farther upstream on the Colorado, jumped from 750 people in 1972 to 3,800 in 1973. On the Middle Fork of the Salmon River, one of the original wild rivers, in Idaho, float-trip traffic has more than tripled in the past five years. Not until 1962 did commercial float trips begin operating on the Stanislaus River in California's gold country, but in 1973 31,807 people ran a stretch that is threatened now by the New Melones Dam project. (I use 1973 statistics because river traffic was down in 1974 due to inflation, the energy crisis, and extremely high water levels on many western rivers.)

---

*The five-day trip actually begins and ends outside the park, but much of its course runs through the park.

Problems related to river running have increased even more rapidly than passenger numbers. During the summer of 1972, serious outbreaks of shigellosis, a type of dysentery, in Grand Canyon caused the abortion of some trips and required life-saving helicopter rescues in some severe cases. In Dinosaur National Monument in the past five years three major fires started by careless campers have destroyed campgrounds along the Yampa and the Green river canyons. Drownings have increased. The aesthetic qualities of the river have been compromised by the sheer numbers of boats and people on the rivers, and the shorelines have been littered and trampled.

As more people flock to the white-water rivers and to the more scenic ones, the problems become legion: congestion at launch and take-out sites and at the heads of rapids; competition for campsites; human waste and garbage disposal; availability of firewood; too many boats on the river; too many campsites along the shore; litter from careless floaters and from wrecked crafts; the abuse of geologic and archaeologic features; overfishing a stream or overhunting a river drainage—the list goes on.

To cope with this increasing traffic and to preserve the river resource, a myriad of federal, state and local governmental agencies have entered the picture. They have set up procedures, programs, and regulations that while constrictive in some senses of the word, are nonetheless necessary if everyone is to continue to enjoy the country's wild rivers. (For more of the history of these programs, see chapter 10.) Therefore, the first step in planning any river running trip, whether on your own or with an outfitter, is to discover the red tape and routine for the river you want to run.

In some areas, regulations include limits on the number of commercial outfitters, or the number of people who can run a river during a season or a week or a day. Sometimes they even specify the date or hour you can launch a boat, or the kinds of boats you can use. They may require specific equipment or outlaw other gear and equipment. They may even assign campsites.

FEDERAL AGENCIES

Among the federal agencies engaged in river regulations are the U.S. Coast Guard, the U.S. Army Corps of Engineers, the Bureau of Land Management (BLM), the Bureau of Reclamation, the U.S. Geological Survey, the National Park Service (NPS), the U.S. Forest Service, the Bureau of Outdoor Recreation, and even such groups as the Soil Conservation Service and the Bureau of Sport Fisheries and Wildlife.

Indirect Control

Largely responsible for administering the Federal Boat Safety Act of 1971 on inland waters, the Coast Guard has jurisdiction over all navigable waters of the United States—and you'd be amazed at some of the waters considered navigable.

Several attempts by the Coast Guard in recent years to enforce on float trips the "Rules and Regulations for Small Passenger Vessels"—those under 100 gross tons—under 46 CFR 175-187 have failed. In correspondence with various Coast Guard officials, I have learned that "the Coast Guard has not in the past elected to enforce these inspection and manning regulations upon non-self-propeller river rafts due to their one-time excellent safety and self-policing record," but that "Personnel at Coast Guard Headquarters (400 Seventh Street, SW, Washington, DC 20590) are reviewing the statistics and operations of the river-rafting floating parties." At this writing no determination has been made concerning the Coast Guard's role in regulating river trips.

The Coast Guard's most direct involvement in river running relates to PFD s, all of which must be Coast Guard approved. Every boat less than 16 feet in length and all canoes and kayaks must have a personal flotation device (PFD) for every person on board. Every boat 16 feet or longer must have one wearable Type I, II, or III PFD for everyone on board plus one throwable PFD (Type IV) for man-overboard situations.

The Savannah, Georgia office of the Coast Guard reports that, "Several special hazard bulletins have been published by the state which were aimed at reducing deaths on the river. Inexperienced traveling on Georgia rivers has resulted in the loss of many lives in recent years. It is possible that the state of Georgia may be developing safety regulations governing the recreational use of rivers."

The Army Corps of Engineers controls many streams, especially those regulated by reservoir release and those that have navigational hazards for power boats, whether pleasure or commercial. The Bureau of Reclamation also controls rivers with power-dam releases that give river runners headaches, but the same agency provides good river-level and flow-rate information.

Direct Control

The greatest direct control seems to be vested in a trio of agencies: the National Park Service, the U.S. Forest Service, and the Bureau of Land Management. None of these has the widespread legal fiat that the Coast Guard enjoys (and might exercise at any time), but each controls vast areas of public land through which many of our more popular rivers flow. Often their authority comes from administrative directive rather than any legislative edict, but as the need for regulations has grown, these agencies have provided important leadership. Especially in the West this triumvirate rules the rivers, often in a vacuum left by state agencies, occasionally in direct conflict with the state agencies, but basically a cooperative attitude prevails.

One of the best things that has happened to river-running regulations in a decade is the Interagency Whitewater Committee (IWC), created in 1973 by the three agencies. Three members from each agency meet periodically, frequently in

The Middle Fork of the Salmon River in the Idaho Wilderness is carefully regulated by the U.S. Forest Service, and the State of Idaho requires any professional guide or outfitter to hold a valid license from the Guides and Outfitters Association. (Verne Huser photo)

conjunction with the Western River Guides Association, to coordinate rules and regulations, to try to develop sensible qualifications for boatmen, and to deal with problems of overlapping or mixed jurisdiction. It seems to be working.

The National Park Service (NPS) regulates the Rio Grande (Texas), the Yampa and the Green (Utah and Colorado), the San Juan (Utah), the Colorado (Utah and Arizona), the Snake (Wyoming), the Current and Jacks Fork (Missouri), and the Buffalo (Arkansas). Check with the proper National Park Service office before you float any of the rivers under its jurisdiction *(see appendix for addresses)*.

The U.S. Forest Service really has its hands full. In the East, this underbudgeted agency regulates parts of the Chattooga (Georgia-South Carolina state line), Black Creek (Mississippi), the Eleven Point (Missouri), the Turtle and the Rice (Minnesota), and the Au Sable (Michigan)—to mention only a few.

In the West, the Forest Service administers boating regulations on the Selway and Salmon (Idaho), the Upper Snake (Wyoming and Idaho), the Lower Snake in Hells Canyon (Idaho and Oregon), the Grays (Wyoming), the Green (Utah), the Upper Colorado and the Eagle (Colorado), the Lochsa and the Clearwater (Idaho), the Rogue, Illinois, and the Grande Ronde (Oregon), and the Kings and Tuolumne (California). Check with local Forest Service officials for river-running information if the stream you plan to run flows through national forest lands.

However, the Bureau of Land Management, still administering much of Alaska, has by far the largest chunk of this nation's federal land under its jurisdiction: the Owyhee, the Bruneau, and the Jarbridge (Idaho and Oregon), parts of the Salmon and the Snake (Idaho), the Rogue (Oregon), the Colorado, the Green and the San Juan (Utah), and the Stanislaus, the Tuolumne, three forks of the American, the Cosumnes, the Mokelumne and the Merced (California), and dozens of Alaskan streams.

Since in many cases various management plans for rivers are still in a state of flux, let me suggest that you write the appropriate agency *(see appendix)* for the current data. Know simply that there are federal regulations on these rivers, that you must have a permit to float them, and that in many cases you will need prior reservations or you won't be allowed to launch.

Other Helpful Agencies

The U.S. Geologic Survey (USGS), like the Bureau of Reclamation, gets involved in river running through its National Water Resources Data Network. This agency can be helpful to river runners by providing information on flow rates and topographic maps, and a number of USGS publications may be of service and interest to the floater. I would especially recommend the 1969 publication *Professional Paper 669: The Colorado River Region and John Wesley Powell,* which includes Luna B. Leopold's "The Rapids and the Pools—Grand Canyon."

A parting word about two quasi-governmental agencies: the Interagency Whitewater Committee, already mentioned, and the Western States Boating Administrators' Association (WSBAA). Both groups are currently working toward more uniform regulations and deserve watching and carefully considered support. The IWC lists four basic objectives: 1) provide for management of rivers so as to assure that the ecosystem and its components are maintained in continuous good condition, thus preserving the quality of the river for future use; 2) provide for optimum use of the resource without destroying the very values for which the area was established or is being managed; 3) assure the opportunity for a quality river experience; 4) establish adequate programs to carry out the above objectives, based on well-documented data. The IWC guidelines deal with capacities and limitations, allotments, commercial operations and private permits, operational requirements and conditions, and research and safety, as well as interagency cooperation.

The WSBAA recently (May 16, 1974 and July 16, 1974) passed resolutions asking various federal agencies to "refrain from adopting any regulations governing equipment, operation, or registration as it relates to the use of vessels and motorboats until and unless such regulations are substantially similar to or identical with state or Coast Guard requirements." This may seem like a power play to some, but

the end result might be more uniform regulations administered from the state level, if the states are willing to
cooperate.

STATE AGENCIES

River regulations vary tremendously at the state level. The
Federal Boat Safety Act of 1971 requires that boats be registered with a state agency. But some states seem to be at a loss
to implement the regulations, at least regarding inflatable
boats. Some states—Idaho, Oregon, Utah, for
example—require professional river guides to be licensed,
but few require such for private floaters.

Administering agencies also vary from state to state:
Frequently it is a department of natural resources or a wildlife or game and fish commission; occasionally it is a parks
and/or recreation department, a conservation commission, or
an environmental protection agency. In a few, it is the division of motor vehicles, the department of transportation, a
tax or finance agency, or department of public, marine, or
boating safety. (In some states, as many as four or five agencies get into the act; in others, no agency seems to claim
responsibility.)

Enforcement of the rules and regulations often lies outside the agency responsible for boat registration, and jurisdiction for river-running regulations is sometimes badly split
among various unlikely agencies, occasionally among state
and federal agencies. The river-running situation has gotten
out of hand in some areas, but we live in a period of positive
response to the void that has existed. Federal agencies have
often taken the lead in controlling river use, perhaps rightly
so, but the states, faced with losing jurisdiction, are responding with new laws and new regulatory agencies, with
an expansion of concern and authority.

To be too specific in this chapter would be misleading because change is the order of the day. However, without

attempting to be comprehensive, but merely representative, let's look at some of the states' river regulations:

Alabama has "no specific regulations in effect for float trips," but all craft "must comply with all existing rules and regulations pertaining to pleasure boats." A 26-page booklet, *Alabama Fishing and Boating Areas,* is available from the Department of Conservation and Natural Resources along with a brochure giving the highlights of Water Safety Law in Alabama, and a list of sources for recreational maps and navigational charts. Much information relates to powerboats.

Alaska is a big state just being discovered by floaters driven out of the lower 48 by too many regulations and crowded rivers. The Bureau of Land Management (BLM) has a head start in providing river information with several brochures on canoe trails, but all I got from any state agency was a list of registered guides sent out by the Department of Commerce. The best source of information about Alaska rivers is probably Bill Kenyon, a BLM employee who has set up the Alaska Whitewater Association (Glenallen, AK 99588) "formed to obtain and disburse river information."

Arizona has a fine synopsis of boating laws and regulations published by the Game and Fish Department, and the Office of Economic Planning and Development sends out a list of the river-running concessionaires in Grand Canyon National Park (which you can also get from the NPS). The Arizona Department of Health Services has worked closely with NPS personnel concerning health problems on Grand Canyon float trips, but the state has not become directly involved in regulating float-trip activities except through standard boating regulations.

Colorado disappointed me with this reply from the Division of Parks and Outdoor Recreation: "Our office is seldom involved with this activity (river-float trips). For the information you are seeking, I suggest you contact either of the below-mentioned addresses." There followed the name and address of an outfitter I know and don't respect and the address for Dinosaur National Monument. River-running activity in Colorado deserves better than that.

Connecticut's Department of Environmental Protection wrote, "River rafting is not carried out extensively in this state. However, all vessels used on the waters of this state are subject to our boating laws and regulations." A copy of the Connecticut boating laws (revised May 1, 1973), a *Digest of Connecticut Boating Laws* for the 1974 season, a 64-page booklet entitled *Connecticut Boating Manual,* and a *Connecticut Canoeing Guide,* all very well done, accompanied the letter.

Idaho's Department of Law Enforcement provides a copy of a 32-page *Safe Boating Tips* booklet that seems outdated since it refers to the Federal Boating Act of 1958 (no doubt it is currently in revision). Noncommercial boating does not come under the jurisdiction of the Idaho Outfitters and Guides Board, which requires anyone who "in any manner, advertises or holds himself out to the public for hire, providing facilities and services for the conduct of . . . boating or other recreational excursions," to obtain an outfitter's license and anyone who, "for compensation or other gain or promise thereof, furnishes services in assisting or guiding any other person in the above named activities," to obtain a guide's license.

As a general rule, boaters in Idaho are required to comply with rules and regulations of those who control the access to and from the stream or any other place the boater might wish to make a landing. Thus, in Idaho a state agency governs the use of the waters along shorelines administered by the Forest Service or the BLM to the extent that a license is required "whenever compensation is received for carrying passengers." A good safety regulation, life jackets must be maintained in good and serviceable condition and must be worn at all times while on the river in Idaho. Idaho has gone a long way in developing state standards for float boaters, as have

sister-states Utah and Oregon. Six Idaho rivers mentioned on
a "classified" list—the Middle Fork of the Salmon, much of
the Main Salmon, the Snake in Hells Canyon, the Clearwater, the Selway, and the Bruneau—have special regulations concerning prior experience for commercial guides and
outfitters.

Iowa's Conservation Commission issues a 16-page booklet, *Iowa Canoe Trips,* that covers a dozen streams in this
state where canoeing is king.

Kentucky provides a map of waterways and recreation
areas along with a campground guide and a highway map. A
Department of Public Information pamphlet called *Canoeing
in Kentucky,* a seven-page account of several dozen streams
runable by canoe, including many in Daniel Boone National
Forest, lists put-in and take-out points, distance between,
and is keyed to the Official Highway and Parkway Map.

Michigan, with no less than four different agencies involved, provides a wide variety of information—from the Department of Natural Resources' *Michigan Guide to East
Canoeing* to maps and boating regulations, the latter published in the "Marine Safety Act of 1967," no doubt scheduled for updating shortly to address the Federal Boat Safety
Act of 1971. At present, "there are no rules and regulations
governing float trips in Michigan" since proposed rules are
tied up in court.

Minnesota's Department of Conservation publishes a
booklet, *Minnesota Voyageur Trails,* that covers several
rivers and canoe trails, and its Department of Administration issues a list of Minnesota state publications, some of
which may be of use to the river runner. A representative of
the Department of Natural Resources writes, "I am afraid
that rafting is not as big here in the Midwest as it is in the
West. There is some of it done on the streams and rivers in the
southern part of Minnesota, however. In particular, the
Minnesota, the Mississippi, and some of those in the southeastern region are probably used the most . . . . Some of the

northern streams could be used for rafting, as they do have fast water and rapids."

Oregon seems to have a handle on the boating situation, though many of Oregon's rivers flow through areas of federal jurisdiction. Beginning in 1974, the Oregon State Marine Board, by legal fiat, required the licensing of all guides carrying passengers for hire. The director of the board (James Hadley, at this writing) works closely with the U.S. Coast Guard, BLM, and Forest Service; with sister-state boating directors (especially from Idaho and Utah); and with the Western River Guides Association, to get a better picture of river running. Oregon also has one of the finest river-preservation acts in the nation in its Oregon Scenic Waterways System. Cooperation seems to be the key to good management.

South Carolina seems largely geared to hunting and fishing and powerboating on the ocean and on reservoirs, leaving the Chattooga to the Forest Service to manage. "South Carolina Boat Landings," one of several pamphlets produced by the Wildlife Resources Department, does list and map a number of put-in and take-out points, but river running seems to be a foster child in the state.

Tennessee has at least two agencies that care about river running: the Tourist Development Division, which publishes a neat little pamphlet, *Canoeing in Tennessee,* that covers 22 rivers in brief, and the Game and Fish Commission, which produces useful river maps, including one on the Buffalo.

Texas, largely through the efforts of several dedicated individuals—Bob Burleson, Emil O. Kindschy, Jr., and Ben Nolen—has a pretty good start toward an awareness of river running. At present a list of some 13 "white-water" rivers and 11 "scenic" rivers is available from the Parks and Wildlife Department, but a much more detailed publication, *An Analysis of Texas Waterways,* is in process and should be available soon. Trail and Waterway Planner Ron Josselet writes, "A license or registration is not required of nonmotorized boats in Texas. This also applies to canoes, kayaks, and rubber rafts, unless they are to be motorpowered. No specific rules or regulations are available for river running in Texas."

Utah, under the leadership of State Boating Director Tedd Tuttle, has long listened to the needs of the river runner (to a large extent, river rafting grew up in Utah). Working closely with the Western River Guides Association, the Division of Parks and Recreation has developed rules and regulations that relate to the float situation. Utah's boating laws are outlined in a publication called *Recreational Uses of Boating Waters in Utah,* and those specifically dealing with float trips are also detailed in a mimeographed supplement entitled "River Running in Utah: Highlights of the Current Laws and Regulations."

The New River in West Virginia offers some of the finest floating in the East. This rocky stretch full of holes and haystacks is part of the commercial run Jon Dragan makes throughout the warmer months. His trips provide an opportunity to learn about river running by doing it with an experienced guide. (Photo courtesy of Wildwater Expeditions Unlimited, Inc.)

A motor-powered Smith-rig tows a triple rig made of three surplus Navy assault rafts on the Colorado River beneath Navajo Bridge on U.S. Highway 89 (Alternate) near the beginning of a Grand Canyon float trip. Grand Canyon float trips are carefully regulated in order that this popular stretch be preserved. (Verne Huser photo)

As I mentioned earlier, I am not attempting to be comprehensive in this section, simply representative. Nor do I intend to denigrate any state, though some do seem to be dragging their feet and letting river running get out of hand. The pressures have not existed in some areas to react to float-trip activity, but they are now growing in every part of the country.

These regulations are subject to change as state legislatures see the need to regulate river use and find better answers to the problems created by overuse. It is important that you know there are regulations of some kind in every state relating to river use and that rivers flowing through federal lands are often governed by whatever agency administers those lands.

If you plan to run a river on your own, let me suggest that you dig out the details for yourself with the aid of the agencies and addresses listed in the appendix. It will mean more to you, and you'll have the most current information available, information that is changing so rapidly that no book could successfully provide it.

Mass produced in Britain, Avon boats satisfy the requirements of many river runners. This professional model is fully equipped for the river: metal frame with plywood floor, oars (including a spare), camp gear in waterproof river bags, foot bellows for pumping boat, food and water containers, safety line, and bailing buckets made from cut-off plastic containers. (Avon photo courtesy Seagull Marine)

3

Equipment

The difference between a safe, comfortable river trip and one that is cold, wet, miserable and frightening rests to a great extent in the kind and quality of the equipment that you pack with you on the river. Adequate cooking equipment, camping gear, appropriate safety equipment, and enough clothing to adapt to the various weather situations encountered are essential to a successful river trip.

WATERPROOF CONTAINERS

The first requirement for comfort is to keep everything dry. You may want a tarp to cover gear under any circumstances, but your best bet is to store everything in waterproof bags and boxes.

River runners have long looked to military surplus for waterproof containers. Military surplus ammunition cans in several sizes have become almost standard for river runners, and though they are becoming more difficult to find, you can still pick them up occasionally at surplus stores. If their original seal has deteriorated, you can easily waterproof them by gluing a strip of soft rubber or sponge to the lid along the seal. Military surplus rubber bags, which come in at least three sizes, are heavy but waterproof. I've used the old "Bag Waterproof Special Purpose," 12"x9"x18", for half a dozen years, packing in it everything I need for a week on the river—including a down sleeping bag but excluding my backpacking tent and camera gear (I use an ammo can—11"x7¼"x5½"—for the camera).

Here at Indian Creek on the Middle Fork of the Salmon, ammo boxes, life jackets, and boat frames are unloaded after being flown in to the launch site. (Verne Huser photo)

A military surplus delousing bag makes a practical waterproof container for carrying sleeping bags, tents, and other basically soft, lightweight gear such as clothing. Note two Dutch ovens sitting in the sand waiting to be packed. (Verne Huser photo)

A variety of other military containers from footlockers to radar-equipment boxes can be adapted for storing food, camp gear, portable toilets, kitchen ware, and personal equipment. Hard containers are almost necessary to protect certain items, but the fewer hard objects you have on the boat, the less likely that someone will be hurt from being thrown about in the action of the rapids.

Since river running has become popular, military surplus containers have become scarce. Many of the commercial outfitters make—or have made—their own gear containers, often fiberglassing them for waterproofing and rigidity, sometimes padding them to prevent injury. Long, rubberized delousing bags make practical containers for much of the gear, but don't put hard objects in them as the action of the boat will no doubt crimp the fabric as the hard object in the bag makes contact with a hard object outside the bag.

Several manufacturers are in the process of developing good waterproof bags. Voyageur Enterprises (Box 512, Shawnee Mission, KS 66201) makes a good line of waterproof bags. An inner bag made of heavy-gauge polyethylene material is protected from external trauma by an outer bag

Klamath Bag made by Ann Dwyer (Canoe California) specifically for river running is one of the best. She makes several other models. (Ann Dwyer photo)

made of woven polypropylene cloth. The whole thing is sealed with a special tube arrangement that rarely fails, if used properly. This "Versa-Seal" closure also serves as a handlebar for carrying the bag. The bags come in three sizes: (V2) the 22"x36" that I've used on numerous trips; (V8) a 17"x40" bag narrow enough to fit into a kayak; and (V16) a 24"x60" expedition model for extended trips. The largest costs approximately $15. Voyageur also sells a handy boat-tape for repairing (temporarily) waterproof gear—even boats, in an emergency.

Ann Dwyer (Canoe California, Box 61A, Kentfield, CA 94904) makes a series of bags and packs that were designed specifically for river trips. I've seen them in use and find them excellent. They are lightweight, with convenient handles (useful for tying them into the craft) and carrying straps, and are made of waterproof material, with seams treated with waterproofing and then enclosed by a waterproof tape. They range from 1,870-cubic-inch food bags and packs to the 3,910-cubic-inch Klamath pack and bag. In dimensions they run

10"x11"x17" and 10"x17"x23". Prices run from about $13 to $20 for the various sizes. One reliable supplier of Ann Dwyer's bags, and much other river-running equipment as well, is Seda Products (P.O. Box 5509, Fullerton, CA 92635).

Klepper (see section on boats) markets an inflatable-float camera safety bag at about $13 and an inflatable-float clothing bag at about $20.

Folbot markets duffel bags and ditty bags at such a low cost (less than a dollar to about $4) that I cannot imagine that they are very waterproof. Various thin, rubberized fabric bags sold at surplus and sporting good stores for a dollar or two just don't get the job done—though they may be adequate for a single trip; but tie-down ropes will often abrade them during the course of a day's action in the raft and render them no longer waterproof.

For years I have used a rubberized bag, made in West Germany, that has proven totally waterproof (it was once submerged for more than 20 minutes when a raft flipped at Big Mallard on the Main Salmon), but I haven't been able to find a duplicate. It cost me about $12 in 1968; it is similar to Klepper's inflatable-float clothing bag.

What is the right bag for you? Let me suggest again that you use your imagination and ingenuity. You can go first class for a little more money, but in the long run it will probably pay off. Or you may improvise and come up with your own best answer. You may be able to adapt to river running the kind of container you use for other outings.

But remember that it must be waterproof. Water can creep into the darnedest places, and many waterproof materials, if subject to abrasion or crimping, to the potential rips and tears of a river trip, won't survive. It may even be a good idea to wrap everything in plastic bags. (In fact, the basic principle behind most of the river bags I've seen is just that: an inner bag of plastic material that is waterproof, protected by an outer bag that may not be waterproof but is tough enough to withstand the rigors of a river trip.)

A trio of guides (Barker-Ewing Float Trips) models three PFDs: the one on the left is a Type I (life jacket), the one in the middle is a Type II, and the one on the right, a Type III. (Verne Huser photo)

SAFETY AND HEALTH EQUIPMENT

Personal Flotation Devices (PFDs)

Another piece of equipment that is vital on river trips is the personal flotation device (PFD). Not only are they required by law, but they are sensible. The vast majority of drownings in this country occur to people who are either not wearing PFDs, not wearing adequate ones, or wearing them improperly. According to a booklet published by Stearns Manufacturing Company (St. Cloud, MN 56301), a major maker of PFDs, 95 percent of all adults require less than 15 pounds of buoyancy (your weight in the water), but children may actually require more.

Personal flotation devices are listed by the Coast Guard in five different categories:

Type I—*life jackets,* big, bulky, often uncomfortable things that usually have about 33 pounds of flotation and are the most capable of saving your life (see the *Consumer Reports* study in the August 1974 issue), because they'll float you face up. They're best to use on real white-water trips.

Type II—*buoyant vests,* smaller with less flotation, usually somewhat more comfortable, that provide a positive righting moment but more slowly than a Type I PFD. They're adequate for quiet water but not for big white water.

Type III—*buoyant device,* more comfortable and often quite stylish; these often do not provide face-up position, and injured wearers may drown. While this type of PFD meets or exceeds the requirements of the Federal Boating Safety Act of 1972, I don't wear one during high water levels or when I'm running a rapid I think might flip the boat. If I have to swim, I want to be wearing a Type I PFD, but for most floating I use a Type III.

Type IV—*throwable device,* includes buoyant cushions and ring buoys, fine for lake boating in warm weather, but cold water renders them useless as a person loses his grip with advanced hypothermia.

Type V—an open classification to provide consideration for specific circumstances (this type is currently not approved for recreational use).

All PFDs offered for sale in the United States must bear

A skilled boatman puts the nose of his craft into the hole, keeping the long axis of the boat perpendicular with the length of the hole and the wave that will almost invariably lie below it. Note the Type I PFDs. (Photo courtesy Wilderness World, Pacific Grove, CA)

the label of "U.S. Coast Guard Approved." They must be in serviceable condition, and they must be of a size appropriate for the person for whom they are intended.

For serious white-water river running, the Type I life jacket is the only one I can recommend as being adequate. If there is even the most remote chance of your ending up in the water in a rapid, you should be wearing a Type I PFD.

For comfort and safety, a number of Type II, III, and IV PFDs are marketed. I've used and especially like Stearns products in this area. They are styled and sturdy, selling for about $15 for children's models, from about $20 to $30 for the various standard models (Sans Souci vests), and from about $28 to $32 for the belted American model. The Gatsby series, especially designed for canoe and kayak users (and certainly for inflatable floaters as well), lists for about $20 to $26. Stearns does not produce a Type I vest, to my knowledge.

Remember that safety is more important than looks. For serious white-water work (in high-water levels, early in the season, when the water is cold, for especially dangerous rapids, etc.), use a Type I PFD.

Wet Suits and Boots

Another safety factor that I will consider in more detail in chapter 9 is the use of the wet suit. For cold water and cold weather, it is a must. I don't own one myself, but I have rented them, spending as much as $40 for a week's use for floating the Middle Fork of the Salmon in early May. As it happened, I didn't need it, though I wore it and was glad I had it along. Imperial (Box 4119, Airport Industrial Park, Bremerton, WA

The safest way to go, especially with children, is to use crotch straps to be sure the PFD doesn't slip off. (Courtesy Stearns Manufacturing Company)

98310), one of the leading manufacturers of skin-diving equipment in the country, produces vests for about $22 to $30 (very practical for white-water floaters, the price depending on the thickness of fabric); ski jackets for about $30 to $50; and full wet suits from the Baby Turtle (about $68-$75) to the King Turtle (about $190). Dacor (Box 157, Northfield, IL 60093) is another leading manufacturer worth checking into for wet suits. Rubatex Corporation (Bedford, VA 24523 and 14715 Anson Avenue, Santa Fe Springs, CA 90670) also produces wet suits used by many river runners.

Just a brief word about wet boots. They are the best footwear I've found for river running, and a lot of kayakers wear them regularly. The best I've seen is Imperial's King Turtle Hightop, which has a tough, felt sole. My main objection to wet boots had always been that they offered too thin a sole to protect the feet against sharp rocks. This model (about $18) answers that objection.

Other Safety Equipment

Other safety equipment should include signaling devices, lights, chemical toilet, a tool/repair kit, and extras of anything you might need in any emergency—matches, oars and paddles, clothing, sleeping bag, even a motor—depending on the type and duration of the trip, the weather, several other factors. For example, on some of the Alaskan rivers you might want a high-powered rifle along as protection against bears.

*Signaling Devices.*If you have trouble and need to call for help, you should have the equipment: dye for the water, cloth signal-flags or banners to anchor in the sand or open meadow; signal flares for nighttime use. Phillips Hardware Company (490 NW South River Drive, Miami, FLA), which caters largely to powerboaters, has a good line of such devices. So does Atlantic-Pacific Manufacturing Corporation (124 Atlantic Avenue, Brooklyn, NY 11201).

On the other hand, river runners are not always sophis-
ticated in emergency signaling devices and may not know
what they mean. Therefore, a simple signal with an upraised
oar may mean more to a passing floater than a commercial
device. A life jacket waved back and forth is a good attention
getter. Mirror signals—if anyone in the neighborhood knows
what they mean—may be useful and will usually attract
attention (I always carry a small metal mirror with me for
several reasons, including emergency use).

*Lights.*Although it is better to plan your trip so that you don't
need lights, you should always carry one for emergency use.
It's still hard to beat the old Coleman lantern, especially with

Put any bail-type lantern on this hanger (manufactured by the Coleman
Company, Inc.) for better light utilization and protection of trees from acci-
dental burns. Adjustable chain included with unit fits trees, limbs or posts.
(Courtesy Coleman Company, Inc.)

the new hanging device for preventing the scarring of trees. (Overall, Coleman Company, Inc. (Wichita, KS 67201) produces more useful camping gear for river trips than any other company I know.) The standard Coleman double-mantled lantern sells for between $13 and $18 (prices vary at different outlets). Numerous battery-operated lights are useful too, but I make no attempt to zero in on any particular model or brand since most outdoorsmen no doubt have their own pets by the time they decide to run a river.

Chemical Toilets

Chemical toilets have been required in the Grand Canyon for several years, not only for commercial parties but for small private groups as well. During the past decade, a number of portable toilets have been developed that are small enough to be practical on river trips. Whether or not they are required, they should, in my opinion, be carried and used on any river trip. To insure their use, an adequate tent for privacy should also be packed.

The Tota Toilet II (Monogram Industries, Inc., 1165 East 230th Street, Carson, CA 90745) is a 100 percent self-contained, six-and-one-half-gallon capacity portable that sells for about $100 (though I have seen them on sale for less than $80). It weighs about 24 pounds. I have seen the Standard Porta Potti (Thetford Corporation, Consumer Products Division, Box 1285, Ann Arbor, MI 48106), regularly about $110, on sale for $90. It has a five-and-one-half-gallon capacity. The smaller Safari model, four-and-one-half-gallon capacity, has been on sale for about $65.

Mansfield Sanitary, Inc. (150 First Street, Perrysville, OH 44864) makes the Porta Potti 947 portable toilet, which sells for about $95. It has a four-and-one-half-gallon capacity and weighs 18 pounds. Write to the company for a list of dealers in your area. Zurn Industries, Inc. (Recreational Products Division, 5533 Perry Highway, Erie, PA 16509) produces the Sani-Mate portable toilet; a little over 19 pounds in

Two different chemical toilets, a Jensen (above), used and recommended by western outfitter, Dee Holliday, and a Zurn (left). (Verne Huser photo)

weight, it has a five-gallon capacity, uses two gallons of water, and sells for about $75. Take your choice, but take one along on your river trips.

Tool/Repair Kit

You should include in your tool/repair kit whatever is needed to repair the fabric of the boat (whether an air chamber or the floor); the rowing or sweep frame; and essential equipment (stove, pump, etc.). Most professional guides carry a knife and a pair of pliers on their person, since both of these tools are used constantly both on and off the river. If they aren't carried on the person, however, they should be available in the tool kit, along with whatever screwdrivers, wrenches, wire cutters, hammers, and saws (including hacksaws) may be necessary for anything that might need repairing in the course of a river trip.

Though the size of the tool/repair kit may well depend upon the length of the trip, a certain minimal kit should be on hand for any trip.

A heavy, curved needle for sewing ripped fabric (use the baseball stitch) should always be carried in the tool/repair kit along with appropriate solvent for cleaning the fabric and patching cement. Not all rips need be sewed, but if you need to do any seamstress work, you had better be prepared. Soft wire and tough cord should be carried, the former for binding broken parts together and the latter for sewing ripped boats. Nails, screws, eyelets, nuts and bolts, and washers should all be handy, as well as extra fabric for patching and a couple of spare D-rings just in case. A fiberglass kit may also be useful to have along.

For information on boat repair, contact any of the following: Gaco Western, Inc. (Box 88698, Seattle, WA 98188); Flexpaint Mfg. Co. (5252 Atlantic Boulevard South, Maywood, CA 90270); Armstrong Products Company (Warsaw, IN 46580); Beacon Chemical Company, Inc. (244 Lafayette Street, New York, NY 10012); or Ron Smith (Inflatable Boats, Box O, Kanab, UT 84741). Write to them for information on their products.

Mike Ferguson (Rocky Mountain River Expeditions, Box 1394, Denver, CO 80201) includes a two-day boat-patching session in his five-day white-water school (about $95 for the patching session, a day of operation instruction, and a two-day float trip) and has developed a booklet on patching that you might write him about.

Extra parts may take up a lot of space and add a lot of weight to your supplies, but they can save your life. You should carry extras for just about everything that has parts. On the brief, three-hour trips I used to run in Grand Teton National Park, on relatively quiet water, we always carried extra oarlocks, plus a set of wrenches to make the change should the metal fail—and it did on several occasions at about 175-180 trips. Many outfitters on the Middle Fork of the Salmon carry small-scale carpenter shops with them to make necessary repairs, since that river—especially in low water—is rough on equipment.

On every white-water trip I've been on, I've carried extra oars, at times only one spare, but on rougher and longer trips two spares. On one Yampa-Green trip in Dinosaur National Monument, with a variety of trainee boatmen, we broke three oars on a three-day trip and had to run Split Mountain Gorge with one good oar and a splinted oar. And several experienced boatmen had similar luck on a white-water trip during high water on the Upper Snake. On a training run they were caught in a hole and broke three of their four oars (both oars in use plus one of the two spare oars). They now call that particular hole the Three-Oar Deal.

Motor-powered float trips in Grand Canyon carry an extra motor and several extra parts. The parties may be several days from help, and they try to carry everything that they might possibly need along with them. Most commercial trips carry extra PFDs in case one fails (many depend upon the waterproof plastic packet for flotation; when they are broken by people's sitting on them or using them for pillows, they have the flotation of a lead balloon).

Most professional guides also pack extra amounts of key food staples. It's bad to run out of coffee, but it may be dangerous to run out of salt. Lots of water jugs should be taken along, even if you plan to drink river water (as you can on quite a number of wilderness streams); if your water supply is cut off for some reason (such as stopping for repairs above the side stream you'd counted on for fresh water), you could be in trouble. Go prepared for the worst.

COOKING EQUIPMENT

Heat Source

One of the major cooking decisions is what to use for heat.

A kitchen setup on the Yampa River in Dinosaur National Monument involves a floorboard resting on two food chests to provide a worktable. Grill on fire is totally portable, constructed of angle iron designed to fit together. The Dutch oven on left and the water buckets, cooler, package of dried milk, pile of firewood (gathered by passengers before they set off to camp) are all part of the river cooking scene on a commercial trip. (Verne Huser photo)

Many people prefer to cook over an open fire when they're out in the wilds, but some areas are running out of firewood (one of the problems of overuse on our rivers). Another solution, especially popular among those with a European background or camping experience, is to use stoves of various kinds.

I like a campfire for social purposes, but I like a stove for cooking. I lived all one summer eating out of a Hawkins (British) pressure cooker using a tiny Svea (Swedish) stove as I camped all over Europe. Carrying a stove takes space and means more weight, but the safety factor, the even cooking, the convenience (no blackened pots and pans to scrub) may make it worthwhile.

For stoves, again I turn to Coleman: the standard two-burner sells for about $20 (give or take a dollar or two, depending on where you buy). It is light and handy. Coleman also produces a slightly more expensive propane stove that uses bottled gas instead of the usual Coleman liquid fuel.

Another heat source, used by a lot of professional river runners—as firewood in many areas has become scarce—is charcoal. Some outfitters have developed their own special charcoal grills; others take along backyard commercial grills. I've used a metal grill a few inches deep by 18"x42" that becomes a cook-table when it is raised on four legs (pipes set by thumbscrews through slightly larger pipes welded to each corner). Pipe legs and support rods for the grill and the grill itself could all be stored inside. It is a heavy beast, but it is great to cook on.

Another neat—and much lighter—arrangement I've seen is four hollow, square, metal legs about a foot long that can be set into four corner holes of a rectangular angle-iron frame to make a serviceable stove for a wood fire or charcoal, used in conjunction with a fire pan. Also, Voyageur makes a backpackers grill that can be a handy aid on a river trip, especially since it comes in a nylon case to keep the soot under control (about $7).

If you do opt to cook over a campfire, you should use it with care. It is a common practice today, especially in crowded areas with heavy use, for administering agencies to require riverside campers to use a fire pan. This reduces fire danger and virtually eliminates the scarring effect. It makes good sense any way you look at it, because it helps reduce the overall impact of campers on the river resource.

Military surplus cook pans make ideal fire pans, but even heavy-gauge cookie pans can be used. Most blacksmiths can devise a reasonably light fire pan that will cool quickly so it can be stowed safely after morning hot cakes have been cooked. But after you pack up, be sure to mark the spot where the fire pan was located or someone may wander through the hot sand and get a bad burn. A woman in Grand Canyon had to be helicoptered out to a doctor after such a mishap.

Whatever you use for stove and/or grill—and many are being provided in newly developed riverside campsites—you will have to dispose of the ashes. Bury them or place them in ammo cans to carry out with you, and keep your soot-gathering gear in burlap bags, using the same side for the inside each time, to prevent the black from getting all over everything. It may not be a bad idea to carry fire-starting materials and even charcoal lighter fluid, in case you have to make camp in the rain. Be careful that such flammable fluids are kept from spilling and causing fire hazards. They are best carried in their own containers or in a plastic bottle in a watertight container.

Jugs and Coolers

To keep plenty of water readily available and to keep food cold enough to be safe (see chapter 9), you have a wide choice of containers. Here again, Coleman products get my nod. Coleman coolers range between $15 and $25 for different sizes; jugs, between $5 and $10. Gott and Igloo jugs I've used have been fine, too.

Ice chests should be sturdy enough to take the beating of white-water trips and well-enough insulated for your purpose (summer trips in the Southwest require superior insulation). Many professional guides have special iceboxes built to fit into their boats. Though a few river runners use dry ice, most use ice to keep food cold. I like to pack all freeze-ables in ice, then superfreeze them the night before the trip (lettuce, tomatoes, melons, etc., of course, cannot be treated in this manner). Help keep coolers cool by using burlap bags and tarps to keep the heat away from them.

Once more, be sure to keep plenty of potable water on hand and in each boat, if there is more than one.

Cooking Utensils

I suggest going light on cooking utensils. Aluminum cooking

kits with several pots and pans and even plates nesting inside one another are ideal for river trips, although they can become messy if they are allowed to blacken. Aluminum griddles for pancakes and eggs are practical, lightweight and even-cooking.

Tin cans may also serve as cooking utensils. I often start a trip with a can of coffee. I open it the first night and transfer the unused coffee to empty (from lunch) Pringle Potato Chip cans, then use the coffee can for heating water for tea. The next morning, I do the same with the Tang and use that empty can for making hot chocolate. I'm not a coffee drinker myself, so I look out for the non-coffee-drinkers on my trips by recycling cans. The cans may be washed along with the regular dishes and used throughout the trip, but be sure to wash them carefully. Using your handy pliers, you can crimp the can slightly at the lip along one side and develop a handy pliers-bite for lifting the hot can off the fire.

Although Dutch ovens are heavy beasts, they are simply great for cooking on a river trip: cornbread, cobblers, cakes, stews, roasts—you name it. Most commercial outfitters use Dutch ovens. It is true that they are generally capable of hauling heavier loads and that they have paying customers to please. But one Dutch oven isn't all that heavy and it can be boxed conveniently for easy handling. Their versatility makes them worth the weight, and I recommend them for river trips—especially if you have a good Dutch-oven cook along.

Other Kitchen Gear

In addition to whatever grills and griddles, pots and pans, and such hardware you take along, you'll probably want to have a supply of other common kitchen tools. A can opener, a potato peeler, pancake turners, ladles, large spoons for cooking and serving, long-handled forks, kitchen knives (using your pocket- or hunting-knife violates basic sanitary rules and can lead to serious disease problems on the river) are all useful. Aluminum foil is also handy to have along, especially if anyone is fishing, and it can be used again if you treat it carefully. Remember to dispose of it properly—carry it out. Garbage bags and baggies and paper towels are all good to have along, and a bar of hand soap should be packed in the kitchen so boatmen can wash up before beginning the chores in the kitchen. The big outbreak of shigellosis in the Grand Canyon in 1972 was traced to lack of personal sanitary practices among boatmen on commercial trips.

Good dishwashing gear is vital. Dishes and cooking utensils must be washed carefully, and at least three different containers should be used: one to wash dishes, one to sterilize them with boiling hot water, and one to disinfect them. For washing dishes, a brush is better than a dish mop or a cloth. Some scrubbers should be included in the kitchen gear. To get dishes out of the hot water, you should have a pair of tongs, perhaps rubber gloves. Some river runners use their bailing buckets as dishwashing containers. Others use plastic pans, buckets, tubs, etc.; still others use nesting aluminum pots. The washing container should be large enough to totally submerge all dishes. Be sure to carry detergent and disinfectant, and don't wash dishes in the river or dispose of wastewater in the stream.

Some floaters prefer to use paper plates that don't need washing, but I tend to lean away from disposable products (including paper towels, handy as they are) because they encourage waste of both energy and natural resources.

CAMPING EQUIPMENT

Basic camping gear includes tents, sleeping bags, ground cloths, air mattresses or sleeping pads, first-aid kit (which will be discussed in detail in chapter 9), recreational equipment, and the personal gear not directly associated with the river trip per se.

A wide variety of tents make their appearance on the beach at the mouth of the Little Dolores River on the Colorado River in Westerwater Canyon. Any lightweight tent that gets the job done is fine for river trips. (Verne Huser photo)

Tents

Depending on the area and the weather, you may or may not want to carry tents. Few river runners in the Southwest bother with tents. But in many areas, during certain seasons you'd be courting a wet trip without one.

If you do take a tent, it should be easy to put up and obviously waterproof (otherwise, why bother?), and lightweight—that's about all.

Lightweight backpacking tents of many shapes and sizes make good river-running tents, as you want to keep the boat loads light, although, of course, you can carry more in a boat than you can on your back. I personally use a Gerry (Box 5544, Boulder, CO 80217) tent that cost just under $100 a few years ago. But everybody's making tents these days, and you have a wide selection in sporting-goods stores, at Sears and

Two tents frequently used on river trips. (Verne Huser photos)

Coleman's Open Air Pavilion may be
ideal for cooking during a rain storm.
(Courtesy Coleman Company, Inc.)

Wards, and other mass-sales outlets and discount stores.

It's hard to go wrong, however, when you buy quality from such outdoor equipment businesses as Recreational Equipment, Inc. (1525 Eleventh Avenue, Seattle, WA 98122); Holubar (Box 7, Boulder, CO 80302); Eddie Bauer (Box 3700, Seattle, WA 98124); The North Face (Box 2399, Berkeley, CA 94702); Coleman, Thermos, Hans Klepper, and others.

In addition to providing sleeping quarters, tents are valuable for saunas (but you can improvise an excellent sauna with oars and a tarp) and cooking shelters in case of rain (Coleman's Open Air Pavilion is ideal but, here again, you can improvise with a tarp and a few extension stakes and some guy-ropes). If you have a portable toilet along—and even if you don't—it is good to have a tent for personal privacy. Where there is plenty of vegetation, natural screens will serve. (Be sure to designate the latrine area so there are no awkward mistakes.)

To keep dampness and chill away from the body, cheap plastic ground cloths are adequate for riverside camping, especially on sandy beaches. Air mattresses have always been more of a bother to me than a help. I personally prefer the foam pad (be sure you get the closed-cell type) that you can buy for $6 or $8, and on a sandy beach, who needs any kind of pad? Just dig out your own form in the sand with a few scoops with the hand, and you'll have the best bed in camp.

Sleeping Bags

Sleeping bags are another matter of personal preference. I have an Alp Sport cocoon bag made with two and one-half pounds of down that wasn't warm enough on an early May trip on the Middle Fork of the Salmon, and I have an $8.88 cheapy purchased at a discount store in 1968 for my first Grand Canyon trip that was too warm to sleep in. Different situations call for different kinds of sleeping bags. Use your regular bag, if you have one, when you go river running, but be sure to use a good waterproof bag or other container to keep it dry.

Down bags are expensive but excellent because they are light and compact, saving both weight and space. You can find an adequate bag for $10, a good one in the range of $30 to $50, and the best down bags for $100 or more.

The latest development in insulating materials—even a more recent development than the use of foam rubber—is Dacron Fiberfill II, a polyester made by Du Pont. Numerous manufacturers are using the material for relatively inexpensive bags. *Train Camping,* a magazine that appeared briefly and then went under (it may be revived—it was a good one), ran a comprehensive article on the product in its June 1973 issue. It said, in part, "DACRON Fiberfill II is plentiful and inexpensive. It is mildew-resistant. It is nonallergenic. It compacts *almost* as well as down, has excellent recovery, and dries quickly." Sounds ideal for river running, doesn't it? Coleman, one of several companies using the product, has a

Fishing is part of the recreation for this group, which is floating the Main Salmon River in a military surplus M-16 raft. (This craft, a bit flexible in comparison to more modern rafts, is going out of style on many rivers.) (Verne Huser photo)

colorful array of sleeping bags made of various synthetic materials.

For Recreation

Recreational equipment for a river trip might include fishing gear (use your standard equipment, buying only for the specific situation you may find on a particular river), Frisbees, volleyballs, footballs, soccer balls—in general, the equipment for whatever games people play. Quoits and badminton and paddle tennis, or variations thereof, are part of many commercial river trips, but others find enough recreation in the natural scene: hiking, bird watching, rock hounding, exploring the area around the campsite, swimming, climbing, enjoying the natural world instead of ignoring it.

Special equipment you might want to include on a river trip includes a river library of books on the area's history and geology, fauna and flora, river maps and checklists of natural features (flowering plants, birds, amphibians, etc.); a survival kit (waterproof matches, fishhooks and line, high-calorie food, a space blanket—one professional guide I know has sewed into the inside of his life jacket a series of pockets in which he keeps such items); gold-panning pans.

If you take along a camera—and I recommend that you do, by all means—be sure you have a good, waterproof container for camera and film, and take along lots of film. The ammo cans mentioned earlier are ideal: Be sure of the seal, pad the can with foam rubber, paint it some light color to reflect the heat, attach a line so you can tie it into the boat, and you're set.

If you want a special river-running camera, the Nikonos II is the only way to go. As far as I know, it is the only waterproof camera available; it enables you to take pictures while you're running the rapids, and it doesn't matter if you get it wet. It sells for between $400 and $500 at most camera shops in this country.

One outfitter I've worked for as a guide, Jim Campbell's Wilderness Encounters, runs an annual nature photography trip with Boyd Norton along to teach people about outdoor photography (he's the author of Snake Wilderness, and his photographs have appeared in numerous national magazines and several books).

PERSONAL EQUIPMENT

In the way of personal gear and clothing, I suggest my constant adage: Check out the local situation, and dress for the trip. You won't need a wool shirt in the Grand Canyon in June, but a down vest on the Cheat in the spring might be useful. Most inexperienced river runners take along far too much in the way of clothing, but it pays to have the right things along.

Clothing

I normally take along a couple changes of underwear (you can always wash it on extended trips) and socks, including a pair of heavy wool ones for my hiking boots and in case the weather turns cold—as it did on the Middle Fork of the Salmon in July one year. I take a tank top, knit T-shirt, turtle-neck, and two shirts—both long-sleeved (one lightweight cotton and one wool, for emergency use).

In warmer weather, I wear old Levi's and cutoffs or a swimsuit (after my legs get tanned—no sense burning them and suffering for a week on the river). For colder weather, I may take along a pair of wool pants, a wool sweater, a Windbreaker or waterproof jacket, and a down vest or even a down jacket. For footwear, I use wet boots (in cold weather or early in the morning) and tennis shoes or running shoes. I usually wear socks only to prevent getting sunburned; once my ankles are tanned, I discard them.

At breakfast in Grand Canyon people are dressed for a hot day. Note that the table has been created by setting a floorboard on food cans. The grill is made of angle iron. (Verne Huser photo)

Wool is good to have along on most cold-weather trips. Unlike down clothing, which is worthless when wet, wool retains heat even then.

Hats can be invaluable on river trips—to shed sun and rain and for identification. Character hats are a fun part of river running; many old river-rats are as well known for their hats as for their cooking or their rigging. It's a good idea to tie hats down with a chin cord (simply cut two small holes at the juncture of the brim and crown, loop a rawhide thong or a nylon cord around the back of the hat, down through the holes, and tie it under the chin). It will save a lot of hats on the river. For cold weather it's good to have a wool stocking cap.

There are two schools of thought concerning how best to dress for the river: 1) wear wet-weather gear so you'll stay dry, and 2) wear as little as possible so you'll dry off quickly after you get wet. I've seen people dressed to the gills in the best wet-weather gear take a wave in the face and spend the rest of the day damp and miserable. Some do manage to stay fairly dry, but unless the weather is foul, cold, and rainy, I prefer the wear-as-little-as-possible school. For really cold weather and cold water, I suggest a wet suit or at least a partial wet suit, even if you have to rent one.

Other Equipment

Wet-weather gear should be adequate to keep you dry if you run into rain for hours or days on end, but it should also give you enough mobility to operate the boat. Loose, flappy rain-gear is bad news as it may be blown about by the wind to interfere with rowing or the boatman's vision. I use a full granny-gown with a hood, the kind you can pick up at most outdoor equipment stores for $30 or so. It ties at the bottom, and the tie can be used around the waist as well.

Gloves or even down mittens may be good for really cold weather, but I prefer the old military-type leather gloves with wool linings that provide some warmth even when wet. I rarely use gloves on the river, but I keep a pair of leather ones

Typical wet-weather gear is in use as river runners watch a boat approach Tappan Falls on the Middle Fork of the Salmon. Note the man on the right is wearing his life jacket beneath his rain poncho and the man in the middle (seated) has his life jacket on over his water-resistant parka. (Verne Huser photo)

handy for handling hot pots and pans and grills and griddles around the fire (they're pretty black from soot, but they keep just about everything else clean).

I like to have a flashlight along for any emergency situations after dark: to check out that noise that may disturb my

10-year-old daughter ("Daddy, I hear a bear."), to go to the bathroom, to check the boats, to spotlight great horned owls calling from the tree above camp, to check the time, or for a real emergency.

It's also nice to have a water bottle within reach when I crawl into my sleeping bag, so that if I wake up thirsty during the night I don't have to venture out into the cold. Many people carry liquor along, but it's best to leave the bottles at home: they break too easily. Decant the liquor into a metal or plastic bottle (often available in select brands at the liquor store for the price of the liquor or at your favorite outdoor supply store for a few dollars).

Cleanliness on a river trip is important, especially on longer trips, and on the river there should be ample opportunity for bathing. Your toilet kit should reflect your needs. Certainly carry a toothbrush and a small tube of toothpaste (salt will do in a pinch), but don't spit in the river. Perhaps a comb and/or hairbrush and possibly shaving gear, for the men (though many of them rough it—I started my own beard the year I ran the Idaho rivers all summer).

Soap is an individual item, but I've found none better than Dr. Bronner's Peppermint Soap, which can be used for hands and face, bathing or dishwashing, even brushing your teeth. It is biodegradable and makes an excellent shampoo as well as laundry soap. A practical soap that is environmentally sound, it is available at many health-food stores throughout the country. If you can't find it, write to Dr. Bronner, Escondido, CA 92025.

I always carry a small metal mirror on camping trips, including river trips, and small packets of Kleenex to use as toilet paper if none is available. I use hand cream (usually Chaphands), but most outfitters carry Bag Balm in their first-aid kits—great stuff for chapped hands. Band-Aids, chapstick, pills and salves, suntan creams, anti-poison-ivy lotion, and insect repellent can all go into the toilet kit.

A Voyageur's Sierra cup (about $1.25) is another handy

thing to have along on a river trip. Patterned after the Sierra Club cup, a utensil of this type is indispensable on a river trip. I always carry one at my right hip, looping it under my belt. It comes in handy for dipping water out of the stream (if the water is safe), for booze or coffee, soup or salad.

One parting shot about equipment: *use checklists.* Make a list of everything you might possibly need on a river trip, organizing the list according to logical groupings: kitchen, camp, first aid, repair, etc. Then add to the lists as you gain experience, and use them for every trip. That way you'll be sure not to forget anything. Add anything you've forgotten on a trip (take the list along so you won't forget to write it down). I've included a checklist in the appendix, to give you an example.

A 25-foot pontoon rigged with two rowing frames and a baggage frame between runs the main Salmon River in central Idaho. Note the distribution of passengers and the post oarlocks for the 12-foot oars. Boatmen are Hank and Sharon Miller, a unique husband-and-wife team who run float trips on several Idaho rivers under the name of Idaho Adventures. (Verne Huser photo)

4

Inflatable Boats and Accessories

The use of improper or inadequate equipment, one of the leading causes of accidents on river trips, may be a function of inexperience—simply a lack of understanding of the forces at work when you enter the natural world and pit your brawn and brain against it. You must learn to work with nature, not fight it, and one of the best ways to cooperate with the forces you'll encounter is to go to the river properly equipped. If, after you have sufficient experience, you decide to mount your own river trip, a sound boat and rigid rig and other accessories will be your most important acquisitions.

BOATS

Rafts

In the early days of river running, military surplus rafts, boats, and pontoons were the primary craft on the river. They were abundant and inexpensive. Though not built specifically for river use and, consequently, not the best, there was little else available, and inflatable floating developed primarily in such craft.

One of the earliest post-World War II surplus rafts used — and by far the most popular in its day — is the heavy assault raft commonly known as the Ten-man. Many are still in use today. This one has had its cross-tubes removed and a wooden floor and frame added (it is not fully rigged). Boat belongs to Stan Miller of Idaho Primitive Area Float Trips. (Verne Huser photo)

However, as float trips became popular, these boats grew scarce and expensive. The old boats got so worn out that patching was no longer effective. And even commercial outfitters, who had a corner on the market, had a difficult time finding good, sturdy leakproof boats. A number of float trips by do-it-yourselfers came to grief—like the Boy Scout group on the Green River a few years ago. There was a great need for good inflatable boats.

Another raft used in the early days and still in operation today is the double-tubed M-16 (I've also heard them referred to as M-5s). This raft is used by Charlie Sands (Flagg Float Trips) for a short white-water stretch just south of Yellowstone National Park. It is an extremely flexible craft. (Verne Huser photo)

A few companies who made the military craft slowly began to react to this need. They built boats specifically for river runners, who designed craft for their own purposes, and numerous models came into being.

One of these companies was Rubber Fabricators, in West Virginia. It began to build Barker-Ewing's Snake River model and various pontoons; the Salmon River model; the Yampa and the Green; the Rio Grande; and the Selway—all for the

Western rivers—and the New River Raft and other models suited to various Eastern streams. Recently this company was purchased by B.F. Goodrich and is now referred to as the Inflatable Division of B.F. Goodrich,* according to Jon Dragan (P.O. Box 55, Thurmond, WV 25933), the East Coast distributor for the company. Ron Smith (P.O. Box O, Kanab, UT 84741) is the western distributor.

Inflatable Boats

I have used various models—Snake, Salmon, Yampa, Green—over the past decade and found that although they are expensive, they are the best in the business. If you plan to do a lot of river running, you can hardly go wrong with one of these boats. Like most good inflatables, they are built of a nylon fabric coated on both sides with a synthetic rubber material, neoprene in this case, (Dupon Hypalon in many other boats). I've used the Snake model—designed by Dick Barker and Frank Ewing (Barker-Ewing Float Trips, P.O. Box 1243, Jackson, WY 83001) specifically for that run—for many seasons running commercial trips in Grand Teton National Park. It is second to none for quiet-water trips. The splash rail almost guarantees a dry trip—if that's what you're after—and with most of the outfitters in the area using this craft, it seems to have proved itself.

I've also used several Salmon models. I have run the Middle Fork of the Salmon, the Main Salmon, and Hells Canyon in the 17-foot Salmon model and was delighted with its stability, its maneuverability, and its toughness. In the Snake River Canyon, below Jackson, Wyoming, I've used the 20-foot model of the Salmon with self-bailing floor and found it excellent, though many outfitters use Yampas and Greens on the same stretch (more Yampas and Greens have flipped at Lunch Counter Rapid, but several 20-foot Salmons have also flipped on that fickle third wave).

---

*Commercial Marine Division, West Virginia Operations, Engineering System Company, B.F. Goodrich.

Two 16-foot
Salmon River boats.
(Verne Huser photo)

I've also used a Green River model in Westwater Canyon on the Colorado. I loved it. In this smaller boat, you really get the feel of the river for a fun ride. It is somewhat less stable than some of the bigger boats, and more maneuverable.

The pontoons offer greater stability, but even they go over in really big water; they also take some of the fun out of the ride, especially if they are run with motors. However, they are certainly able to carry a lot of people.

Ron Smith also sells the hard-hulled Sportyak, a 3½-by-7-foot boat weighing a mere 38 pounds, that has been used in some of the biggest water in the West (Grand Canyon, Cataract Canyon, the Green River). Made of vacuum-formed rigid polyethylene, this remarkable craft is almost unsinkable and can be used in small streams as well as heavy water. Try Bill Belknap's Fastwater Expeditions (Box 365, Boulder City, NV 89005) to learn how to use the Sportyak on a Green River float trip (more of that in chapter 5).

In 1959, an independent British company, called Avon Rubber, began making inflatable craft, starting with an 8-foot and a 12-foot dinghy that they marketed in 1960. As World War II faded into ancient history and military surplus craft became expensive and scarce, the various Avon models took hold in this country. The Craighead brothers, John and

Frank, Jr., who had begun rafting with Navy survival craft during the war, began using Avon boats—you saw them in the National Geographic Society TV special on wild rivers. I've never personally used an Avon raft, but I know a lot of people who do and swear by them.

Avon currently produces four boats in the dinghy range: the 8'2" Redstart (about $370), the 9'3" Redcrest (about $450), the 10'3" Redseal (about $500), and the 12'3" Redshank MKII (about $575). These boats are excellent for small, tight rivers; they are sturdy and light and have great maneuverability. They've been used by experienced boaters on such streams as the Middle Fork of the Salmon, the Main Salmon, and the Colorado in Grand Canyon with no real problems. In 1971, responding to the growing demand for boats, Avon produced the White Water River Runner in two models: the Adventurer (13' long, 6'6" wide with a 17"diameter tube, which sells for about $875) and the Professional MKII (15' long, 6'8" wide with 18"-diameter tubes, which sells for about $1200).

The Avons are virtually the only mass-produced inflatables I can recommend. Avon headquarters are in Great Britain (Avon Rubber Company Limited, Inflatable Products Division, Dafen, Llanelli, Carms., South Wales). U.S. distributors include the following regional offices: *Western States*—Seagull Marine Sales, 1851 McGaw Avenue, Irving, CA 92705; *Eastern States*—Imtra Corporation, 151 Mystic Avenue, Medford, MA 02155; *Midwest and Central Eastern States:* Inland Marine Company, 79 East Jackson Street, Wilkes-Barre, PA 19701; *Alaska*—Alaska Marine & Equipment Inc., Box 6208, Anchorage, AK 99500.

Consumer Reports (March 1974) had a section on inflatable boats in which the Avon Redcrest was recommended, along with the Zodiac Simplex and the C-Craft CD 9. The Simplex was rated at the top, with the Redcrest in the runner-up spot. *Consumer Reports* made a few comments about inflatable boats that may be of interest to you: "Inflatable boats can be taken out of a closet, carried in your car's trunk, and

An Avon raft on the Stanislaus River in California is powered by oars on post pins. Note that every passenger and the boatman is wearing a PFD and that everyone is holding on as the boat enters a rapid. (Avon photo courtesy Seagull Marine)

set up at waterside. They're virtually untippable and unsinkable. But they handle less precisely than hard-hulled boats. They can be exhausting to row." I would suggest that "virtually untippable and unsinkable" is a bit strong, but basically the comment is accurate.

I do not know the Zodiac boats from any personal experience. One owner of a major boating distributorship which sells several different brands says that the dinghy is the only Zodiac he can recommend, and that is the model that *Consumer Reports* recommended. Zodiac headquarters in the United States is Zodiac of North America, Inc., 11 Lee Street, Annapolis, MD 21401, but numerous dealers throughout the country sell Zodiac boats.

Outdoor Adventures (688 Sutter Street, San Francisco, CA 94102) handles Avons, Zodiacs, Newcos ("an inexpensive line of nylon rafts that have proven to be the most reliable boat we have tested," says Outdoor Adventures' managing partner, Bob Volpert), and American Safety products. The latter company is relatively new to the recreational-boat scene, but Volpert anticipates it will soon be a leader in the field.* You might want to check with them before you buy your craft: American Safety Equipment Corporation, Recreation Products Group, 16055 Ventura Boulevard, Encino, CA 91316. Its new raft series is scheduled for mass production for the 1975 season.

Outdoor Adventures also offers a unique customer service: booking float trips with a commercial outfitter for his customers so they can test their own equipment. Bob Volpert offers this service on a commission basis and for the sales he may make, but he wants his customers to learn how to operate the boats they buy. I've talked with Bob, and his appraisal of various outfitters generally agrees with my own—he doesn't book with every outfitter, since he wants to be sure that his customers have a positive experience. By the way, for safety reasons he sells only nylon boats, and he recommends Type I life jackets for most white-water trips, the SEDA for comfort and safety as a Type II PFD (particularly for kayakers). He gets his paddles from Feather, Iliad, Canon, and Smoker, and his oars through Feather and Smoker. I believe he's a man whose counsel you can trust when it comes to white-water boating.

Perhaps the most active seeker after the best boat in the business, however, is Vladimir Kovalik, who operates Wilderness World, one of the most imaginative and environmentally oriented commercial-river-trip operations in the country. I've known Vlado for years, and I've never met him when he didn't have a new boat to tell me about. He wrote me recently, "I have been traveling this year (1974) a lot in the

---

*They've been making military craft for years.

United States and overseas, working on the design of several boats presently being manufactured and which I'm now testing. I'll be distributing these boats under my own personal name. They will be approximately 14, 16, and 18 feet long in heavy-duty commercial designs, and lighter models for private use." His address is 1342 Jewell Avenue, Pacific Grove, CA 93950. It might be worth your while to contact him before you make your decision about a boat for your own use. He'll have the latest information on the best boat available, and he'll probably be selling it himself.

Inflatable Canoes and Kayaks

Another recent development in the United States is increased use of inflatable canoes and kayaks. Long popular in

This inflatable kayak does well in Double Hydraulics on the Youghiogheny in Pennsylvania. I've seen similar craft on rapids in Grand Canyon, but I also know of a few drownings in them, more the result of inexperienced boaters than the boat. Several white-water schools use them for training white-water boaters. (Photo courtesy Mountain Trails and Streams Outfitters)

Europe, they have come into more common use in this country during the past decade. Among the craft available to the general public are the Sevylor products that Jerry Bentley uses for his Orange Torpedo Trips in Oregon (see chapter 5) and northern California. Sevylor began making inflatables in 1948. I first saw one in 1968 when Dr. Roderick Nash paddled a Tahiti through several of the minor rapids of the Colorado River in Grand Canyon. He ran Tuna time and again, carrying the lightweight craft back upstream for each new run; he also ran one of the rapids below North Canyon and broke a paddle in heavy water. I used the craft at the mouth of Havasu.

Sevylor makes several inflatable boats that might be fine for mild rivers, but I would not use them in anything like white water (I'm sure many people do and get away with it, but they're not for me). The Tahiti comes in four models from 7'8" to 12'6"; it was the smallest of these that Dr. Nash used in Grand Canyon. While this type of craft might be fine for short runs, it is by no means a worthy craft for any kind of extended trip without a support craft. Sevylor headquarters for the United States is on the West Coast: Sevylor U.S.A., Inc., 4476 E. Washington Boulevard, Los Angeles, CA 90023.

Leisure Imports (104 Arlington Avenue, St. James, NY 11780) with a branch office in the North Central area (2625 South Greeley Street, Milwaukee, WI 53207) also has a canoe series from France used by at least one commercial outfitter for do-it-yourself training trips. Made of vinyl urethane, the Pyrawa and Sea Eagle series have become popular recently, with the Sea Eagle 300 getting the highest rating from river runners I've talked with. None of these boats, however—neither the Sevylor nor the Sea Eagle-Pyrawa series—have the safety factor of rip-stop nylon as a base, and they are subject to tearing to a much greater extent than nylon-based boats. Use them on quiet rivers unless you become an expert, and be extremely careful about sharp twigs and branches and rocks and any man-made sharp objects that might easily cut such a fabric.

A canoe takes the rapids in races down the Wolf River in Wisconsin. (Photo courtesy of the Wisconsin Natural Resources Department, Madison)

Hard-hulled Kayaks and Canoes

Although they are not the principal subject of this book, kayaks and canoes are nonetheless popular white-water craft. To satisfy the curious, I would suggest one or more of the numerous books, written specifically for the kayaker or canoeist, which cover the subject well. Peter Dwight Whitney's *White-Water Sport* has a good chapter (3) on "How to Choose a Kayak," and the Arighis touch the subject lightly but soundly in their *Wildwater Touring* (chapter 4: "Wildwater Boats"). John T. Urban does much the same in the Appalachian Mountain Club's (AMC's) *White Water Handbook for Canoe and Kayak*. Bill Riviere's *Pole, Paddle & Portage* is another excellent source of information specifically on canoeing; his first two chapters deal with how to select a canoe, and he lists more than 40 sources for canoes. John Malo's *Complete Guide to Canoeing and Canoe Camping* also devotes two chapters (4 and 5) to the selection of the right craft for you. And Stackpole's *Introduction to Canoeing*, by Bradford Angier and Zack Taylor, offers basic information on "Choosing the Canoe" in the opening chapter. Jenkinson's *Wild Rivers of North America* also lists 10 canoe builders and/or distributors.

Let me suggest that probably the best bet for selecting a kayak is to contact one, or several, of the American White-water Association (AWA) affiliates (address in appendix) and get some personal input from members. Kayak sources include White-Water Sports, Ltd. (Box 9406, Denver, CO 80209); High Performance Products, Inc. (25 Industrial Park Road, Hingham, MA 02043); Old Town Canoe Company (Old Town, MA 04468—both kayaks and canoes); Phoenix Products, Inc. (Tyner, KY 40486); White Water Sports (1203 NE 65th, Seattle, WA 98115—canoes and inflatables as well); Natural Progression Kayaks (Box 1017, Sun Valley, ID 83353); and Surf-Kayak Company (Box 218, Encinitas, CA 92024).

Folding boats—primarily the Folbot and the Klepper—are close to kayaks in principle but are built of a fabric stretched over a wooden frame. They can be convenient carrying units and assembled at the riverside without inflation devices. Hans Klepper Corporation (35 Union Square West, New York, NY 10003) and Folbot Corporation (Box 7097, Charleston, SC 29405) both produce craft of this type that sell for anywhere from about $75 (factory direct price for Folbot's junior) to about $1,000 (for Klepper's Master, with complete sailing equipment). A 15-foot single seater ("Sporty") from Folbot varies from $135 to $350 in different models; Klepper's single seaters range between $200 and $320.

As for canoes, I own a Grumman, myself, an 18-foot aluminum, which is better for lake use than for river running. But I will leave the selection of the canoe to you and the experts. On the West Coast, try Canoe Trips West, Inc. (Box 61, Kentfield, CA 94904) or Easy Rider (200 SW Michigan Street, Seattle, WA 98106). In the South, Feather Craft, Inc. (450 Bishop Street, NW, Atlanta, GA 30318). In the Midwest, Smoker-Craft (Smoker Lumber Company, Inc., New Paris, IN 46553), Water Meister Sports (Box 5026, Fort Wayne, IN 46905), Sawyer Canoe Company (234 South State, Oscoda, MI 48750). In the East, Grumman Boats (Grumman Allied Industries, Inc., Marathon NY 13803) and Old Town Canoe Company (see above).

A good way to become acquainted with boats and other equipment is to read the publications on the sport: *Canoe,* the bimonthly magazine of the American Canoe Association; *American Whitewater,* the journal of the American Whitewater Affiliation (see Appendix A for address); *Down River* (Box 366, Mountain View, CA 94040); and *Oar and Paddle* (Box 621, Idaho Falls, ID 83401), two new publications (both initiated in mid-1974) about boating.

Another service worth mentioning to the potential canoeist is Grumman's Rent-a-Canoe Directory (write to Grumman Boats, Marathon, NY 13803), which provides a list of hundreds of canoe-rental liveries throughout the country, plus a listing of scattered information sources in several areas.

POWER SOURCE

Obviously the most important item once you have the boat is the means of propelling it, the source of power and control. Basically there are two means of propelling a craft: motor and manual. Many weekend boaters and a good many commercial-float-trip operations use motors, some as high-powered as possible. While I can justify the use of motors for running out onto a reservoir at the end of a white-water float trip and the use of small motors on slow rivers, this book will not address itself to the use of motors. Let me merely suggest that you contact your local sporting goods dealer for a better discussion of the subject than I could provide.

It may also be good to check with your state boating director for rules and regulations regarding the use of motors (in some states, if you put a motor on a raft or canoe, you suddenly are thrust into a whole new class of crafts known as "motorboats," with entirely different regulations). Also, check with federal, state, and local authorities, because many waters are closed to the use of motors: the Allegash in Maine, the Middle Fork of the Salmon in Idaho, parts of the Upper Snake in Wyoming, the Chattooga between Georgia and South Carolina, etc.

The three means of propelling a craft that involve manual methods are the sweep (an oar at bow and stern), the oar, and the paddle. All three systems have advantages and disadvantages, and there are emotional involvements among boaters concerning one or the other. There is no universal right answer, only a best answer for any individual. Objectively speaking, the sweep boat is probably the safest craft, but it is difficult to row. Probably more paddle-powered boats capsize than others, but they are certainly the best from the participation point of view. Oar and sweep-powered boats require rigs for mounting, which is obviously more expensive than no rig at all. My advice is to make up your own mind as to which system is best for you and the rivers you'll run.

Sweeps

Since I know of no source of commercially available sweeps, I will not address them in this section. They are almost in-

(Facing page) The three manual methods to propel an inflatable are by sweep (top — on the Owyhee River in Oregon), paddle (middle — on the New River in Virginia) or oar (bottom). (Photos, from top to bottom, courtesy of Dave Helfrich of Prince Helfrich and Sons, Wildwater Expeditions Unlimited, Inc., and O.A.R.S. Inc.)

variably built by a specific outfitter or boatman for his own use, or he may have the sweep built by a local blacksmith or welder who has some expertise in that area. But basically they are homemade.

Paddles

Many of the commercial float-trips in the East use paddle power. Jon Dragan explains: "Due to the roughness of the turns and the narrowness of the rivers here in the East, we feel that is the safest way to run a trip. This also gives passengers a chance to participate." I've used oar-powered rigs to run some pretty fast Western rivers, with some pretty tight turns and narrow chutes, but I can't argue with Jon—he knows the Eastern rivers.

My personal feeling is that a rowed raft responds more quickly because all power is tuned in to the same brain, and with a rigid frame there is less lost motion. While paddling passengers may produce more power, there is less coordination than there is with one strong oarsman working from a fixed frame. Also, the paddles are not fixed to the craft as the oar is, and the paddlers, with nothing to hold on to but the paddle, may more easily be bounced out of the boat. (Some groups run with oars *and* paddles for participation and control.)

If paddles are used, the specific type of paddles generally depends upon personal preference. However, they should be long enough to reach the water from an inflatable boat, which may be much higher above water level than a canoe (contrast a person straddling the 24-inch tube of a pontoon with someone kneeling in the bottom of a canoe).

Paddles made of ash and maple and, occasionally, birch are the old standbys for the canoeist. They are heavy—especially the maple—but sturdy and limber. Lightweight spruce paddles have come into greater use in recent years, especially in wide-bladed models, but spruce is brittle; it doesn't seem to take the beating of white-water paddling as well as the heavier woods.

Aluminum paddles developed during World War II have also sneaked into the market. Many of the early ones were flimsy and easily broken, often leaving a party with no paddle power; I've rescued parties in this situation on the Upper Snake. Of those available today, Iliad aluminum paddles seem to be considered the best on the market by many floaters. They are expensive ($37 each), but they are light and sturdy, and they float just like wooden paddles. On the other hand, they are less flexible than wooden paddles, an important factor on longer trips.

Iliad paddles weigh 1.8 to 2.8 pounds and come in a variety of blade sizes (22", 25", 28" widths) and overall paddle length (51" to 72" in 3-inch intervals). They are guaranteed as follows: "If an Iliad paddle fails in proper use due to defective materials or workmanship, it will be replaced or repaired without charge." Dealers have indicated to me that the company makes good on that offer with few questions asked. Numerous dealers throughout the country handle them, but for the name of one in your area, write to Iliad, Inc. (168 Circuit Street, Norwell, MA 02061).

Cheaper paddles are readily available at any boating-equipment store; check the canoeing guides mentioned elsewhere for more detailed information on paddles. One of the biggest producers of both paddles and oars is Swanson Boat Oar Company, Inc. of Albion, PA 16401 . Swanson paddles sell for around $10 to $14 each, in white ash and northern hardwoods, in lengths from 54 to 72 inches. Shorter paddles are slightly cheaper but probably not practical for inflatable-boat use. A canoe-paddle maker on the West Coast, Ralph Sawyer (8891 Rogue River Highway, Rogue River, OR 97537) makes a fiberglass-covered paddle with an 8-inch blade and a 25-inch tapered length that sells for about $15 and comes in lengths from 50" to 69". Another model, 10 inches wide, comes in lengths to 60 inches and sells for slightly more.

Oars

Of the three manual-power methods for inflatable craft, my

This pontoon's wooden rowing frame is chained to the boat by D-rings. Its plywood floors are also suspended by chains from D-rings on the outside of the pontoon. Wooden boxes are used for storage of food and camp gear; coolers provide plenty of water since little is available on this Yampa River run in Dinosaur National Monument. (Verne Huser photo)

personal preference is for oars. Not only does the oarsman have more control and more to hang on to than the paddler; he also has an easier time rowing than if he were in a sweep-powered craft. And, though oars are heavier than paddles, the weight is supported, not by the hand and arm, but rather by a fulcrum point at an oarlock mounted rigidly on the craft or on a rigid frame attached to the craft. On the other hand, with the rigid material of both oar- and sweep-frame, there is greater potential for injury and added stress to the fabric of the boat. Operators of oar or sweep rigs must be careful to pad or bevel corners and edges, to avoid protruding bolts, and to alleviate the wear and tear of chains or ropes on the boats.

Oars. Oar size depends upon several factors: the size of the boat, the size and kind of river, and the strength of flow. But you must keep in mind that part of the oar length is lost, so to speak, through the fulcrum point: that is, if you use a 7-foot oar mounted 3 feet from the end of the handle, you have just 4 feet of oar out over the water. To determine what size oars you need for your boat, do some testing, ask some questions, make some observations. The Selway boat, only about 12 feet long, might require an 8-foot oar for relatively mild water, but a 10-foot oar for running the Grand Canyon (and a Selway has done it all the way, without a flip, under oar power). For a 16-foot Salmon River boat on the Middle Fork, I've used 10-foot oars and for a 20-foot Salmon River boat on the upper Snake, 12-foot oars. I've used 12-foot oars on the quiet upper Snake for the 18-foot Snake River (Barker-Ewing) model, and 10-foot oars on a Green River boat in Westwater Canyon on the Colorado. Keep in mind that, on the one hand, you don't want them overlapping in your lap, but that if you have too much oar hanging out over the water, your leverage will be too greatly compromised, and you may not be able to pull any water.

Long oars (eight feet or more), made of white ash or hard maple, may sell for about $20 to $80, depending on length. Many commercial outfitters buy longer oars, then cut them down to suit their own needs; this means a thicker oar less likely to break in a tight situation. They may even cut down the oarblade length, as well as the handle, to achieve a sturdier shaft that will withstand the power of white-water rowing.

One of the first things a rower learns is never to stick the end of the downstream oar into the bottom of the river. Oars are expensive, and breaking too many oars, as I've noted elsewhere, can be not only inconvenient but really hazardous.

Oarlocks. If you use oars, you'll need some kind of oarlock. Oarlocks vary from the hard rubber ones built into some of the small inflatables to the specially designed metal ones developed by commercial outfitters for their own specific purposes, but there are three basic designs: pin, ring, and pressure.

The pin oarlock has a pin or bolt through the shaft of the oar or a grip of some kind which provides absolute articulation, ready response, and solid contact. However, the pin or bolt through the shaft will weaken the oar unless it is wrapped at the articulation with fiberglass fabric for strength. (Many professional guides also wrap the oar tips with fiberglass to reduce splitting.) Some pin oars are rigged to pop out under pressure; others are held fast. Another variation on this theme is the post oarlock (see photo). Each has its advantages and disadvantages. With a pop-out pin you may lose the oar momentarily at a critical moment, but in doing so, you may prevent the breaking of an oar or a frame.

The ring oarlock allows for withdrawing and feathering the oars, an impossibility with a pin arrangement. This may be an important consideration on tight rivers with narrow chutes, steep cliffs at the water's edge, or lots of tall rocks in the water.

Pressure oarlocks hold the oar in place much like a ring oarlock, but pressure will cause the oar to pop out of the oarlock, a feature that may save the oar or paddle but may put the boat in jeopardy at a critical moment.

RIGS

Once you know how your craft will be powered you can determine how to rig it for operation. One of the first considerations is the frame.

Frames

Both oar- and sweep-powered craft virtually require the use of frames for rigidity, and they are used on a few paddle-powered rafts as well. Some kind of frame is also necessary for motorpowered rafts to serve as a motor mount. A frame

A U-shaped, pin-type oarlock mounted in a wooden block. Oar shaft is fiberglassed at the pin for greater strength. (Verne Huser photo)

The post-type pin oarlock in which a piece of conveyor belt is bolted to the oar shaft so that it fits over the post that serves as oarlock. Note the chain used to anchor the rowing frame to the boat. (Verne Huser photo)

This type of oar and ring oarlock arrangement prevents loss of oar but still allows feathering and shipping of oars. Note the bath-curtain ring used to secure ring pin to rowing frame. (Verne Huser photo)

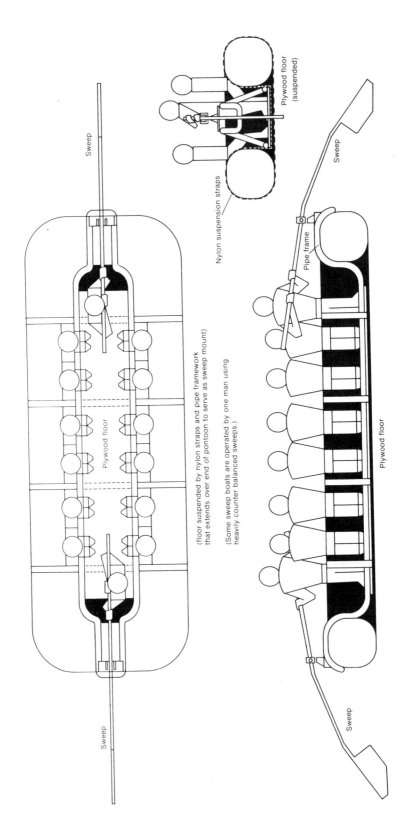

(floor suspended by nylon straps and pipe framework
that extends over end of pontoon to serve as sweep mount)

(Some sweep boats are operated by one man using
heavily counter balanced sweeps.)

Sweep

Sweep

Sweep

Sweep

Plywood floor

Plywood floor

Plywood floor
(suspended)

Nylon suspension straps

Pipe frame

Figure 1. Single pontoon sweep rig.

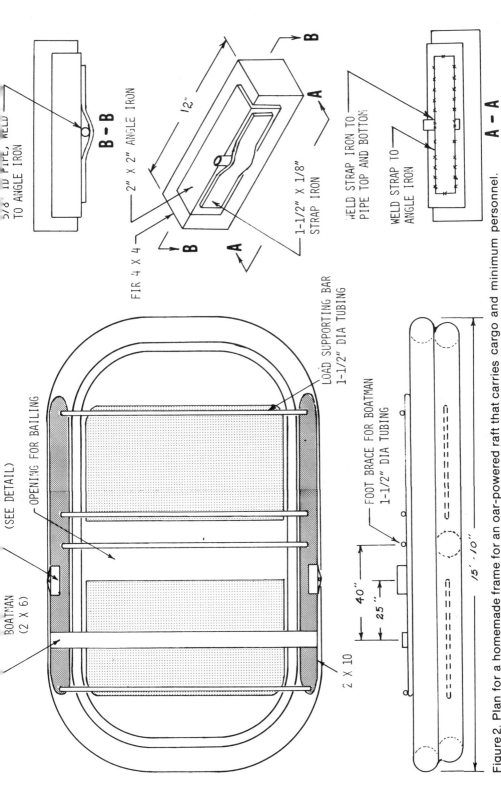

5/8" ID PIPE, WELD
TO ANGLE IRON

B - B

2" X 2" ANGLE IRON

12"

FIR 4 X 4

1-1/2" X 1/8"
STRAP IRON

WELD STRAP IRON TO
PIPE TOP AND BOTTOM

WELD STRAP TO
ANGLE IRON

A - A

(SEE DETAIL)

OPENING FOR BAILING

LOAD SUPPORTING BAR
1-1/2" DIA TUBING

FOOT BRACE FOR BOATMAN
1-1/2" DIA TUBING

BOATMAN
(2 X 6)

40"

25"

2 X 10

15' - 10"

Figure 2. Plan for a homemade frame for an oar-powered raft that carries cargo and minimum personnel.

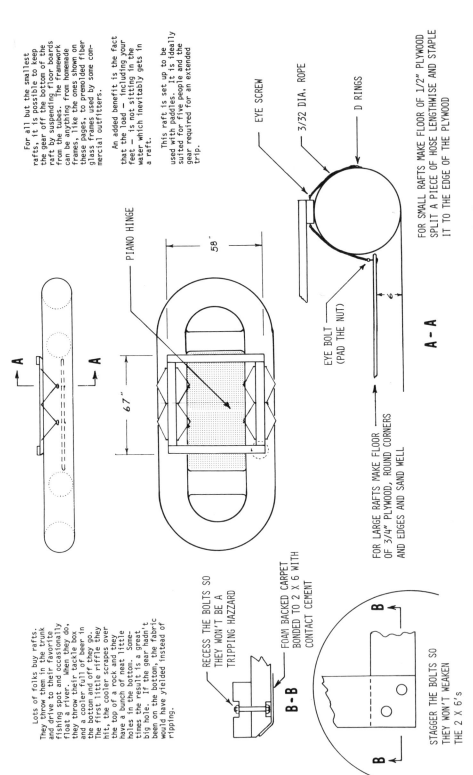

For all but the smallest rafts, it is possible to keep the gear off the bottom of the raft by suspending floor boards from the tubes. The framework can be anything from homemade frames, like the ones shown on these pages, to premolded fiber glass frames used by some commercial outfitters.

An added benefit is the fact that the load — including your feet — is not sitting in the water which inevitably gets in a raft.

This raft is set up to be used with paddles. It is ideally suited for five people and the gear required for an extended trip.

Lots of folks buy rafts. They throw them in the trunk and drive to their favorite fishing spot and occasionally float a river. When they do, they throw their tackle box and a cooler full of beer in the bottom and off they go. The first little riffle they hit, the cooler scrapes over the top of a rock and they have a bunch of neat little holes in the bottom. Sometimes the result is a great, big hole. If the gear hadn't been on the bottom, the fabric would have yielded instead of ripping.

Figure 3. Plan for a homemade frame designed for a paddle-powered raft.

A contoured aluminum rowing frame is strapped onto the D-rings with nylon webbing, but weight of gear on floor suspended from rowing frame and the contours of the frame help keep it in place. Valve for inflation lies just left of and below D-ring. Waterproof river bag is stowed beneath boatman's seat (right), and ammo cans are tied in. (Verne Huser photo)

provides a positive articulation between boat and whatever means of power and control is used so that the boat reacts rapidly and has a sturdy unified dependable response to the applied mind of the boatman. They are usually attached to D-rings on the craft with chains, rope, or nylon straps.

Frames may be made of wood or metal, and numerous different types have been devised. Wooden frames are inexpensive and easy to build. Though they splinter under stress, they are practical for many milder waters. One commonly used wooden frame is built of 2-by-6 or 2-by-8 pine or fir and bolted together at the corners (never use nails). It should fit the inflated boat's upper tube surface. The bolts should be set with their heads (round or smooth hexagonal) beneath the frame (tube side) and recessed to reduce abrasion. A padding of cloth or carpeting or an extra layer of boat fabric may be used to cushion the frame at contact points.

Metal frames have come into common use in recent years. They are usually made of small-gauge steel pipe or large-gauge aluminum pipe. Metal is more expensive and harder to work than wood. And while they last longer and resist shock

An old assault boat (military surplus) rigged for rowing with a wooden frame and metal oarlock seat. The broad part of the frame is a baggage area, but it comes off and becomes a table (screw pipe legs into corners) for overnight cooking activity. (Verne Huser photo)

A 20-foot Salmon River boat rigged for rowing with a metal frame and wooden floor in center section. Oars at rest are tucked in and tied down. Nylon straps hold frame in place. End sections have self-bailing bottom. (Verne Huser photo)

better, metal frames are more difficult to repair on the river should anything go wrong (which is less likely, however).

On the other hand, metal frames can be built to conform to the contours of the boat, a distinct advantage in providing a true marriage of boat and frame for better response. At least one aluminum frame I've used is so built that it has enough lateral play to flex with the action of the boat in a rapid; it is so form-fitting that the craft reacts as though boat and frame were one.

Even on a wooden frame, the oar or sweep mount (see photo) is usually made of metal, sometimes with a block of oak (or other hard wood) used for the actual oarlock seat. For sweep boats the two sweep mounts—one at each end—should be attached to the same frame, for the best response. A sturdy frame must then run the length of the boat, a heavy arrangement, but sweep boaters insist that the weight doesn't matter: "I can carry five times as much weight more safely in a sweep boat than I can in an oar-powered craft," says Idaho outfitter Stan Miller, of Salmon.

Floors

Though the existence of floors on inflatable craft may be taken for granted by the uninitiated, not all boats have bottoms. Some boats have standard bottoms with floors suspended well above, and others have simple self-bailing bottoms that let the water run out. But many of the larger commercial rigs have had the bottom cut out and run with artificial floors suspended from D-rings or tubes by means of ropes, chains, or nylon straps.

Suspended floors may be used in any of the three types of craft: those with no bottom (in which case floors are almost necessary), those with self-bailing bottom, and those with standard floors. Nylon straps may be arranged around the tubes in the first two cases with the floor supported by straps crossing from one tube to another. Chains may be used to

A Salmon River boat with metal-and-wood rowing frame and wooden floor suspended from the rowing frame by chains. Note the recessed eyelet bolts. (Verne Huser photo)

A detailed view of the self-bailing bottom shows a large envelope of waterproof material surrounding a hard foam layer laced into the flap that is part of the boat. Water simply flows in or out, the air chambers of the pontoon providing the flotation. Double rope down the middle is for passengers to hold onto in heavy water and big rapids — it keeps them from bouncing about too much.
(Verne Huser photo)

keep the two sides of a pontoon from separating, with the floor hung from or suspended by this chain. Another common arrangement is for the floor to be suspended by chains attached to the frame.

Whatever the suspension system used, if you have a standard bottom be sure the floor is hung high enough so that a rock hitting the bottom cannot crimp the fabric against the floorboard (usually made of plywood). Such action cuts holes in the bottom of the boat, and you'll overwork your bailers.

In a boat with a standard bottom bailing is important, and if suspended floors are used, some arrangement must be made to provide bailing access: either a bilge pump or leaving one portion of the boat open to the bottom. Water weighs roughly eight pounds per gallon, and a boat gets heavy and hard to handle unless it is bailed. Self-bailing bottoms, usually a sturdy floor laced to a flap full of grommets , allows the water to pass right through, but it also lets water in, assuring a wet trip.

Other Rigs

I've been dealing with what I call the standard rig in these last few pages, a basic inflatable boat used as such: the Avons, the military surplus assault boats, any of the Rubber Fabricators products, even pontoons. However, commercial outfitters use a number of other rigs. Since most of them are too big for practical use by do-it-yourselfers, I'll mention them only briefly. Standard rigs may run to the 33-foot pontoons, but my personal opinion is that when you get over 20 feet in length, you're in a different class, the barge—safe perhaps but less fun.

G-rig. Named for Georgie White, the remarkable woman who began running Grand Canyon float trips when she was almost middle-aged, the G-rig is created by fastening three pontoons together side by side and running the rig with a motor on the middle rig.

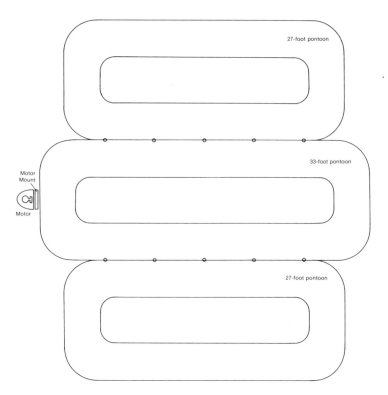

Figure 4. The G-rig is named for Georgie White.

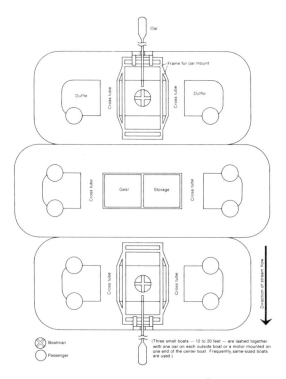

Figure 5. The triple rig is an adaptation of the G-rig using smaller boats.

Triple-rig.The triple-rig is a variation of the G-rig, using smaller boats, and I'm not sure which came first. It is commonly used in Grand Canyon and Cataract Canyon today with Green or Yampa River Boats or similar craft. Parties often run single boats to the head of the big rapids, then lash into a triple rig (obviously there must be at least three boats in the party) for the big stuff. My first trip through Grand Canyon was in one of these rigs, and I really got a ride, especially in Crystal.

J-rig.Jack Currey's use of single "sausage" tubes (in contrast to the "donut" type) lashed together was an innovation copied by a number of outfitters in a number of variations. Five tubes lashed side by side, the J-rig has tremendous stability and carrying capacity and is usually run by motor.

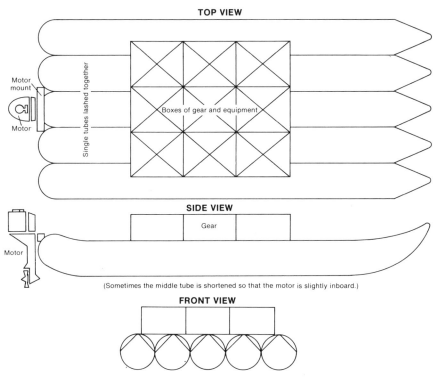

Figure 6. The J-rig is named for Jack Currey.

Smith-rig. Ron Smith developed what he considers an improvement on both the G-rig and the J-rig by using single "sausage" pontoons as outriggers on either side of a 37-foot pontoon. I've been through Grand Canyon with Ron on one of these rigs and consider them safe and exciting.

There are probably as many different rigs used on the rivers of this nation as there are river runners. If you run a river or two, no matter what your own craft may be, you'll see something new. In the spring, there are numerous river races

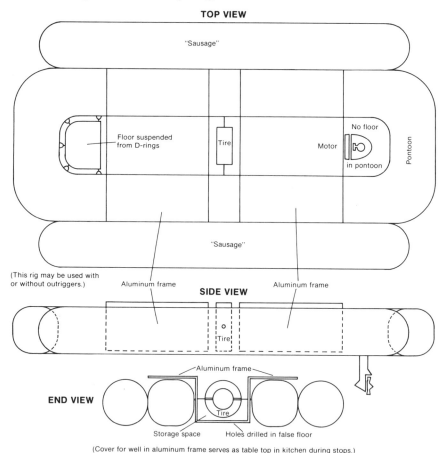

Figure 7. The S-rig is named for Ron Smith.

A vacuum cleaner is often used for pumping boats — if you have an electrical outlet handy or a generator to produce electricity. This arrangement is used more at the launch site than on the river; few river runners want to carry that much gear on the river. (Verne Huser photo)

around the country for unique rigs, but if you stick to the standard pattern, then improve on it with your own innovations for your own use, you can develop a highly personal river craft.

PUMPS

To pump up inflatable boats, river runners use a variety of devices, from vacuum cleaners in reverse to hair driers, from electric-powered pumps to hand pumps. The problem is twofold, because not only must the river runner find a way to inflate his craft initially, but he must also have a way to adjust the air pressure in his boat while he is on the river.

It may be possible to inflate a boat before you head for the river, if you have a trailer for the boat. And commercial outfitters who run short trips—only a few hours duration and perhaps several trips in one day, with the same boat, or trips day after day—usually keep their boats inflated, merely adjusting the pressure during the day each day.

But if you must rig by the river, it may pay to have an electric pump of some sort along, especially if there are several boats in the party. And since not all launch areas will have electricity, you may have to bring your own portable generator, too. However, these are relatively expensive—several hundred dollars.

If you have a source of electricity, you can use any kind of blower mechanism to pump up the boat. Coleman makes a portable inflator you can plug into a car's cigarette lighter, but it takes a while to pump a boat with it. (I might add at this point that a vacuum cleaner used as such is useful at the take-out point to get all the air out of an inflatable boat. It's easier to roll up and store that way. Also, various foot bellows are available from $5 to $10 that can be used either way.)

Since you're going to need a hand pump along on the river anyway, and may not have access to electricity, it may be worthwhile to use it for initial inflation. Certainly pumping is good exercise to condition you for rowing. Military surplus pumps are available but hard to find and usually too old to be practical. A number of the white-water boating stores and equipment companies offer good pumps, the standard being a 6″ by 19″, high-volume, low-pressure pump (Type I) that usually comes with a 48″ hose (you can get longer hoses, but this length is practical for most use). This pump sells for roughly $75, a good investment.

Smaller pumps in the same style (Type II) are available in two sizes: size 1 is 3″ in diameter and just under 7″ long; size 2 is also 3″ in diameter but 10″ long. They are handy to have along for any on-river pumping that may be necessary, but the larger pump should also be carried for topping off

A standard high-volume, low-pressure pump for inflatable boats is used each morning to inflate boats (adjust pressure). Note wooden floor suspended by means of chains and eyelets from a wooden rowing rig. (Verne Huser photo)

boats in the morning of each day you're on the river.

You'll get better performance on the river and longer life out of the boat if you take care to keep air pressure relatively constant. Since air expands when heated and contracts when cooled (Boyle's Laws), air pressure varies during the day, and inflatable boat users must be aware of the fact and adjust to it. Boats pumped tight on land at the river's edge will go soft when placed in the cooler water; boats pumped tight in the cool of early morning will sometimes get tight enough to burst in the heat of the day. Many river runners have practiced painting their boats with light colors (many of the rafts are made of black material and tend to absorb heat) especially silver, to help reflect the sun's heat and reduce the adjustment necessary. It pays in maneuverability and control to keep boats tight while in operation on the river, but when pulled up on land at the end of the trip or day, you must be careful they don't get too hot and too tight. Average pressure for operation is usually between two and three pounds per square inch.

The experienced boatman may be able to gauge the pressure of his boat merely by pounding the tube, but the novice will find a pressure gauge of some kind helpful in keeping his boat properly inflated. For the most part, these gauges are not commercially available but must be rigged for your specific purpose. One outfitter, for instance, has developed a pressure gauge that fits right on the pump so he can pump boats to the desired pressure automatically (Barker-Ewing). Perhaps your favorite service-station attendant or gasoline dealer can help you.

This Green River boat is fully rigged and loaded and tied up at a rest stop. Notice the "chicken" lines strung down both sides for holding on to in the rapids. (Verne Huser photo)

You've got the boat, and you've got the means of power, control, packing, and inflation. Now add rope for safety lines—nylon may be more expensive, but it is the only way to go. Use quarter-inch for the waterline safety rope that goes all around the boat on the outside; half-inch for bow and stern lines; something in-between for "chicken" lines to hold on to in the big, bucking rapids and for lashing gear into the craft.

What's next? Planning a specific trip.

By the time you get to the river, the planning should be done. (Verne Huser photo)

5

Planning

Before you head for the river, you have a lot of decisions to make and a lot of work to do. This preparatory stage may last months, even years before you take a particular trip. You read a lot and write for information, study the alternatives in boats and equipment, and finally take the plunge. If you are a more advanced rafter and plan to buy and run a boat with sweeps or oars, you have the time and expense of building a rig, but you have the satisfaction of knowing you'll be in the safest craft on the river.

READING

You've heard about floating from friends who've tried it; you've seen *Deliverance* and some of the TV specials on river running. You want to know more about it, and with books hitting the market every day on some phase of river running, you have a wide selection from which to choose. Magazine articles on river running appear more and more frequently, and you'll want to augment your reading with related books on specific rivers, history and geology, fauna and flora.

Westwater Books, which published my first book, *Snake River Guide,* sells more than 80 books related in one way or another to river running. Leonard Hall's *Stars Upstream,* about floating on the Current River, in Missouri, and Gay Staveley's *Broken Waters Sing* are delightful reading. Boyd Norton's *Snake Wilderness,* several Sierra Club books, and Edward Abbey's *Desert Solitaire* deal in part or *in toto* with rivers and problems related to rivers. For history, there are the *Lewis and Clark Journals;* John Wesley Powell's *The Exploration of the Colorado River and Its Canyons;* Wallace Stegner's *Beyond the Hundredth Meridian;* Washington Irving's *Astoria;* and *Battle Drums and Geysers,* by the Bonneys.

Several magazines—two of them first published in 1974—deal with river running: *American Whitewater,* journal of the American Whitewater Affiliation; *Canoe,* official publication of the American Canoe Association; *Oar and Paddle* (new); *Downstream* (new); and numerous publications of local river-running groups.

Several books dealing specifically with river running are scheduled to be published about the time this book reaches the public, and a few are already out: Scott and Margaret S. Arighi's *Wildwater Touring* and Michael Jenkinson's *Wild Rivers of North America;* and Bill Riviere's *Pole, Paddle & Portage,* primarily for canoeists, is one of the best I've seen.

A number of books on natural history will be mentioned in chapter 8, and numerous titles are listed in the appendix. Various river guides used in the chapter (11) on where to float make good reading, too, as do Dr. Roderick Nash's *Wilderness and the American Mind* and a Sierra Club book edited by Nash, *Grand Canyon of the Living Colorado.*

WRITING

Part of your preparation for running rivers on your own involves gathering information about the rivers you'd like to float. Write to the federal and state agencies listed in the appendix for information on rules and regulations, for maps and natural-history data, for general information on the area. Write to the outfitters for brochures and schedules and information; even if you don't take a trip with one, they can supply you with useful information—you can learn a great deal by studying their data packets. Write to the manufacturers of river-running equipment and to the distributors and the producers of river-running gear for information that will help you in making your selection. Write to the mapmakers and conservation organizations, the white-water affiliates and outing clubs listed in the appendix, and develop a file of specific information on the areas you want to explore. The more you write, the more reading material you'll have.

Do be considerate of your potential correspondents. As a courtesy, send along a stamped, self-addressed envelope for the reply, if you request information. Many of the best sources of information are not in business to supply information nor do they have the budget or personnel to supply requests for unlimited data. And in the name of paper conservation, share the data with others.

DECISIONS AND ARRANGEMENTS

The third step—planning—takes longer, for it involves making basic decisions about what kind of trip you want to go on and what you want to take.

Kinds of Trips

Of primary consideration is whether to go floating with an organized group, on a river trip with friends (who know what they are doing), or even to a school. Or perhaps your ultimate plan will involve several of these and other alternatives, in sequence.

Commercial float-trips have sprung up all over the country—wherever there seems to be a demand for white-water boating. Probably the best single source for information on the commercial float-trip is Pat Dickerman's *Adventure Trip Guide,* revised in 1974. Also, the Automobile Club of Southern California publishes a concise list of outfitters on 13 western rivers in a pamphlet called *Riverboat Trips,* and many state and federal agencies and local chambers of commerce will be happy to furnish you with a list of outfitters in a particular area.

Several national organizations listed in the appendix sponsor float trips on various rivers, and numerous outing groups—including local chapters of national conservation clubs and affiliates of the American Whitewater Affiliation—offer river trips. Some universities even offer credit for float trips as environmental-education workshops, and a few offer river-running courses.

White-water schools, like commercial-float-trip operations, have appeared everywhere, especially in the West. In many parts of the country the American Whitewater Affiliation local chapters offer weekend white-water training, and participation trips are, in a very real sense, white-water schools, even if they aren't billed as such. You learn fast.

Specific white-water schools I can recommend include Ann Dwyer's Canoe Trips West (P.O. Box 61, Kentfield, CA 94904); Bill Belknap's Fastwater Expeditions (Box 365, Boulder City, UT 89005); ARTA's American White-Water School (1016 Jackson Street, Oakland, CA 94607); Gay Staveley's Canyoneers ROWorkshops and Follow-Me Floats (Box 2554, Grand Junction, CO 81510); Jerry Bentley's Orange Torpedo Trips (Box 1111, Grant's Pass, OR 97526); and Vladimir Kovalik's Wilderness World White-water School (1342 Jewell Avenue, Pacific Grove, CA 93950). This list is strictly for western rivers; in the East, try Jon Dragan's Wildwater Expeditions Unlimited, Inc. (Box 55, Thurmond, WV 25936) and Ralph McCarty's Mountain Streams and Trail Outfitters (while they aren't white-water schools *per se*—though McCarty offers a kayak course—they are good learning experiences as participation trips).

Most ARTA trips have an instructor and training raft along for people who want to learn the skills of white-water sport. (Courtesy of American River Touring Association)

Hiring a guide to run your boat or lead your group is another good way to get an idea of what river running is all about. But it can be ticklish because of specific regulations in some areas—you might end up being classified as an outfitter and need an expensive license (in Idaho, for example). Check local regulations carefully with the appropriate authorities, and don't necessarily take the guide's word for it. Contact the various guides' associations for suggestions.

Planning the Menu

To eat well on the river, you have to plan and pack carefully beforehand. Kayakers often feed on backpacker fare to keep load-weight down—unless they are followed by support rafts—and canoeists like to go light if any portaging lies on the route. Inflatable floaters, on the other hand, can usually haul heavier loads and consequently may eat better.

One of the best ways to be well-fed on a river trip is to keep a detailed list of all items you use on a trip, indicating what you ran out of and what you had too much of. After a year or two, you will have a list indicating just how much you need of numerous food items for a given number of people. By developing such a dynamic food chart, you can plan more accurately, keeping weight down by leaving at home unnecessary items, yet eating well and rarely running short.

There is no need to use expensive backpacker food, but you may want to use such items as instant hot cereal, packaged corn bread or muffin mix, Bisquick, and other standard "instant items" such as Tang, sour cream, gravy, etc. that can be made quickly by adding water to a mix. Fresh fruits and vegetables make good salads and help keep people "regular" on the river, an important consideration on extended trips.

It also pays to premix many foods before you pack. For example, the dry mix (baking powder, salt, and sugar) that goes into pancake batter, the flour, and the dried milk can all be packaged ready for a batch—or two batches or three, depending on the size of the party. Just mix the milk with water,

A kitchen setup, again a specially made box to carry basic kitchen utensils and staple foods. It folds up into a convenient box to carry in the boat and opens to provide a worktable for cooking, with everything handy. Note the trash bag hanging from far side of box, griddle by fire spit, and grill made of angle iron. (Verne Huser photo)

use the 2-2-2 rule (eggs, cups of flour, cups of milk), and add the dry mix, and you've got almost instant batter. You can do the same for several fine desserts.

Meat and any other perishables should be handled carefully.

Proper pretrip planning and packing can help assure healthy traveling. The large ammo cans still available at many military surplus stores are ideal for packing food for river trips and, except for certain staples, it is best to pack by the meal or by the day.

In one can, pack everything that you will need for lunch, except the perishables and items that should be kept refrigerated—which should be packed conveniently close to the top in the ice chest. Most river runners have a rather standard lunch fare: sandwiches of cheese and sliced meats, tuna fish and sardines, peanut butter and jelly, and some olives and pickles, potato chips and Fritos, maybe fresh fruit, lettuce and tomatoes, something cold to drink, and perhaps cookies and candy bars.

Plan a balanced menu for the cooked meals—dinner and breakfast—and pack breakfast items on the bottom, as they will be used after the dinner items on top. Again, perishables should be refrigerated, perhaps even frozen when you start the trip, but each night's meat should be thawed during the floating day.

Pack food items in a logical manner, and you'll save a lot of frustration on the river. It is also a good idea to mark cans with a key to what each contains: drinks, lunch, breakfast, snacks, extras, etc. And cover your ice chest to keep it away from the heat but don't bury it so you can't get to it easily.

Keep careful records of what you use on various camping trips, and you can develop a valuable checklist. Careful planning before you head for the river will assure you of good food on the trip—if you pack it carefully in waterproof containers.

Transportation

You will also need to make transportation plans, not only to get your party and rafts to the river, but to have everyone and everything picked up downstream at the end of the trip (since rivers don't run in circles). Kayaks and canoes must be hauled on racks, and some floaters—especially professional guides on short trips of only a few hours duration—have trailers built for their inflatable boats. However, many inflatables will fit into the trunk of your car.

As for transportation at the end of the trip, you will need a shuttle or ferry so you can get home when you're off the water. This may mean that someone in the party cannot make the trip or that you take someone along to serve as driver. Or you waste good river-running time shuttling the cars.

If several cars are involved, you may simply shuttle—either before or after the float trip—using one car to haul all the drivers back to the launch area; this method works better for short shuttles, and you do have to leave at least one car at the take-out point. For longer shuttles, you may want to hire someone to drive a car around, an expensive business because it usually involves two drivers (one to pick up the shuttle driver so he won't have to spend several days waiting). It may seem very complicated at first, but work out the details so that the final plan goes smoothly and don't forget the car keys.

An ARTA party camps and cooks — it's chow time — at Elk Bar on the Middle Fork of the Salmon River, my own personal favorite campsite on one of my favorite rivers. (Courtesy of American River Touring Association)

6

River Routine

Though river trips are led and taken by a variety of people, in a variety of crafts, for a variety of reasons, to some extent they all follow the same basic format. And when you have assembled your boat, gear, and food, checked out rules and regulations, laws and licenses, made all final arrangements for transportation and guidance, and have actually arrived at the river, your trip will probably follow a somewhat preordained course.

RIGGING

The first step is getting ready to go out on the river—or rigging. This involves unrolling or unfolding the boat, inflating it, attaching the frame and floors, and getting it ready for the river. Then the boat must be packed and everything tied down before you are finally ready to launch.

Launch areas may be crowded unless you've picked your time carefully. Some heavily used rivers even have a starting-time schedule just like your favorite golf course, so

103

Busy launch ramp on the Middle Fork of the Salmon. (Verne Huser photo)

don't take up too much space or time or you'll be part of the problem. (If you've practiced rigging a few times in your basement, garage, or backyard, you'll have it down to a system.) Be organized and be considerate. You'll have an opportunity to learn from watching others because there are as many different rigging procedures as there are rigs.

Unload your rigging gear and river baggage, keeping the two separate but close together so they won't get lost or be in the way. Spread out boats and pump them up. If you have a source of electricity or a portable generator—or can borrow one—you may be able to pump the boat with an old vacuum cleaner with the hose reversed. As an electrical source, it is also possible to use the battery of the vehicle that brought you to the river, if you have a converter or if you use the Coleman portable inflator (better test this at home too; I've run a battery down in this manner). Be sure you have at least one hand or foot pump, the one you plan to carry along on the river for topping off boats every morning.

You might want to send a rigging crew of two or three people to the launch site early so that the basic work is done by the time the party arrives with personal gear, but if you have the man- and womanpower standing around watching, put them to work to reduce the time you need at the launch site. The boat can be pumped while the gear is being unloaded (if you've packed carefully), and rowing frames can be put together (if they are the break-down kind) by one group while another sorts gear. But keep the party together as much as is practical so that you don't get in other people's way.

Plan your trip as much as possible to avoid conflict with others. Don't occupy the launch ramp itself with your rigging operation, especially if it is crowded. Let other parties play through rather than cause them delays if they are ready to launch before you are.

Know your order of rigging priorities so you won't waste time. It's a good idea to mark all equipment by boat and by position. For example, B-ff might mean Bevo (name of boat), front floor. Be organized, even to the point of being absurd; it will save time on shore and give you more time on the river.

When you are inflating your craft, it is best to position the frames and floors when the boat is slightly soft; then the top-off pumping tightens the whole rig. Most floors will have to be placed in the boats before the rowing frames are positioned, even though the frames will normally have to be in place before the floor can be attached. You may want to put the boat in the water before you put the frames and floor in place—it will depend upon your rig and the crowd at the launch site—but most people rig on shore and then wait until the boat is on the water to actually load gear, party equipment, personal bags.

Check all fastenings. Tighten every bolt. Snap every gate. Tighten every strap. Secure every chain. Make sure that everything is tight and ready *before* you load. Also be sure to tie on at least one line. Boats should have both a bow line and a stern line, and it's a good idea to run a small line, preferably

Boatman assembles contoured aluminum frame to fit Salmon River boat in background (top), prepares to place completely assembled frame in boat (center), and then completes the rigging and loading process.

In the loaded Salmon River boat (below) ammo cans with food are tied down in the foreground, providing a foot brace for boatman; ice chest is tied in beneath seat for boatman; boatman's waterproof gear bag is wedged in next to ice chest — all on suspended wooden floor. Note wooden floor in front of compartment, resting on a network of nylon webbing (under the floor).

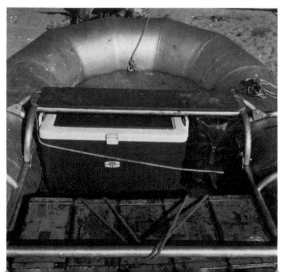

This aluminum frame, contoured to the boat, has enough flexibility in its joints to absorb most of the motion of the boat in a rapid. (Verne Huser photos)

nylon (goldline), around the boat at water level or just above for people to grab if they do get thrown out or the boat capsizes (a wet boat is hard to hold if there are no ropes). The boat should have plenty of D-rings to tie all the necessary ropes on to. You'll probably want to attach the spare oars or sweeps or paddles where they will be handy but not in the way, where they won't be broken or come loose in heavy water.

Now you're ready to load and secure gear. A bit of advice on loading gear. Pack heavier gear low, the more waterproof bags in the potentially wet spots, and the soft gear near the top of the load (it's usually lighter), especially if you expect passengers to ride on the load. Be careful to keep abrasive surfaces free of causing damage and sharp corners well padded. You should pack a first-aid kit on every boat and the repair kit in the sweep (last) boat along with emergency signalling equipment.

My rule is tie everything down, everything. Some of the sweep-boat operators tie down nothing, relying on the hope that they won't flip, but I've seen some mighty big rigs tossed about like matchsticks in the big rapids and folded like toy balloons when they hit an obstacle.

Some people simply tie down the load and leave it open to the elements, but most river runners prefer to tarp the load. I like to tie down the load, then tarp it, and then tie down the tarp. That may seem like a lot of trouble and call for a lot of rope, but it pays dividends in dry sleeping bags and clothes when you get off the river. And if you pack carefully, the day-bags can be kept handy, even under the tarp, so people can get to their personal items without much trouble during the day when their other bags may be packed at the bottom of the stack of gear.

There is one thing, however, that should never be tied down: the people. In no way should a person ever be tied to the craft. The 18-month-old daughter of a ranger in one of the national parks was nearly drowned on her first float-trip when, tied to the boat, she was sucked underwater when the boat was swept under a tree. Only mouth-to-mouth resuscitation—after she'd been cut loose from the raft—saved her life, and her parents still had a five-mile walk out with the infant barely breathing. One of the recent drownings on the Chattooga resulted from a man's tying himself to his boat, which flipped. The eight minutes it took for friends to right the boat was a little too long.

Never wrap a rope around your hand or foot; never put your hand or foot through a loop or in any way make yourself fast to the boat—to do so is to invite disaster in certain emergency situations. There have been a number of drownings resultant from a person's being dragged underwater simply

A typical launch site, this one on the Yampa River at Deerlodge Park in Dinosaur National Monument, is a good place to get to know various kinds of boats, rigs, and equipment. The box in the foreground holds food and kitchen gear plus ax and hammer. Note the checklist and menu taped to the lid of this specially built box for river running, measured to fit just right into the boat, where it serves as a foot brace for the boatman of a rowed rig. (Verne Huser photo)

by the force of the flow and because he was tied to an un-yielding object by rope or strap or even by his own life jacket. This is not a chapter on safety, but one can never be safe enough on a river trip, and it pays to be alert to possible problems.

One thing more: use a checklist. Check the list before you leave home, then double check it at the river to be sure you have everything. Some of the rigging gear may go home or on to the take-out site, but keep a list and check off each item as it is loaded. That way, there should be no left-behinds (there always will be, of course, but you add these items to the list for the next trip).

When you launch will depend on several factors: the length of a trip and the distance to travel to the launch site, the shuttle arrangements, the proximity of a campground near the put-in point, whether or not you are assigned a starting time. And though lunch may come before or after launch, it may pay to take a sack lunch the first day of a several-day trip to save time.

ON THE RIVER

Floating

The first boat on the river should be operated by someone who knows the river well, the last boat by the most experienced and responsible person. Each boat is responsible for keeping adjacent boats in sight; no boat should pass the first boat or leave the last boat behind. And everyone should be wearing a PFD; law requires that they be aboard, but common sense says wear them. In some areas, regulations require that they be worn, and passengers and boatmen alike may be fined if they don't. When everything is ready and everyone is seated where the boatman tells him to sit (this depends on the kind of boat and load), untie the bowline, shove out into the current, and feel the force of the river.

A basic routine soon emerges on river trips, short or long:

They're on the river. Every passenger is wearing a PFD, and most have paddles on this New River float trip in West Virginia. Note bailing bucket made from a cut-down plastic Clorox bottle and the river bag marked "Lunch Container: This End Up." (Photo courtesy Wildwater Expeditions Unlimited, Inc.)

launch, exciting chatter, floating, rest stops (stops to explore, sightsee, fish, swim, scout rapids, have water fights), running rapids, and finally landing for the night or at the end of the trip. On extended trips a day's shedule might look like this: breakfast, break camp, float a few hours, lunch, float a few hours, camp early, unload boats, set up camp, cooking and cocktail hour, dinner, cleanup, campfire (singing, storytelling, talk about tomorrow's plans and sites, sights and rapids), bed. Whenever you launch, plan a rest stop every hour or so. The experienced guide can manage this to coincide with side trips to see petroglyphs or pictographs, a

Two good rest stops: Whitie Cox grave just off the Middle Fork of the Salmon (a war hero who left civilization to look for gold in the wilderness, Cox died in a rock slide and was buried here beside a hot pool full of tadpoles) . . .

and an outlaw cave on the Colorado River in Westwater Canyon (stove and bedsprings remain in the riverside hideout used by thieves a few decades ago). (Verne Huser photo)

waterfall, cave, or spring, a good birding area or historical site. Or it may be to scout a rapid. I'm convinced that some boatmen scout some rapids as a psychological buildup for the passengers. Looking at big rapids gets the old adrenaline pumping.

A swim stop is sometimes called for, especially on one-day trips on which you won't be camping overnight, but on many rivers during warm seasons, passengers go right into the water to drift along with the boats. It's lots of fun. However, on at least one float trip, a man drifted away from the boat in the swift current and was picked up hours later on the

At lunchtime on the Middle Fork of the Salmon, a log serves as table for luncheon meat, cheese, peanut butter, and jelly. Punch in pot is made from water right out of the river, but you can't do that on many rivers today (Verne Huser photo)

reservoir below, suffering from acute hypothermia. Another man died of a heart attack in a similar situation. So be careful.

The boatman will brief passengers along the way about bailing, paddling, and landing. Even bailing, a necessary activity to keep the boat light enough to maneuver, gives the passengers a feeling of participation, and if passengers are paddling to control the craft, they really feel a part of the scheme of things.

It's also necessary to know how to slow down and stop, once you've got started. Eddies can help—if you learn to use them. An eddy is a reverse current, slow water, so to speak, that enables the boatman to maneuver more easily.

Landing

Attempt to stop the boat in relatively slow water whenever

possible. It is difficult to land in fast-moving water. And select an open area, preferably a sandy beach, if you can. If you have no experience at landing, you may want to practice a few times in the quiet waters of a lake or mild stretch of river beforehand.

The basic landing procedure is to approach the shore, slowly, at an angle so that a rear corner of the boat, the stern (back) near one side, nudges the shore. At precisely the right moment—and knowing that moment comes only with practice—jump ashore (or have someone else do so) with the stern line and either snub it around a post or rock or tree—or simply provide an anchor yourself. Be sure to keep the landing line ready, carefully coiled and free of obstructions, especially people in the boat. As you jump out, watch your footing. Also watch the shoreline for hazards. Warn your passengers to anticipate a sudden stop as you ease the nose of the boat onto shore. Tie the boat securely, and help the other people off the boat, warning them to watch for slick or sharp rocks, poison ivy, snakes—whatever hazard there may be.

If you are tying up for any length of time, check the shoreline carefully for sharp rocks, broken glass, beaver-cut twigs—anything that might puncture or abrade the boat. If you're landing for the night, be sure you have a safe anchorage, and if you are on a fluctuating stream below a dam—Grand Canyon, Hells Canyon, numerous streams in the East—try to allow for the rise or fall of the river. Watch it carefully and be prepared to retie the boat as the river level dictates.

Precautions

On the river it pays to adjust the tube pressure in your boats, as necessary. During the heat of the day, you may have to let air out of the boats, due to expansion, but be sure to top them off again in the morning so they're tight for the day's run, especially if there will be big rapids.

As for rapids, there are certain ones that most boatmen

A deadman is a log buried in the sand to serve as an anchor for tying boats when there is no tree or rock or sturdy object available. Place a small log in a hole with the boat lines tied to it (top). Bury it in the sand with a rock at one end to offer additional weight (middle — note ropes to boats fanning out from deadman).

Boats tied to the deadman (bottom) are safe for the night — unless the river should suddenly rise, but at this season on this stretch of river there is little threat of that. (Verne Huser photos)

scout every time they run them: Crystal (Grand Canyon), Warm Springs (Yampa), Skull (Westwater), Wild Sheep and Granite (Hells Canyon). Know your river well enough to know which rapids need scouting, and if you're running the river for the first time or at a water-level you've never run, it's a good idea to stop and look it over. As you approach the rapid to scout, don't forget that most accidents happen on shore. Be careful clambering over boulders and look out for snakes, poison ivy, any hazard—don't lose sight of safety in your anxiety to see the rapid. And scout it—if possible—from water level as well as from above. Throw sticks and bark into the river to study the current. Watch other boats go through, if you have the opportunity.

Then choose a route and talk it over with other boatmen. Once you select a route, stick to it, unless it becomes obvious that your choice is a bad one. Indecision (changing your mind or heart in midrapid) may be disastrous, but so may be the wrong decision followed to its illogical conclusion. Sometimes you will see from the tongue of the rapid something you missed from the shore that will cause you to alter your plan, but if you have studied the situation carefully, chances are that your initial decision is a good one. If the boatman ahead of you waves you toward another route, heed his advice; he no doubt sees something from his vantage point that you may have missed, and you should take advantage of his information.

Mistakes in judgment do occur, in spite of careful scouting. The first time I ran Redside Rapid (that's the one with the big rock at the tip of both the left and the center chutes) on the Middle Fork of the Salmon, the crosscurrent at the head of the rapid got misread, even though we'd stopped to scout it. We were pulled too far right by the lateral current and had to cartwheel, running the center chute backwards so that we were out of position to miss the lower rock at the tip of the tongue. We rammed it broadside. Fortunately, we had a tight boat (we'd pumped when we stopped to scout), and I was able

Paddlers stick to their route at Rivers End at moderate water levels on the Yough in Pennsylvania. (Courtesy of Mountain Streams & Trails Outfitters)

to keep the boat moving by letting my right (upstream) oar catch the current above the rock. We cartwheeled off after smashing the rowing frame and taking on a good bit of cold water. A few years earlier there had been a drowning at that very spot when a boat wrapped around that same rock and the current washed a boatman without a life jacket into the icy current.

So use good judgment—and good judgment on the river comes with experience—and be ready to make a quick decision or alter a plan instantaneously. Don't be afraid to change your mind if the situation calls for it, and be ready to act quickly.

CAMPING

Camping adds another dimension to overnight trips, and when and where to camp are important considerations. You may be assigned a campsite on some of the more crowded rivers. There is an advantage to assigned campsites since on crowded rivers without assigned campsites you may actually find yourself racing other floaters for a favorite campsite or being disappointed at finding it already occupied.

But if the choice is up to you, you'll get to play the campsite game, described in Gay Staveley's *Broken Waters Sing*. A good campsite has wood and water, level areas (grassy or sandy are ideal) for sleeping, trees for shade and screen and privacy, perhaps a good fishing hole or an interesting historic or geologic feature. Plan to camp early enough to enjoy it, especially the first day out on an extended trip, because the passengers may be tired from the drive and excitement, the exercise, and just being outdoors.

Military surplus waterproof bags (silver-painted to reflect heat) lie scattered at the campsite at the mouth of the Little Dolores River on the Westwater Canyon trip on the Colorado River as parties set up camp. Note the variety of tents going up. (Verne Huser photo)

Hells Canyon campsite: the kitchen is set up mighty close to the river, which is controlled by reservoir release, constant at this time of year so there is no concern about inundation. For the most part, campers sleep on a grassy bench above the river. The Forest Service maintains an aesthetically pleasing outhouse at the Lookout Creek site. Shelter has been constructed of tarp, tent poles, and rope to protect kitchen from brief thunderstorm. Lone tent on beach is for a sauna. (Verne Huser photo)

When you land for an overnight stay, be sure the boat is secure and at a reasonable anchorage. Don't let anyone get away until they've helped unload the boat(s), and brief them on camp routine before they head for their separate camps.

Setting Up Camp

Float trips leave virtually no impact upon the river itself, particularly if no one litters the water with so much as a cigarette butt, but they do affect the shore, especially at campsites. The less impact you leave at each campsite, by camping carefully, the more people the river can handle before it succumbs to overuse.

A common latrine or toilet should be used. Some campsites will be equipped with an outhouse or john, but cathole sanitation is archaic in this age of heavy use and available chemical toilets. Whatever toilet arrangement is used, a tent

A portable chemical toilet in the shelter of the toilet tent provides the privacy that will encourage people to use it. (Verne Huser photo)

or at least a tarp screen should be provided for privacy—and observe the angle of the sun when setting it up or the camp will be treated to some interesting "lantern shows."

Plan to cook together and share one fire. Individual fires and individual kitchens should be discouraged because of fire danger and their much heavier impact on the river resource. The common kitchen should be near the boats. Cooking chores may be assigned by meal, by day, by boat—whatever plan you like.

Dee Holliday (Holiday River Expeditions, Inc.) has developed a routine I'd like to see adopted on every river in the country: when he finds fire pits at a beach campsite, he gets a

Dee Holliday (center) and one of his boatmen clean up a fire pit left by a careless and thoughtless camper on the Colorado River in Westwater Canyon. Everything from the fire pit goes into a bucket of river water, and everything that isn't natural or that floats is placed in the tin can to haul out with trash and garbage. Ashes and burnt sand are disposed of at the river. (Verne Huser photo)

bucket of water from the river, shovels the fire-pit trash and ashes into the bucket, skims off everything that isn't natural, stowing it in a closed container to carry out with his own trash and garbage, then finally disposes of the burned sand and ashes to leave the beach fresh and clean. The tragedy of it is that he has to do this every time he hits the beach, because too many river runners have too little respect for the resource and spoil it for others.

In general, people don't like rules and regulations, but such restrictions become necessary when people don't use common sense. As people learn to respect the river resource and care for it, there will be less need for new controls and restrictions. If you are assigned to a campsite, stay there. Take good care of it.

River etiquette also says that you never crowd in on another party's campsite. I've seen as many as five different parties camped at Hardings Hole on the Yampa River in Dinosaur National Monument, a really devastating scene that can sour people on river running.

Set up your camp, concentrating activity to reduce impact. This isn't to say you can't go wandering off to fish or watch birds or do your thing, but there is no need to cut boughs for a bed or to ditch a tent or to dig for worms. And don't cut growing vegetation, pick wildflowers, or scar trees. Plan to carry out all your garbage and trash—everything you brought in and then some—and use only dead and down wood for your fire. Take care of the place that enables you to have a unique experience so someone else can have that, too.

After camp is set up and the chores are through you might try some of the activities that have grown up on the river, including stone-skipping contests, the Olympic rock throw (throwing a rock forward between your legs by crouching and holding it with your arms behind your knees), Hells Canyon Frisbee (a little like dodge ball, often played with two Frisbees), even burling (logrolling), and wood-chopping contests.

Floating party hauls a load of wood into camp. At some campsites firewood has become scarce due to overuse. (Verne Huser photo)

Morning Routine

Few people carry alarm clocks on river trips, and most parties go by Indian time (whenever you're ready). During floating season, days are usually long with the sun up early, and parties often find time for a layover day because the river is high and fast.

But if it's river running you're after, you'd better get up early so you can get on the river early. This is especially true in late summer, when the water is low and the daylight hours grow short, so that you may have to work hard to make your destination unless you've planned carefully. The wind can be a factor, too, since it usually blows upstream in the afternoons—better to be off the river in slow-water areas by 2 P.M.

Breakfast on the Colorado River in Westwater Canyon starts with melon and juice (top) set up on a low table created by using water jugs as legs and floorboards as table top. Eggs, bacon and English muffins (bottom) are next. Boats are already pumped for the day. (Verne Huser photos)

Serving line at Geneva Bar in Hells Canyon: Pancakes on the griddle cook evenly on a charcoal fire in a raised fire box supported by pipe legs held in place by thumb screws at corners (note carrying handles also). Guide has typical river runner's knife and pliers in back pocket. Coffee pots keep hot on charcoal in same fire box. (Verne Huser photo)

The first one up should probably start the fire, even if you're cooking with commercial fuel. Get hot water and/or coffee on early—many campers depend upon that first cup of the day to get rolling in the morning. Others may want tea, hot chocolate, hot Tang—any number of early-morning hot beverages. Cold Tang or juice helps as serving time nears, but by then the kitchen crew will have organized the meal: bacon or sausage or ham, eggs and hotcakes, biscuits or muffins, perhaps a few pork chops left over from dinner the night before, if the 'coons didn't get into them (you did remember to store your food overnight where prowling animals couldn't get at it, didn't you?).

If you are in a hurry to get on the river, have everyone pack personal gear before breakfast. Set one gang to work

A boatman pumps in the cool of the morning, using a standard river runner's pump on pontoon with a wooden floor suspended by chain from D-rings outside the pontoon. Note ammo cases and oars, one reinforced with tape. (Verne Huser photo)

pumping boats and another to cleaning up the breakfast things, striking the kitchen. Don't rush things, but get organized so everything gets done and you don't have a bunch of people standing around doing nothing. Again, it pays to have someone in charge, to be organized.

On a layover day everyone can sleep in or get up early to fish or hike or whatever, but each day's plans should be announced the prevous evening over cocktails or around the campfire so everyone knows what to expect. On the last evening plans should be made for the take-out and return trip.

TAKE-OUT AND DE-RIGGING

It usually pays to get an early start on the last day of an extended trip, and on shorter trips to reach the take-out well before dark. In both cases this may help avoid congestion at the landing and enable participants to get wherever they're going by a reasonable hour. Whenever possible, make use of passengers for the de-rigging operation; it saves time and makes an appropriate parting gesture. It also helps reduce the possibility of someone's leaving something behind.

When you land at the take-out, consider other parties already there or those who may arrive shortly. Take up as little space as possible and move as quickly as possible. Once again, it helps to be organized. First, secure the boat to the bank, perhaps pulling it as far as possible out of the water (but not into the path of traffic). Untie the load and unload, making use of a baggage brigade line to get everything ashore—all personal and party gear, all equipment, and anything not part of the rig itself.

Then deflate the boat slightly and start to de-rig: Remove the spare oar or sweep; untie the safety lines and coil them for next time; detach the floors and frames, washing both before stacking them on shore. If rigging is the break-down kind, put someone to work breaking it into components.

After everything is out of the boat, assemble a crew of as many people as are handy to tip the boat on edge and use a bailing bucket to slosh it with water from the river to wash out sand, wash off mud—in general, to clean it up a bit. Then carry it out of the river to a place where it can be totally deflated and carefully rolled without its getting all dirty again—if that is possible. (You may have to reroll it at home to get it as clean as you'd like it to be.)

Keep all gear in one place, pack everything in trunk or truck or trailer, tying it down for the trip home, tarping it to keep the dust off or to protect it from rain. You may want to dispose of trash and garbage at the take-out point if there is adequate service, but more river runners are getting into the practice of taking it home to dispose of. Whatever you do, be sure you haul out everything you took in.

STORAGE

For storage between trips or between seasons, be sure everything is clean and dry. Paint and repair before storage, and use boat talcum powder inside the air chambers of the inflatable craft. Store in a cool, dry, well-ventilated area, and plan for the next trip.

7

How to Do It

It pays to understand the river and learn what it does, and my best advice is to watch a river to learn. Just sit on the bank and watch it roar or roll or ripple by. It doesn't even have to be a very big river. You might throw a bit of bark or some twigs or branches or even logs—depending on the size of the river and the violence of the current—to see what the river does with them. What happens to them will vary with the force of the current, with the obstacles (both underwater and above the surface), and with the contour of the river (both its bottom and its banks).

You can even learn from flowing water that isn't a river. One of the most enlightening experiences of my life was playing in my daughter's sandbox with a hose. We made a mini-

(Facing page) A triple rig at the brink of Big Drop (top) in Cataract Canyon of the Colorado River in high water — everyone on board is tense with anticipation, not an eye looking anywhere but downstream. The downstream oarsman pulls hard as the upstream oarsman takes another bite of muddy white-water. As the rig drops into the big hole in Big Drop, it moves smoothly through the swirling water before havoc breaks loose (below). (Photos by Eric Grohe, courtesy Holiday River Expeditions, Inc.)

ature river in the sand with three big looping bends. The water cut banks and deposited sand bars. My daughter was delighted, and I learned a great deal myself, seeing erosion and depositing going on at the same time, as they constantly do on real rivers. On another day, walking down the sidewalk in downtown Salt Lake City, I noticed a stream of water flowing down the gutter. There were a few holes in the paving adjacent to the concrete gutter and a few patches that didn't quite match the street surface. Suddenly I saw eddies and constrictions, convergences and ledge systems—everything I might have observed on a white-water river. So keep your eyes open and your mind working.

You may see a current flowing upstream (called an eddy) or water piling up around an obstacle. Rivers flow downhill, but water does flow upstream, and it does pile up. Though both phenomena seem to break laws of gravity and logic, they do follow fundamental laws of physics.

Rivers offer some other interesting phenomena. For example, in the ocean, the waves move but the water stands still (any given molecule merely bobbing up and down as a wave passes through); but in a river, the water moves and the waves stand still, created by underwater obstacles.

You will also notice that waves and curlers, holes and haystacks remain fairly consistent at the same water level, but as water levels fluctuate with the seasons or with the release of water from an impoundment, the surface features may vary greatly. In general, the higher the water, the faster the flow; the lower the water, the slower the flow. But in low water, more obstacles may appear, causing more surface turbulence. Some waves or holes grow bigger as the water rises, but others are drowned out at high water levels. Some rapids are tougher to run at low water levels because more rocks are showing, but at high water levels, the current is faster and rapids may become more dangerous due to the speed and power of the current and the difficulty of moving a craft rapidly enough to avoid disaster.

The current is no enemy unless you misuse or misread it. If you learn to read it properly—and that includes knowing when not to venture onto the river—its vagaries can be used to your advantage.

RAPIDS

Rapids are created by the river's being dammed by an obstacle, which in effect raises the water level until ultimately the water flows over the obstacle. The obstacle may be a ledge of particularly hard rock, a pile of rock rubble brought into the river by a tributary stream, or a wall of water created by the conformation of the riverbed. Water pools behind the obstacle and eventually reaches a height that enables the water to flow over, through, around, or between the obstacle(s). The increased declivity causes the water to speed up and flow rapidly over the obstacle(s). This increase of velocity may in turn cause a reverse current, commonly called an eddy, in which the water actually flows upstream to fill the hole created by the obstacle's damming effect. Water literally piles up behind the obstacles, and the differential creates waves and holes—irregular piles of water known as haystacks and more regular waves, often breaking continuously upstream, known as tailwaves. A wave that breaks upstream is called a curler. A curler breaking into a hole may create a situation that can hold a boat in place for minutes at a time.

Rapids are classified on a scale of I to VI according to their difficulty. Although a scale of I to X is sometimes used to classify western waters, it is gradually giving way to the other scale.

An interesting account of the various actions of a river in different situations is given by Dr. Luna B. Leopold in his article "The Rapids and the Pools—Grand Canyon" published as part of Geological Survey Professional Paper 669: *The Colorado River Region and John Wesley Powell.* He says "Four types of waves can be distinguished in rapids . . . de-

A series of ledges influence the flow pattern in the Snake River Canyon (Wyoming). (above) Forced into a narrow chute, the water forms a downstream Vee indicating the safe route. A back eddy forms on each side below the Vee. (Verne Huser photo) (right) Forced through a narrow passage, the current spreads out into a pair of back eddies as the river banks recede. (Verne Huser photo)

scriptive of the hydraulic form rather than the geomorphic cause of rapids." And he goes on to describe them (I'm paraphrasing here):

Waves below large rocks or outcrops. These rock masses or blocks force water to pass over and around the obstruction; the water speeds up on the downstream side, causing a hole or deep trough in the water surface: Immediately below that, a standing wave occurs, characterized by water leaping upward at the wave crest and continually breaking toward the upstream side.

Deep-water waves caused by convergences. When a narrowing of the channel forces water from along the side toward the center, often simultaneously from both sides, water piles up near the center, creating the wave series often called tailwaves.

Figure 8. *Constriction waves:* when the current is squeezed in by the banks so that the same volume of water must flow through a narrower slot, it tends to pile up and accelerate. Where the river widens below such a pinched-in place, a reverse current known as an eddy often forms. The eddy line appears at the sheer zone between main current and reverse current. Occasionally, especially in high water, the high waves in the main current contrast sharply with the whirlpools of the eddy to create a dangerous differential.

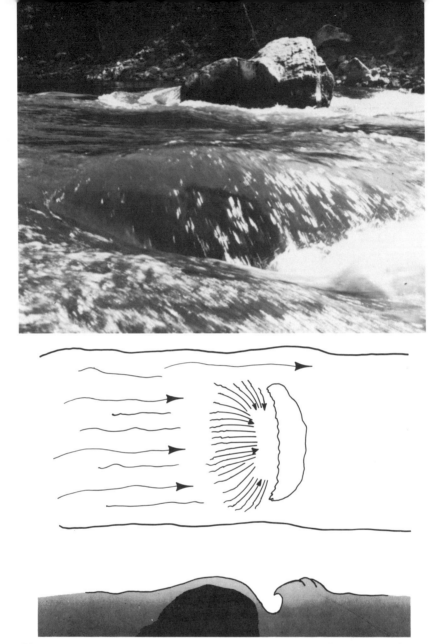

Figure 9. *Hole created by submerged rock:* the current is forced up and over a ledge or boulder, falls sharply over the downstream face creating a hole or trough; downstream water curls back upstream to fill the hole, frequently building into a haystack. Created by underwater obstructions, these waves are basically stationary, but they seem to be moving upstream because of the optical illusion, and the wave may in fact break back upstream into the hole, in which case it is called a curler.

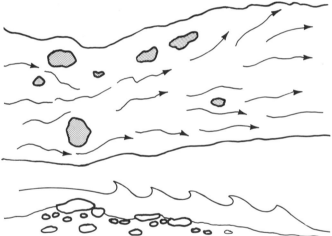

Figure 10. *Series of waves created by shallow water:* the current is forced up and down by the bedrock of the river and/or by rocks along the bottom. The river is wide with no real lateral constriction and has to be read carefully to avoid shallow rocks.

Waves and riffles in shallow water. When water from a deep pool flows out over the obstructing bar, it will flow in a shallow and more or less uniform sheet at higher than usual velocities owing to the steep water slope on the downstream side of the obstructing bar.

Figure 11. *Velocity differential waves.* Fast-flowing water hits deep area where the difference in velocity causes waves to build up due to friction of surface water with deep water. Photo shows water accelerated by partial damming of current by mid-stream rocks. A series of waves is formed downstream (especially in foreground) as fast water hits deep pockets. Notice also that a Vee pointing upstream indicates an obstacle while a Vee pointing downstream usually indicates a passage (often called a tongue).

Waves in deep but high-velocity water. Large waves can occur in very deep water not associated with convergence (my own feeling about this is that here again we have a convergence situation, only the current rather than the canyon's walls are creating the convergence). Leopold explains the pattern of rapids in the Grand Canyon as resulting from a quasi-equilibrium situation in which the river is in a dynamic state of adjusting.

The subject of what rapids are and do is discussed in several books: John Urban's *White-Water Handbook for Canoe and Kayak;* Robert McNair's *Basic River Canoeing;* Peter Dwight Whitney's *White-Water Sport: Running Rapids in Kayak and Canoe;* and Bill Riviere's *Pole, Paddle & Portage.* But at some point you'll have to leave the books long enough to look at a river. You'll have to learn to read water.

READING THE RIVER

For someone who has never been on a river, the term "reading the river" may seem like a put-on, but it is the key to river running. You've got to know what's coming, and the surface of the river offers numerous clues. So does the very conformation of the river—both the riverbed, which makes itself known in areas where it matters, and the shoreline, which—for the most part—will be obvious.

The river knows two basic boundaries—its bottom and its banks—both of which it may be capable of altering if the material is susceptible to erosion. Since almost all materials that compose river banks and bottoms are erosible to some extent—even the Vishnu schist (very hard, very ancient rock) at the bottom of the Grand Canyon—rivers are constantly subject to change. The force of flood waters is fantastic, and given geologic time that force, repeated century after century, has helped carve some of the earth's mightiest canyons.

When riverbeds are composed of several kinds of rock, one may be more erosible than the others. Powell and his men, for instance, dreaded the harder layers of rock in the Grand Canyon because they came to know that this more resistive rock formed barriers, natural dams that created rapids. "The dip of the rocks is to the north and we are running rapidly into lower formations . . . we shall soon run into the granite. This gives some anxiety. At nine o-clock we come to the dreaded rock. It is with no little misgiving that we see the river enter these black, hard walls."

Sighting Obstacles

Sometimes potentially hazardous obstacles are difficult to see. The most difficult obstacles to sight are those that run more or less parallel to the current flow. These are often the most dangerous, not only because they are difficult to see but also because they tend to be sharp (can-openers, they're called on rivers where jet boats operate). Note that a "V" pattern on the water with the point of the "V" upstream usually means an obstacle (rock, tree branch, steel rod from submerged concrete debris), while a smooth "V" pattern pointing downstream means—usually—a chute between obstacles, a tongue, a route to follow.

Ledges, which can create huge suck-holes or holding hydraulics, and diversion dams are also occasionally difficult to see. The water may not build up but flow easily over them, dropping abruptly below the ledge or dam. Certain rocks and logs have the same characteristic and are called sleepers because if you're asleep—that is, not paying attention—you may be caught by one of these subtle hazards.

Barbed wire constitutes a primary nemesis to floaters, perhaps more to kayakers, many of whom carry a handy pair of wire cutters taped to their craft to use in emergencies. A major point should be made here: Rocks are solid barriers; fences and trees are not. Water will literally pile up against rocks, often providing a buffer that will prevent a boat's being swept into or onto the rock or cliff. But water will flow through a fence or the roots or branches of a tree. The current in such situations may pull a boat right into the obstacle. The boat, being held, is in a dangerous position because the force of the current is still playing against it.

White water tells you that something is causing a disturbance. Surface turbulence results from either subsurface

Rocks in river create "white water" as water piles up against them, then flows rapidly around or over the "dam" created by the rock. Current is constricted by the rocks to form a Vee which marks the route to take — unless other obstacles downstream cause other problems. (Verne Huser photo)

or obvious barriers and obstacles. You may be able to see the source of that disturbance if it is a rock ledge extending from the bank, a tree in the water, a previously wrecked boat or a barrier of junk left by someone who lives by the out-of-sight, out-of-mind philosophy of dumping unwanted material into the streams. It's when you can't see the source of the disturbance that you need to develop a keen sense of river awareness which only comes through careful observation and experience.

The Second Time Around

Once you've run a river, don't think you know it. The same stretch of river may be entirely different at a different water level, and as pointed out before, a river can change overnight, especially during high water periods. Always be alert for changes—new snags and trees, rapids and wrecks. I once came around a tight, blind corner on the Middle Fork of the Salmon to find a recently wrecked driftboat lodged on the rock I always had a hard time missing; the wreck narrowed the chute even more.

On a 1959 commercial float-trip on the Upper Snake when I was still a trainee boatman on the rear sweep, we came around a corner and swept quietly into what we called "Spruce Ditch" for the leaning spruce tree that partially blocked that channel, an intimate route. To our horror, we found the tree had fallen during the night and blocked the narrow channel completely. Fortunately it was low enough so that we weren't swept under it. Ramming it, we stuck fast, held against the tree by the swift current. But we were lucky. It was deep enough to find a route without wrecking us. We took the passengers ashore without a mishap, floated the lighter boat over the tree, reloaded the passengers, and went on our way. The captain that day was Frank Ewing.

Spring floods may alter the entire course of a stream—as the floodwaters recede and leave new channels or have perhaps cut through old bends to form oxbows. Flash floods can bring about change even more quickly as when a wall of water roared down Crystal Creek in the Grand Canyon of the Colorado the fall of 1966 and overnight created the worst rapid on the Colorado.

In some instances, quiet water can tell you as much as roaring rapids. Elmer Keith, the packer and guide of Salmon,

Idaho, who has written many books about guns and big-game hunting, was also a river guide for many years in the 1930s, running huge wooden barges down the River of No Return (the Main Salmon) with Capt. Gulicke. On one such trip he recalls running into quiet water where there should have been fast flow. A few miles downstream he found a barrier of rock debris from a landslide that had quite literally created a lake. They ran a chute through the steep face of the dam that was the worst rapid he'd ever seen.

The best way—in the final analysis, the only way—to really learn to read a river is to experience a river trip, preferably with a person who knows something about reading water.

RUNNING THE RIVER

Actually operating a boat by oar or paddle or sweep on the river comes only after you learn what to expect. The object of all these means of locomotion is to move downriver on the surface without hitting obstacles, flipping or swamping the boat, or losing anyone overboard. This involves two basic things: power and control.

Power

The first of these, power, will normally be furnished by the river. On a true float-trip, you simply float along with the current. However, if the current is too slow or if the upstream wind overpowers the downstream current, you'll need to use the means of control to move you downstream. With a sweep boat, that is most difficult, especially on a windy day since the sweep boat must turn broadside to the current (and usually the wind) to perform the power stroke. With oars and paddles, it is a simpler matter: Just push the water upstream with your oars or paddles, and the boat will move downstream.

With one man using an oar as a rudder and other passengers paddling like mad, an ARTA party runs some white water. (Photo courtesy American River Touring Association)

Control

For control with paddles, you simply move the water in the opposite direction from which you want the craft to move. But it is difficult to coordinate several paddles, each held by a different pair of hands and each controlled by a different brain. Performing an action as a unit may be difficult. Paddle trips involve greater individual participation, but more of them end up with the participants in the water than for either oar-powered or sweep-powered trips. In some rivers, during some seasons, that factor should be weighed carefully.

With oars, for the most part, control is achieved by positioning the craft broadside so that the oar, in effect, becomes a sweep. Rowing the craft back and forth across the current, you select the proper part of the current and position the craft correctly to run chutes and catch tongues. Once the boat is in the proper position, however, it is best to hit the slot head-on, that is, with the long axis of the boat into the waves (which, remember, are stationary, though they may seem to be moving upstream). If there are angular waves, it is best to hit them at right angles, as long as such a position won't get you

A well-loaded boat approaches Tappan Falls on the Middle Fork of the Salmon at a slight angle, still getting into the exact position. At this water level, with the fin (rock just off the far shore) showing, there may be only six inches to spare on either side of the boat — the narrow way — but to properly position the boat, you have to broadside it until the last few seconds. Swung parallel to the current, the boat hits the slot with its long axis into the hole and the wave with little room on either side. Broadside, the boat might have flipped and might have been cut by the underwater fin. You've got to know what you're doing to run the Middle Fork. (Verne Huser photos)

into trouble—such as forcing you broadside into a suck-hole. You have to play each situation as it comes, but the basic principles apply: Maintain the broadside position for maneuvering, if you need to reposition the craft within a rapid—unless to do so breaks another principle. Hit big waves and big holes with the long axis across the length. If you must hit a rock or hole or snag, try to do so in such a manner as to bounce off or cartwheel—keep the boat moving or you'll be in trouble.

Avoid obstacles and hazards whenever possible. Avoid hitting rocks, especially rocks that might damage the craft or on which the craft might hang up. Avoid hitting snags and trees, especially those with overhanging limbs or with the potential to damage or hold the boat. Make up your mind early if you have a choice of channels; indecision may lead to your being swept onto the dividing point, which is more often than not littered with logs that have suffered the same fate.

Also, avoid holding hydraulics or suck-holes that might stop a boat and drag it down, capsize it, hold it for several minutes with water pouring into the boat by the freezing ton. Don't let the oars get caught in whirlpools or hit by big waves—take them out of the water—and don't stick the downstream oar into the river bottom.

A sweep boat will have its long axis parallel to the current, and to control the craft so as to miss rocks, the shore, other obstacles in the water, you push the sweep in the direction you want the boat—or one end of the boat—to move. (The sweep handle has a fulcrum point just like the oar; by pushing the handle to the left, you force the sweep blade to the right, an action which pushes the water to the right and forces the boat—or that end—to the left, the direction in which you pushed the sweep handle.)

The sweep boat has the advantage of being lined up for the narrow chutes or slots as it is maneuvered into position—unlike the oar-powered craft, which must be turned to meet the waves once it is in position. The sweep

A pontoon rigged as a sweep boat for hauling gear to accompany a party of drift-boaters on the Middle Fork of the Salmon. One man can handle the counter-weighted sweeps. (Verne Huser photo)

boat is usually capable of carrying a heavier load, and is the least likely to flip—but once it does, it is the most difficult to right, and the damage may be considerable, the loss of equipment and gear, almost total.

Hands and feet may be used to propel or even control a small craft—air mattress, inner tube, some really tiny boats—down a stream, but the water had better be pretty mild in both temperature and temperament.

Motors I have rejected earlier as unbecoming on a float trip, but if the trip ends on flat water—Lake Powell at the end of the Cataract Canyon trip, numerous trips in the eastern United States—it may be wise to have a small motor along.

The motor can be used for power or control, and the individual motor will dictate its use for both.

FLOATING TECHNIQUES

Using the Current

On most floating waters the current will provide the power. Let it. There is no use fighting the force of the water. Learn to use it. If you watch a stream take driftwood, you'll soon notice that the wood moves along with the current. So will the boat if you'll let it.

Of course you will want to control the boat to the extent that it doesn't smash into an obstacle or go aground, but if you learn to read the river carefully, maneuvering can be kept to a minimum. An inexperienced boatman will work five times as hard as an old-timer at the oars or sweeps, simply because he hasn't learned to use the river to his advantage instead of fighting it.

A trio of do-it-yourselfers, who know what they're doing, run the Stanislaus River in California's gold country at the western edge of the Sierra Nevada. (Ray Varley photo)

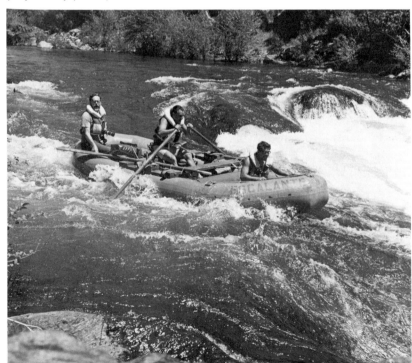

On my first Grand Canyon trip I was a passenger, but I'd already had several years of experience on the quiet water of the upper Snake. I thought I knew something about handling a boat, but when I was given the oars in the relatively slow-moving water at mile 212 or so, I found myself rowing back and forth across the current, fighting eddies and exhausting myself while Don Neff roared with laughter. Since then I've run a lot of white water, and I've learned to let the river work for me, not against me.

Obstacle currents, as I've said before, are caused by the water's piling up on the upstream face of an obstacle of some kind—a ledge, a rock outcrop at the shoreline or in midriver, even a dam or log if it is big enough and the river playing off it has sufficient current. You can head for the obstacle with the boat under control, read the crosscurrents carefully, and catch the swift flow of water around the obstacle that occurs because the water above the rock (upstream) is higher than the water below the rock, and wants to reach equilibrium.

You'll want to be careful not to hit the rock or not to get caught in the back eddy below the rock, unless you plan to use the eddy to stop or slow the boat. (If you are fishing, you may want to hold position to hit the hole where big trout may be lying, and you can also use the eddies below such obstacles to slow down, stop to wait for the next boat, to scout the next rapid, or to land.)

Many simple rapids might be called swing rapids in which a line of rocks from a tributary stream delta forces the current away from that shore. Trying to fight the strong current that takes the boat away from the point you may want to reach is not only frustrating but futile. If you want to continue in the current, simply head for the row of rocks: The current will keep you from hitting them, and as you swing the craft to parallel the current, you will likely follow the flow of water. Pushing with the oar on the eddy side may help keep you in the current, and backwash from the opposite shore may help keep you from swinging too far to the outside of the turn.

If you want to stop below the row of rocks, where there will likely be an eddy and a sandy beach, the best way I can suggest is to back toward the end of the row of rocks that protects the eddy, and as soon as you've passed the last rock, pull hard a couple of strokes and you're in the eddy, which you can ride to a desired point for pulling in to shore.

The eddy line or sheer zone is the churning water between the downstream flow and the back eddy. From this line you can get back into the current or slide off into the eddy with relative ease. In fast-flowing rapids with deep current you may have strong whirlpools that prevent your doing what you want to at this point, but if you feel the water with the oars, sweeps, or paddles—you can't always see it because it changes too abruptly—you may be able to prevent the river's taking you where you don't want to go.

A back eddy is as real as a curve ball. If you've ever played baseball and tried to hit a curve, you know they're real. So are back eddies, so real that they can take a two-ton boat upstream at five miles an hour in a really strong whirlpool. But if you get caught in one, don't panic; just ride it out. You may go 'round and 'round a few times, but it simply doesn't pay to fight the river—unless it's a life-and-death situation, and then chances are good that you'll lose. Avoid critical situations by looking ahead, reading water carefully, planning your moves, and executing them properly.

Using Obstacles

You may also use the obstacles themselves, but you must use them carefully so as not to lose passengers or damage the boat. On the Middle Fork of the Salmon, particularly the upper 25 miles from Dagger Falls to Pistol Creek, you don't miss all the rocks; you can't, especially when the water level begins to drop. You learn to play rock shots: If your boat is tightly pumped—but not too tightly—you can readily carom off this rock to miss that rock, off this outcrop to miss broadsiding that snag, off this wall to avoid plowing into that

A 25-foot pontoon noses through the rocks in Devil's Teeth Rapid on the Main Salmon River. What looks like a tough rapid from this angle is actually "a piece of cake" for experienced river runners, but it does take some maneuvering. (Verne Huser photo)

gravelbar. Avoid sharp rocks and tight spots where you might get a boat caught on a rock and avoid rocks so close to water level—either just above or just below—that you might hang up.

It may seem like a sloppy way to go, and sometimes it is. But in fast, rocky water it is sometimes impossible to miss everything, impossible to maneuver quickly enough to avoid all obstacles. So don't be afraid to use them, especially if you get caught short. And a little experience playing rock shots can be mighty helpful if you get into a tight spot; it may save you if you haven't been reading the water carefully enough.

Once you know what you're doing out there on the river, it pays to practice a little, not showing off, but learning the capacity of the boat, or your own skill, learning what the boat and the river will do in certain situations. I'm not suggesting you be reckless, careless, or foolhardy, but the more different situations you get into and out of, the better you'll know the river and yourself.

Getting Out of Suck-Holes

Suck-holes or holding hydraulics are perhaps the second greatest fear to the river runner (the first, being swept into a partially submerged tree—being caught in any situation where you are held fast with the river still playing upon you). Prevention is the best bet, but even the best boatmen will sooner or later get caught, and it's a fearsome experience.

The story of Three-Oar Deal, mentioned earlier to emphasize the necessity of packing spare oars, is the story of a suck-hole—today called Three-Oar Deal. A party of professional guides and their wives were running a reconnoitering trip down the Snake River southwest of Jackson Hole, in 1972, at a high water level prior to beginning their commercial run. They ran a neat wave created by a tilted underwater ledge, but that ledge created a powerful back eddy with a mass of water 50 feet wide and 100 feet long, rushing upstream to fill the hole below the wave. They ran it correctly, long axis into the wave, but that mass of water stopped them dead, swung the boat broadside, and forced them into the wave. Held by the water and pounded by the wave, they remained in the hole for eight minutes. They broke three 12-foot oars, both regular oars and one of the spares, trying to work their way out of the hole, but the force of the river was too great. It finally spit them out, and they limped downstream for half a mile before they were able to pull out of the river.

With water temperatures 42 degrees at the time, they might have been in serious trouble. Had they not been in a boat with a self-bailing bottom, they might have been flipped into the river.

Now, how do you get out of such a monster? One thing that often happens is that the boat capsizes and washes out of the hole. This usually precipitates the passengers into the river, which may be dangerous, especially if the water is extremely cold. Try to stay with the craft, but don't get caught between the craft and an obstacle; it is wise to stay on the upstream side of the boat. Hang on to the ropes, even climb up on the craft's bottom, but don't get tangled up in the craft. The only time I've been flipped in such a situation, I washed out of the hole and found myself some 20 feet upstream from the boat. I tried to swim, but the river had me, so I simply drifted with the current. In a few seconds, I felt myself swirled out of the mainstream into a small eddy, my feet touched bottom, and I walked ashore.

Waves and canyon walls make quite a scene. (Ray Varley photo)

8

Natural Information

Knowing the nature of the river and its environs not only makes a float trip much more interesting and exciting but also is necessary for safety. Wind, lightning, sun, and even wildlife can be dangerous as well as exciting. The more you know about how to handle natural situations and what to look for in the wilds, the more enjoyable your river trip will be.

Much natural information—specifically data relating to the river and what it does, factors relevant to navigation—has already been discussed. This chapter deals with natural information that relates to safety and also with natural history.

SAFETY FACTORS

Wind and Rain

Wind is a definite factor to consider in river running, because upstream winds are the rule rather than the exception in the afternoon on almost every river you'll run. That means you'll be paddling or rowing—hopefully not sweeping—against the wind during the heat of the day when you're tired and want to reach camp.

Wind can be just a nuisance, but it can also be a danger. Seven of 12 boats that flipped in Lunch Counter Rapid on the Upper Snake River in Wyoming during the high water season of 1972 did so primarily due to wind that held boats long enough for the current to swing them broadside. Wind causes steering difficulties as well, and when you have a tight chute to run, it may become an upsetting factor.

Thunderstorms especially are usually accompanied by strong, gusty winds. Storms don't come up so suddenly that you don't have enough time to prepare for them if you watch the simple signs. (Bill Riviere devotes a whole chapter—worth reading—of his *Pole, Paddle & Portage* to "Canoeman's Weather.")

On one-day or part-day trips you can avoid the weather by not launching. You can also prepare for bad weather to a certain extent with wet-weather gear, and if you like to run rivers in the rain or in the teeth of a gale, have at it, keeping in mind that wind may make it a bit more difficult to maneuver and to get downstream (you should judge your time accordingly).

On extended trips, you may simply have to put up with it. I've floated during snowstorms (usually gentle) and sleet, through hailstones and rain, any of which may be accompanied by thunder and lightning. You may try to wait it out in camp (keep in mind the possibility of the river's rising from heavy rains, especially in narrow canyons) or call it off if you're near a take-out point or a road. On many of the western rivers, this is impossible or impractical, and you need to prepare for the worst kind of weather.

On one mid-July trip on the Middle Fork of the Salmon it rained for five hours, noon till late afternoon, with snow in the high country visible from the river when the clouds thinned. We had two cases of hypothermia on our hands in the heart of the wilderness. On another, a late-March Grand Canyon trip, it snowed on the Rim and we nearly froze to death at river level. We stopped after every rapid to warm up and dry out—and three days later when I left the river party to hike out, I had icy trail conditions for the last mile up to the South Rim.

Lightning

Lightning storms can bring disaster but rarely have. Usually there are better targets for the lightning, but don't tempt the watchful gods. On a big, wide river with a metal sweep in my hand, I've been scared to death, knowing that I was the highest point for a quarter mile in any direction and a perfect conductor, but there was no place to go for protection.

Avoid being the high point. Don't offer sharp points to the skies, especially if they are metal. Lightning has been known to follow the heat of a campfire, so don't huddle around a fire, and don't huddle beneath tall trees. Green trees are better conductors of electricity than are dead ones, but dead trees don't offer much shelter, and the wind from the storm may blow them over or knock down dead branches. Caves may offer reasonable shelter, but a person standing at the mouth of a cave may create just the spark gap needed for the dispersal charge to ground itself.

With lightning there are two things to worry about: the initial strike and the dispersal of the charge. If you receive the initial strike, there's not much to worry about—you've usually had it. Your best bet is to try to avoid the dispersal charge which follows all kinds of natural conductors: wetness, rock, metal, etc. Don't tempt lightning—avoid it if you can; anticipate it and plan accordingly. Your best bet may be to stay on the river, or it may be to go ashore and find shelter—the situation and your knowledge of the outdoors will dictate your choice.

The Sun

The sun on a river trip is more powerful than in other circumstances because you are subject not only to the direct rays but also to the reflected rays beaming off the surface. If you are not properly tanned, wear a sunscreen lotion. Use dark glasses, preferably Polaroid. I've heard some talk of Polaroids being dangerous because they don't actually stop certain rays and actually damage the eyes. Be that as it may, I prefer them. Whatever glasses you use, tie them on with an elastic band so you won't lose them in a rapid.

Wildlife

One more factor to consider in the realm of natural information is potentially dangerous wildlife: bears and buffalo, moose and alligators, perhaps crocodiles in some exotic areas (crocs lie in wait in the quiet pools below rapids to feed on fish and animals battered about by the rapids). On Alaska's rivers, bears may be a problem, and elsewhere in the wilder parts of the United States you may run into bear problems ashore. Anticipate them and go prepared. Keep a clean camp and store your food out of reach and range of nocturnal visitors. Moose and buffalo (a real rarity but present on a few rivers, such as the Upper Snake in Jackson Hole, Wyoming) should be approached with caution on the river, I've been within 30 feet of both species on the Upper Snake without spooking them, but be sure to let them know you're there—don't surprise them or they may panic and attack. Alligators might be found in several of the Gulf Coast states.

The moose cow may be considered dangerous in the late spring-early summer, when her calf is young. Never get between a cow and her calf—any more than you'd get between a sow bear and her cubs—and don't approach too closely. The cow will generally move out of the way of approaching rafts, but if the hair on her back rises and her ears go back, get out of there as fast as you can. The bull is more likely to be dan-

Skunks are common along many rivers, especially if you don't keep a clean camp. This young fellow taking a defensive position among the sagebrush swam the river shortly after this shot was taken. (Verne Huser photo)

gerous in the fall when the rut (breeding season) is on. Bull moose have been known to charge locomotive engines at this time when they consider almost anything that moves a possible rival. I know of no case in which a moose has charged a raft or boat, but I've had some amazingly close to the craft, even frighteningly so.

Always remember this simple fact when you are in wild country: It belongs to the wildlife; you're only a visitor. Respect the animals' home, and you'll be safer and so will the animals. Leave a filthy camp that attracts animals, and you are threatening them. If they become a nuisance, chances are good that they will be killed or "controlled" (a euphemism for killed or removed). If you behave yourself, they will be more likely to leave you alone, and you'll both be safer.

Basaltic columns along the Snake River in Hells Canyon tell the story of ancient lava flows. Much of Hells Canyon is carved from volcanic rock. (Verne Huser photo)

Cactus blooming along the Yampa River in Dinosaur National Monument. (Verne Huser photo)

NATURAL HISTORY

To me, one of the most important features of a river trip is the fauna, flora, and natural formations that one experiences along the way, not only on the river itself but along the shore during stops to explore or camp or scout rapids. A great deal of misinformation concerning plant and animal life runs rampant along rivers, often perpetuated by untrained guides who think they know what they're talking about or don't but try to dupe the tourists who run rivers with them. A good river guide not only knows the river (its currents and obstacles, its campsites and danger spots) but he knows the geology and history, the wildlife and the wildflowers, the trees and shrubs, as well.

For the do-it-yourself floater, I suggest a study of nature along the way, preferably with someone who knows the natural scene, someone who can teach you if you don't know. Field guides are an important aid in this exploration. One of the best field-guide series is the Peterson Series, published by Houghton Mifflin Company, of Boston. It now includes more than 20 guides in handy format available in both hardback and paperback editions. The various books cover everything from birds (including specific guides to western birds and the birds of Texas) to butterflies, from minerals to mammals, from animal tracks to reptiles to amphibians, from rocky mountain wildflowers to stars and planets—all valuable to have along on a river trip where you may discover for the first time in years that there are stars up there and that salamanders live along the river.

I personally prefer the Golden Press (New York) book by Robbins, Bruun, and Zim for bird watching (*A Guide to Field Identification: Birds of North America*) because of the maps and the fact that it covers the whole country better in my opinion than the Peterson *Field Guide to the Birds.* Let me say that I grew up using Peterson and have all of the bird books in his series and use them too, but when I go on a river trip, I take the Zim book along as more practical.

I've used several of the other books in the Peterson series as textbooks when I taught high-school ecology courses in California, in the 1960s: Stebbin's *Guide to Western Reptiles and Amphibians;* Burt and Grossenhider's *Guide to the Mammals;* the Craigheads' *Guide to Rocky Mountain Wildflowers,* Peterson's *Guide to Western Birds;* and Murie's *Guide to Animal Tracks.* All of these are excellent, though some of them deal too specifically with western species (in most cases there are eastern equivalents in the series). For wildflowers in the northern Rockies I find *The Plants of Yellowstone,* by McDougall and Baggley more useful, but the Craighead book, which covers a wider area in less detail, is probably a more useful book for the river runner in the West, especially since the Craigheads—river runners themselves and experts on edible wild plants—give useful information of wild-food sources.

Ewell Gibbons's *Stalking the Wild Asparagus* and *Stalking the Blue-eyed Scallop* are useful to have along on a river trip. I have frequently added miner's lettuce, lamb's quarters, watercress and cattail parts to green salads on river trips, and that hardly scratches the surface of Gibbons's repertoire. A number of good books on wild, edible plants are available at most bookstores, but be sure they deal with the part of the country where you plan to eat out.

Animals

*Amphibians and Reptiles.*River trips are a natural for amphibians and a frequent habitat for many of the common reptiles, some of which are dangerous but many of which are delightful to have around, to observe and study, on and off the river. It may be wise to check with a local or regional naturalist (in person, by mail, by phone) to get advice on the best book(s) on the subject in your area or in the area where you plan to float, if you want to dig more deeply into the subject.

Salamanders come in a number of different sizes and colors and are delightful to observe. Most species of sala-

manders are not as active in the open as other amphibians—except at night, during rains, or during the larval
stage of development. Some larvae may not complete their
transformation, may actually breed in the larval condition.
Found under logs or rocks, in rotten vegetation, in the open in
damp woods, at times, newts especially move about during
breeding season. Pacific giant salamanders and tiger salamanders may grow to six inches in length, but most salamanders are much smaller—only a few inches long (some less
than two).

Toads are, generally speaking, short-legged, rough-
skinned, slow-moving amphibians, in contrast to the long-
legged, smooth-skinned, fast-moving frogs, though many
uninitiated laymen fail to differentiate among them. Basically, frogs are moist and toads are dry; many toads secrete a
substance with an offensive · odor—in some species,
especially some exotics, this may even be toxic—as a protective mechanism. Frogs rely more on their quick, long jumps
and protective coloring for defense. The western toad is the
most common toad on most of the western rivers. Tree frogs
(chorus and cricket) sound off at night or during or just after a
rain or a high-water flash from an upstream reservoir release. They are for the most part small and long-legged; many
are jumpers and/or climbers.

Turtles are especially prevalent in the East, much of the
West being too high and dry for the clan. Snapping turtles are
strictly an eastern phenomenon—east of the Rockies, that is.
Painted turtles range widely north and east of a rough line
from the Louisiana-Texas state line, on the Gulf of Mexico,
to Puget Sound, with a few scattered areas south and west of
that line reporting the species. Sliders and softshells are basically eastern, southern, and midwestern; softshells largely in
the Mississippi River drainage; spiney softshells largely in
the southeast.

Lizards are more common in the west than in other parts
of the country. I've seen the chuckwalla and the collared
lizard on Grand Canyon trips (the collared will run on its

hind legs like some of the dinosaurs apparently did). And fence lizards—both eastern and western—commonly called blue-bellies because their undersides turn a bright blue when they are excited are sometimes sighted. The whiptails, slim-bodied, long-tailed alert lizards that are active diurnally (this species includes the six-lined racerunner common east of the Rockies all the way to the Atlantic Coast) are also seen.

Mammals. River trips are ideal for finding mammals because wildlife finds sustenance and refuge—food, shelter, water—along the streams, and floating with the current is usually quieter than the current itself. If people want to see wildlife and are willing to remain quiet, they will usually be repaid for their efforts. A bunch of loudmouths can spoil a river trip for many people, so it's important to select the right group to go with and to avoid the crowded sections if you're looking for solitude and wildlife.

Deer are probably more numerous today than when the Pilgrims landed, and they are common along most river corridors, East and West. The elk is locally common in many parts of the West. Other members of the deer family—the moose and caribou—are rare in the eastern United States except along the Canadian border. In the West, the moose (Shiras, subspecies) is common along the backbone of the Rockies in Idaho, Montana, Wyoming, Utah, and Colorado with a few in extremely eastern Washington and Oregon (a lone straggler wandered back and forth across the Snake River in Hells Canyon in the fall of 1971, then disappeared). Woodland caribou are known in the Idaho panhandle and adjacent areas in northern Washington and Montana.

Pronghorn, a strictly North American mammal, commonly called antelope, but actually the only species in its family, is common throughout the Western states but is rarely seen on river trips except for approach trips and shuttling. Bighorn sheep, both the desert bighorn and the Rocky Mountain variety, on the other hand, are seen on many western

Bighorn sheep are commonly seen along many of Idaho's rivers, especially the Middle Fork of the Salmon and the Main Salmon. (Idaho Fish and Game Department photo)

river trips: Grand Canyon, Hells Canyon, most of the Idaho river trips, and a few others. Mountain goats are also seen in Idaho, Oregon, and Washington, and the South Dakota-Wyoming state line in the Black Hills Country.

I've seen bison (commonly called buffalo) on the Upper Snake River, in Grand Teton National Park—one swam the river a hundred yards ahead of my raft, another was bedded down on the river bank. But few areas can offer these huge native ungulates.

Bears can be a problem or a hazard, but usually they're delightful to see. I've seen them on the Middle Fork and Main Salmon, on the Upper Snake (a sow with triplets on one rare occasion). The bear's near cousin, the raccoon, is more com-

Beaver, common along rivers throughout the nation, may be most evident through signs — dams and lodges and fresh cuts along the bank — but they do appear at dusk to work throughout the nocturnal hours (R. Morris Brown photo)

mon in the South and East; in the West and many northern climes the air is too high and cold, even for his well-furred coat. Squirrels and marmots and other rodents, such as the porcupine, liven up river trips in many areas, as do bats at dusk and flying squirrels. (Carry a strong light to observe their nocturnal activities.)

Beaver, more than any other animal, change the landscape and make their presence known with their dams and lodges, their cuttings and canals. I've found them in the Grand Canyon and in Hells Canyon, on the Upper Snake (numerous) and on the Yampa and the Green, in southern California and in central Wisconsin. They're found in every corner of the nation with the exception of most of Florida and

A beaver lodge in Jackson Hole, Wyoming, where more than a hundred thousand floaters run the river every summer. Note the cow moose in the background. (Verne Huser photo)

the extreme Southwest—though I've seen them in some pretty unlikely areas even there—and in parts of Alaska. Both beaver and otter are delightful to watch, interesting to study, and on many river trips, you'll have an opportunity to see one or the other or both.

Coyotes are common on many of the western rivers and are extending their range eastward. Coyotes are perhaps more adaptable than any other canine. Only in Alaska and the northernmost contiguous states might you see wolves; they are relatively rare south of Canada. Foxes—grays and reds, and in the West, swift and kit—are bonuses on river trips. They are not commonly seen except during early-morning hours at campsites or late in the afternoon.

Cats are even more rare than the foxes, especially the larger felines. Mountain lions (cougars) still live in much of the West and parts of the South, but they generally stay in the most remote country.

Several members of the weasel family frequent river habitat: otter, mink, long- and short-tailed weasels (ermine in winter), and various skunks. Wolverines are rare, and badgers are less likely to be on the river, though I've seen them on more than one occasion from the river in Jackson Hole.

Rabbits and hares, everywhere; armadillos and peccaries, in the Southwest; opossum in the South and East, and aplodontia (mountain beaver) on the Pacific Coast streams; bats, voles, mice, pack rats, all of these may be part of your river trip.

Birds

Birding on river trips can be fantastic. You have the advantage of reaching a rich bird habitat quietly, unobtrusively. You can't stop when you're on the river to check out a particular bird, and binoculars are worthless on the water, but if you're interested in birds, you can land your craft as often as you please—consistent with your schedule. I used to conduct special birding trips in Grand Teton National Park, stopping at many places along the Upper Snake to check out a marsh or a beaver pond, a heron rookery or an eagle nest, but as river traffic exploded, the park service was forced to post specific areas off limits to intruding man.

I've seen as many as 47 species of birds on a three-hour float trip, as many as 56 on a six-hour trip (I wrote about this in the October 1968 *Audubon* magazine). In Hells Canyon, on a week-long, springtime float-trip, I once logged 73 species, including dozens of Lazuli buntings.

Osprey and bald eagles are common on many rivers. The bald-eagle nest on the Upper Snake in Jackson Hole was destroyed in 1974 when the ancient, dead cottonwood tree in which it had perched for decades blew down in a storm. The

This bald eagle nest on the Snake River in Grand Teton National Park was destroyed in the summer of 1974 when a storm blew down the ancient dead cottonwood tree in which it had been built some two decades earlier. During an 18-year period, a total of 32 eaglets — like the one you see here from the 1969 season — were raised in this nest. Three eaglets died when the tree fell. (Dick Barker photo)

adult birds had raised at least 32 eaglets in the previous 18 years, but a trio of young eaglets died when the nest crashed to the forest floor. Hawks and falcons are also often seen.

Waterfowl are obviously present on many river trips. Canadian geese, sometimes during migration, even snow geese, dozens of ducks, shorebirds, herons and cranes, gulls and terns—all follow the rivers. I've seen the colorful avocets in Hells Canyon; great blue heron on almost every river I've ever floated; the loon and the grebe, and heard their haunting call; the great white pelican; the trumpeter swan.

The green heron, common in the East, I first saw on the Rogue River in Oregon, in 1961. I nearly got thrown out of a boat in Grand Canyon at the head of Horn Rapid when I broke Don Neff's concentration with my identification of a green heron ("Helluva time to be talking about birds").

The American bittern adds its weird cry to night noises on the river. And the sandhill crane, locally common every-

A great blue heron in a Southern swamp, elegant in the plumage that once decimated its numbers as hunters killed the species to adorn women's hats, lives on fish and frogs and other water-dwelling creatures. This magnificent bird is found on many rivers throughout the United States. (Willard E. Dilley photo)

where west of the Mississippi, can be readily identified by its rattling call or its outstretched neck in flight.

Mourning doves are as universal a bird as we have in the United States and the most common and widespread of the native doves. Other hunted species include the bobwhite (east of the Rockies); several western quail; the imported chukar (so abundant in Hells Canyon and on the Salmon river

The great horned owl, one of the more common members of his clan and one of the largest, is frequently heard at dusk from riverside campsites. (Verne Huser photo)

it's like floating through a barnyard); the ring-necked pheasant; several grouse (largely northern and western); and the widely scattered turkey, gone from much of its natural range but transplanted in more than half the states in the southern half of the United States.

Owls may not be seen much during the river day, though I've seen lots of great horned owls on the Upper Snake and even a few great grays. However, they make their presence known at dusk, during the evening hours, and early in the morning, if anyone is up at that hour.

Of the goatsucker clan, only the common nighthawk is found throughout the nation. Known as the bullbat in Texas, where I grew up, this nocturnal insect-eater is common on most rivers at dusk and just before storms—whenever insects are active. (On a Hells Canyon float-trip several years ago, I was reading up on nighthawks one evening and learned for the first time that, "They sit lengthwise on limbs," and the very next day when we stopped to pan gold, we actually saw a bird perched in a pine tree, lengthwise of the limb; sure enough, it was a common nighthawk.) In the East, you'll find the whippoorwill; in the West, the poor-will; and in the southeast, you might also find Chuck-will's widow.

Swifts are common in many western river canyons, and swallows are locally common, especially along rivers in agricultural lands. Jays also frequent rivers.

Flickers—yellow-shafted in the East, red-shafted in the West—and yellow-bellied sapsuckers, hairy and downy woodpeckers, are among the more common piciformes seen on river trips. On the Middle Fork of the Salmon, in the spring of 1974, I saw my first pileated woodpecker ever; a few days later I saw another on the Main Salmon. These spectacular black and white birds with a vibrant red crest are hardly common anywhere in the United States but are found on many eastern rivers and on a few northwestern streams, a thrill to anyone who loves birds and appreciates nature.

Two birds cry for special attention: the water ouzel or dipper and the belted kingfisher. Both birds are common on every western river I've floated. Unfortunately, the dipper is strictly a creature of Western streams, a dark slate-gray bird, wrenlike in body form but about the size of a bluebird, stocky and short. An insect eater, the ouzel will walk along the bottom of the fastest-flowing stream to gather aquatic insects. The name "dipper" comes from its habit of doing deep-knee-bends every time it lands on a stream-side boulder or mid-stream rock. Its favorite nesting place is in the spray of a waterfall, though I've found their nests under bridges crossing fast-water streams.

The kingfisher is known nationwide, north and south. Its sound may attract attention before it is seen, a loud rattling call as it flits on irregular wingbeats from one riverside perch to another. The blue and white birds (the female has a cinnamon belt around her belly) sit on dead branches overlooking the water, then dive for fish in the water below. They will hover before diving, at times, but they catch lots of fish—one reason this beautiful bird is sometimes shot by fishermen who find it a competitor for trout or bass or perch. The kingfisher nests in a bank burrow, one of a handful of birds that build underground dwellings.

The perching birds (passerines)—a few I've already discussed—include most of the smaller birds, impressive for their color or song or unique behavioral patterns rather than for their size. They may be more difficult to identify for the nonbirder, but you don't have to know the name to enjoy the beauty. There are flycatchers and larks, the wrens and thrashers and thrushes, the waxwings and warblers, the blackbirds and finches, the tanagers and the grosbeaks, the sparrows and the orioles. Half the bird book is devoted to these often colorful, frequently songful creatures.

Plants

Vegetational patterns vary tremendously on river trips in different parts of the country—from arctic tundra to dismal swamp, from coastal rain forest to desert, from midwestern farmland to tropical paradise. Wildflowers break through the snow in the spring, and others still bloom through the first frost of fall. During the height of the summer, a dozen species a day may spring forth to blossom along the river, from cactus to violet, from wild rose to domestics gone wild. Many of the Salmon River campsites are old homesteads where or-

Balsam root blooming in early May at Goat Creek on the Middle Fork of the Salmon River less than a mile from its confluence with the Main Salmon. This flower, so common to the arid West, especially in the northern Rockies, paints whole hillsides yellow in the spring and early summer. (Verne Huser photo)

chards still produce fruit (at least one still grows rhubarb for cobblers whenever we camp there). Let me suggest you learn the trees and shrubs and flowering plants of an area before you float its rivers. There are more detailed guides to the flora of most areas. Check with the government agencies and with local natural-history museums or nature groups or botany clubs; check the local libraries and bookstores. Talk with friends and neighbors and local experts, and you learn as you study and float. Most national parks provide checklists of flowering plants as well as of faunal species. It may be worth your while to write for them. But your river trip will be more enjoyable if you know what you're seeing along the way.

Geology

A working understanding of the earth sciences will enlarge your knowledge about what you're experiencing and make clearer why a river behaves as it does in certain situations. Basically, there are three kinds of rock: sedimentary, igneous, and metamorphic, and you'll run into all three on various river trips, often in a matter of a few feet (many of the boulder fields in the Grand Canyon, for example, will have samples of just about everything you could imagine).

Sedimentary rock is laid down by wind or water in layers known as strata, upper layers usually representing more recent periods than the lower layers that they overlie. Igneous rock is fire-formed, the result of molten magma (liquid rock) that has cooled and hardened, either within the earth to be later exposed by erosion, or through volcanic activity on the surface. Metamorphic rock may have originally been either sedimentary or igneous, but through heat and pressure, it has been changed to some other form.

Cucumber Falls on the Youghiogheny in Pennsylvania. (Photo courtesy Mountain Streams and Trails Outfitters)

In general, the story of the earth is most easily read in the sedimentary layers, and it is through this type of rock that so many of the nation's great canyons have been cut. Many of them have also been cut through igneous rock, and a few have reached some of the oldest rocks exposed on the surface of the earth. Metamorphic gneisses and schists are visible in deep cuts such as in the depth of the inner gorge of Grand Canyon or in Westwater Canyon, both on the Colorado River.

Rivers constitute one of the greatest forces continually at work, changing the face of the earth. It is interesting to observe these changes and to decipher the clues to previous changes, to anticipate more changes to come. Wouldn't we have a fantastic film if someone, two billion years ago, had begun taking a time-lapse movie, a frame every hundred years?

Float trip passengers look at a rubber boa discovered on a trip on the Middle Fork of the Salmon in early May. (Verne Huser photo)

You can dig a lot of good geological information out of a library. You might even want to take a basic geology or earth science course at your local college or high school. A number of good geology texts are available at college bookstores, and more popularized introduction-to-geology books find their way into the market every year. Since recent geology also holds many clues to man's short period of time on earth, you may want to move into archaeology and anthropology. Reading such magazines as *National Geographic, Smithsonian,* and *Natural History* provides good background in these areas and offers interesting material for exploration on river trips.

It is possible, I suppose, to become too involved in the sciences on a river trip, to become too pedantic for some people to enjoy, but it seems to me that if you have an active mind and a bit of natural curiosity, you'll want to learn as much as possible about the surroundings through which you float. Here again, it is up to you to make of the experience and opportunity whatever you want it to be—within natural limits. You're not going to find a grizzly bear at the bottom of the Grand Canyon nor a neolithic village on the banks of the Chattooga—but then again, you never can know for sure unless you look.

9

Safety and Health

Nothing can destroy a float trip more quickly than a drowning. Yet every year there are a number of drownings on river trips, most of which could have been prevented. Accidents and illness ruin dozens of river running opportunities every year, but most of them could have been avoided. According to the Stearns Manufacturing Company booklet (mentioned earlier, in chapter 3), from which I quote, with permission, there are several major factors that contribute to death by drowning: 1) injury, 2) poor physical condition, 3) exhaustion, 4) lack of swimming ability, 5) inaccessibility of lifesaving devices, 6) lack of lifesaving devices, 7) improper use of lifesaving devices, 8) inadequacy of lifesaving devices, 9) failure to use lifesaving devices, and 10) water conditions.

(Facing page) Rod Nash relaxes in his inflatable kayak in the still waters of Havasu Creek at its mouth on the Colorado River in Grand Canyon. (Verne Huser photo)

175

Prevention—cautious care to avoid the avoidable—remains the key: good equipment, good skills, good judgment. Safety involves careful planning with an eye to the weather and the water level and necessitates adequate experience in a variety of circumstances. The selection of proper equipment is a function of experience, as is the decision to run a rapid or portage it or the choice of a campsite. Knowledge of a stretch of river or a rapid, and wisdom enough to scout a bad one, may be vital; it is wise to run certain rivers with an experienced boatman the first time through.

PREVENTION

Equipment

The quality of the equipment is essential to the safety of the passengers. It doesn't have to be new, but it should be in good repair. Repair equipment between trips and have it riverworthy when you launch.

The boat itself should be airtight in its flotation chambers and watertight in its bottom—unless you use a self-bailing bottom. A boat full of water may be too heavy to manage and difficult to get to shore. Boats should be pumped tight and tested before launch. Air pressure—between two and three pounds normally—should be checked periodically, keeping in mind that cold water will cool the air in the tubes and reduce the pressure, that hot sun will increase the pressure and expand the tubes. A flabby boat won't respond as quickly or as accurately or bounce off rocks as well as a tight boat, and a too-tight boat may burst. Adjustments should be made to keep the air pressure stable, and boats should be topped off every morning, perhaps before running major rapids, and in response to abrupt changes in temperature, as when a thunderstorm hits.

The floors and frames should be in top repair with no splinters or cracks, weak spots or sharp edges (rough spots can quickly wear a hole in the flotation chambers). You can

This inflatable boat is dangerously low on air; the paddler is almost sitting in the water; the boat will not respond readily to paddle power and is difficult to control. (Verne Huser photo)

wrap damaged gear with fiberglass fabric, but don't expect such repair work to stand alone: replace broken equipment if it can't be adequately repaired. Oars and paddles and sweeps should be in good condition. Always carry a spare oar or paddle or sweep if you're on potentially dangerous waters.

The ropes and chains—whatever you use for rigging—should be sound and set so as not to rub holes in the craft. For rope, nylon is the only way to go if you're concerned about safety. It is stronger and has a resilience lacking in other kinds of rope. The rope used at both ends—bow and stern lines—should be long enough for easy landing and strong enough to hold the boat against the force of the flow. The safety lines should be strong enough to hold the weight of a person against the force of the water or the force of the flipping action of the boat in a heavy rapid.

Personnel

Equal in importance to the condition of the equipment is the condition of the boatman—his mental attitude and assimilated experience coupled with his physical strength and general competence. He must realize fully his responsibility and accept it. His choice of route, his attention to detail, his observation and concentration are vital to the safety of the whole party.

Boatmen need extensive practical knowledge. They should know how to read water, how to position and maneuver a boat to avoid obstacles, how to launch and land and handle the overnight chores in camp. A boatman should prepare himself for a trip in several ways. He must study the river itself, through maps—specific river maps as well as USGS topographic maps of the whole area—and data provided by administering agencies. But he should also talk to other river runners about current conditions. He should know where the nearest phone or radio is located in case of an emergency, and the nearest ranger station, road, and take-out point.

Drinking is part of most river trips, an evening cocktail hour and lots of beer on the river in the heat of the day. Accidents have occurred as a result of a boatman's having one too many, and a good practice is for boatmen to drink only after they're off the river for the day. I don't mean to moralize—just talk common sense.

EMERGENCIES

The most common emergency situations on the river, for which the boatman needs to be prepared, are capsizing in rapids, having someone go overboard, being caught in a hole, and being caught on an obstacle in the current with the full force of the river bearing down. The best account of what to do in these various circumstances that I've seen in print is in the American River Touring Association's (ARTA) *River Guides' Manual* (not for sale but available free to ARTA members—and membership is open to you for $10 individually, $15 for a family). Pages 14 and 15 of that succinct document cover the subject in brief.

Two suggestions from the booklet bear out my advice: "Always wear life preservers," and "never tie a rope to your

This tiny inflatable boat was used by this trio of fishermen to cross the Snake River below Hells Canyon Dam — and not a PFD in the bunch. (Verne Huser photo)

body in any way while on the river." A number of drownings on river trips have resulted from boaters' not wearing life jackets (their other PFDs weren't adequate or weren't used) or from wearing them improperly (several bodies have been found with the life jackets binding the arms of the victim or actually choking him).

Capsizing

A lot more boats capsize than people would like to imagine, but amazingly few people get into trouble when boats flip. An upset can happen to the best boatmen and occasionally does. Bob Yearout, river manager for the Colorado River in Grand Canyon, told me recently that while more small boats flip in the big rapids of that magnificent gorge, injuries are more likely on the larger, usually motor-powered rigs because they are heavier and generally have more hardware banging around to hurt people. Tip-overs, he says, are not necessarily injury- or drowning-related, at least in Grand Canyon.

The only time I've ever flipped in a boat—and I wasn't driving at the time—was the experience I described earlier in which an eddy carried me into shallow water. In Big Mallard on the Main Salmon River in Idaho, in late July on a warm

A 33-foot sweep boat wrapped around the Bump Stump in the Snake River in Grand Teton National Park. No one was injured in this mishap, but they were lucky. This wreck may help to illustrate the power of the river. (Verne Huser photo)

day, we hit the big hole and simply rode the curler up and over. I was thrown free, clear of the boat. Wearing a Type II life jacket, I remained under for several seconds in the cold, churning waters but presently popped to the surface. It is difficult to swim in a Type II PFD since it provides a positive righting moment, but the current had me and I couldn't have done much good swimming anyway. After we all got out, it took 10 men to right the capsized boat, well loaded with tied-down gear. It is the kind of experience you don't like to have but you do appreciate having had—because it is a good learning experience.

Advice on what to do when a boat capsizes varies. Some say "stay with the boat," while others insist that you should "get clear of the boat." Both make sense at certain times. You don't want to stay with the boat if you're being swept down a fast current in cold water. You have a good chance of being struck by sweep or oar or rowing frame as the boat flips, so it may be wise to stay away from the boat as it goes over. There's also the possibility of being trapped beneath the boat, which may be frightening but is often not as dangerous as you might think—though there have been drownings in this situation. One thing almost everyone agrees on: you should get upstream of the craft so as not to be caught between it and a rock, an extremely dangerous position.

But what *do* you do when a boat flips? ARTA's booklet (*River Guides' Manual*) lists these priorities: yourself, other people on your raft, other people on your trip, other boatmen, equipment—in that order. Get away from the raft in the rapid, but try to keep track of everyone, suggests the *Guide,* and check beneath the raft if anyone is missing (on my own flip in Big Mallard, the boatman at the oars when we went over was momentarily caught under the craft but got out with no trouble). A logical step—once the excitement is over—is to right the boat.

One boat-righting technique that you can use after you're out of the rapid, is to climb onto the overturned boat and, using a strap previously tied around the boat, simply stand on one side and fall backward into the water, pulling the boat upright with your own weight. Another method is to get the boat ashore, then tie a rope to the outer edge and have everyone pull while you kick the inner edge out from shore. If water or air temperatures are low, build a fire and dry off, warm up—people could be suffering from hypothermia (discussed later in this chapter).

If anyone is missing when you finally get everything ashore and have time to count heads, start a search immediately, and if it is feasible, send someone for help. Coordinate your efforts so you don't have lost people all up and down the river. Seek assistance from other boating parties, and hope. (See Tom Brokaw's newspaper article listed in bibliography.)

If you have everyone, you'll probably want to get everyone warm and dry before you get back on the river; you may even want to abort the trip if you are near a logical take-out point. If you must go on or decide to continue, be sure that all equipment is in good-enough condition or repair it on the spot. Each flip will teach you a new lesson; each upset is unique and only basic advice makes any sense: Don't get caught by the boat; get the craft and all the people ashore as soon as possible; right the boat and warm and dry the people; then decide what you want to do—after everyone is relatively warm and safe and dry.

Man Overboard

I've only had two people leave my boat on the river in 15 years of floating: a girl sunning herself on the edge of the boat just as we approached Velvet Falls on the Middle Fork of the Salmon and a man walking on the edge of the rowing frame as we entered a rocky stretch of the Snake in Hells Canyon. Both were frightening experiences—for me and for the victims—but both happened on warm days. In the girl's case, the boat nudged an underwater rock, and the sudden contact sent her tumbling into the water; her husband and another passenger had a tough time pulling her aboard because she was well greased with suntan lotion. They had her sprawled out over my oars as we approached Velvet Falls, a real touch-and-go situation for a moment, but we made it in fine style. The man was immediately pulled back into the boat by other passengers, but his wife really gave him hell.

Most man-overboard situations occur when someone is bumped out of the boat in a rapid or washed out by big water. A sudden jolt when the boat hits a boulder or rock wall (a rock shot), or the powerful force of a giant wall of water, or a huge haystack's hitting the boat may be enough to wash passengers overboard if they aren't holding on tightly enough. Often the passengers can be helped into the boat by those who have remained aboard, and occasionally the next wave actually puts them right back into the boat.

If you find yourself in the water because the boat has flipped or because you've fallen or been thrown out, use the same procedure you would use in a capsize situation. Keep

A triple rig works its way through Hance Rapid on the Colorado River in Grand Canyon at the entrance to the Granite Gorge. Two men are actually overboard in this shot, but both were recovered on the next wave. (Verne Huser photo)

your feet tucked up and off the bottom, pointed downstream; this enables you to ward off any rocks and cushion the blow and also prevents head injuries because you're not leading with your head. Don't try to swim in the normal sense, but using a sidestroke or sculling movement, try to work your way to the boat or the shore, depending on the situation. However, don't wear yourself out if the current has you. Ride with it until it lets you go by swinging you into an eddy—unless, of course, you're heading over the falls.

Several books have worthwhile sections on safety and rescue. John T. Urban's *A White Water Handbook for Canoe and Kayak* has a chapter (9) with that very title; and Bob McNair's *Basic River Canoeing* devotes two chapters (6 and 7) to rescue, dividing the subject into a safety code and rescue methods. Bill Riviere's *Pole, Paddle & Portage* devotes chapter 7 to canoeing safety; and the introduction to most guidebooks at least mentions the subject in passing.

Caught in a Hole

One of the main dangers of being overboard or capsized occurs when the person overboard is caught in an eddy or hole and the boat goes booming on downstream—or the other way around.

To get a boat out of such a situation, first, keep the passengers away from the hole so the boat's opposite side is heavier—usually downstream—and the boat is light on the side facing the hole. This allows the boat to ride up and over the major turbulence—hopefully. Next, try to angle the raft so an end or a corner is out of the fierce backwater and can catch the current. Caught in a small hole on the Upper Snake in 1973, I was able to nose the boat into the current by shipping my upstream oar and applying both hands to the downstream oar, but the hole held us for a minute and a half.

You might be able to use the very obstacle creating the hole for leverage to pry your way out of it. Hells Canyon is full of giant eddies, some of them terribly powerful at high water levels. I've known a boatman to circle such an eddy for half an hour and finally jump into the current holding a rope to serve as a sea anchor to finally pull them out into the current. If nothing else works for getting you out of the hole, you may have to resort to that technique, but be sure you are wearing your Type I life jacket and are not tied to the rope.

When a person is caught in such a hole, hopefully another boat will come by and pull him out. If it isn't too far from shore, someone may be able to work a rope out to him. If a boat is caught in the same hole at the same time, there is the danger of the person getting trapped beneath the boat in the swirling currents; check this possibility by sticking an oar or paddle under the boat, but do so with great caution as the force of the water will likely be tremendous.

As dangerous as it may seem—and it could well cause a drowning—sometimes the only way to get out of such a hole is to go overboard, if you're still in the boat, or slip out of your lifejacket if you're already in the water, the idea being to be swept on downstream by the deeper current beneath the swirling waters of the hole. But this technique should be used only as a last resort—like a tourniquet.

A Wrapped Raft

If a raft strikes an obstacle—tree, rock, bridge abutment, snag—and is held there by the current, you could be in big trouble. Chances are good that you'll have people going out of the boat, perhaps to be caught underwater by the current's force against the obstacle. Water flows through the branches of a tree in the water, and people—even those wearing Type I life jackets—could be pulled into the death trap. Ropes and wires and anything that might catch a person in the water are extreme hazards. People have a slightly better chance if they are trapped against a solid object from which the water flows off.

ARTA's *River Guides' Manual* suggests: a) keep off upstream side, stay on rock (downstream) side; b) move all weight to one end of raft and try bouncing; c) try standing on the floor; d) try using oars as levers; e) if possible to do so safely, stand in water and try to lift raft; f) if all the above fails, try pulling the raft off the rock with rope, using the current to its best advantage; and g) if all else fails, wait for the water level to change—if feasible.

A few summers ago I saw one of the cheap yellow rafts caught on the high point of a ledge system across the Upper Snake; the two men in it tried everything. It was a warm day in August, and the water was not particularly cold. I suggested they abandon the raft and swim for it, which they finally did. Sometimes all else fails.

I've had success with shifting weight, bouncing, and prying. On the Middle Fork of the Salmon, where much of the first 25 miles is a rock garden, we play a bounce-me-off game. If a raft becomes lodged on a rock, the raft behind tries to hit it a glancing blow to free it without itself becoming caught. The last raft is out of luck.

A good way to get to know how to react to an emergency on a river trip is to watch other boats run a hazardous rapid. Sooner or later someone's going to make a mistake, and you can learn from that mistake. As you gain experience on rivers, you will no doubt come in contact with other river runners who will be glad to share their experiences with you. For that matter, you can pick the brains of the professional guides with whom you take your first trip or two. You can also learn a lot by reading some of the books I've suggested. (The American Canoe Association draft copy of *Basic Rules for Safe River Running with Rafts, Canoes, and Kayaks* is a good reference.) You'll soon learn that not all the experts agree, and your best bet is to gain some experience yourself.

FIRST AID

I have no intention of offering a first-aid course in this chapter, but I can suggest remedies for several of the common problems you may experience on a river trip. A number of them have already been alluded to in previous chapters. More accidents occur off the river than on, probably because you are likely to spend more time off than on. Then too, people tend to be more careful when they are out of their own element.

Common Diseases

Food- and waterbourne diseases have probably wiped out more float trips than all other injuries combined. Whole parties have quit the river, and some people have even had to be helicoptered out to save their lives. Most of these diseases could be prevented by careful handling of food and water. The Arizona Department of Health Services (Bureau of Acute Disease Control, 1740 W. Adams, Phoenix, AR 85007) document entitled *Communicable Disease Control on River Trips* covers this subject expertly. Let me say here that such common practices as the food handlers' washing their hands before beginning their work in the kitchen; their using kitchen

The tent contains the portable chemical toilet, and the table created by the toilet carrying box serves as a wash basin so people can wash their hands — a simple setup but important to the health of the whole party on a river trip, especially on extended runs. (Verne Huser photo)

knives instead of their own buck knives; even the careful attention to ice chests and coolers can prevent an outbreak. Common sense and careful practices can go a long way in assuring a healthy, happy river trip.

During the past decade, a number of practical "portable johns" small enough to be carried for river trips have been developed. Chemical toilets have been required in the Grand Canyon for several years, not only for commercial parties but for the small, private group as well. Whether or not they are required, they should be carried on any river trip. I've seen too many campsites ruined by cathole sanitation. A prime example is the campsite on the Colorado River in Westwater Canyon just above the mouth of the Little Dolores; barely inside Utah, this BLM administered area is the favorite campsite in the canyon. It is used nearly every night of the season, and there is no outhouse there.

Nor do I want one. It would destroy the wilderness character of the place, but it's being destroyed now by the scattered toilet paper and human feces in every private place within a quarter-mile of the beach. If every party carried a chemical toilet and dumped the treated waste in a particular area (or hauled it out as some outfitters do), the problem could be solved and the wilderness character of the campsite saved.

Common Injuries

Among the most common injuries on float trips are insect bites and sunburn, poison-plant irritation and the normal cuts and scratches, sprains and strains, bruises and occasional breaks of most outdoor activities. Rarely is there a concussion, but serious injuries are always possible as are such conditions as heart and diabetic attacks, heatstroke and exhaustion, and simple fatigue. It is wise to have a doctor along if possible, but it is imperative to have someone well-trained in first aid. Many agencies that license professional boatmen require that they hold a valid Red Cross First-Aid certificate. Before you go into the wilds on a river trip, know something about basic first-aid procedures and practices.

Ticks, bees, wasps, hornets, yellow jackets, mosquitoes—all are abundant on most river trips. Watch carefully for ticks (they can carry diseases); bring along your shot if you're allergic to bee stings; include insect repellent to ward off buzzy critters (I find Cutters the most effective). Keep a sharp eye out for black-widow and brown-recluse spiders, especially under toilet seats and picnic tables and in sleeping bags and shoes—any place dark and undisturbed for a time. Snake bite is always a possibility though I've not heard of a single case on any river trip. Know that the old cut-and-suck method is generally regarded as archaic, that the current concept is to chill the area of the bite (the icy water of some of the streams you may float might be good, but you'll have ice to chill the food you take along, so use that).

Poisonous plants you'll just have to learn to identify and avoid, but take along the medication that works best for you. Calamine is the old standby, but several new products seem to be very effective, and you can now get shots that will prevent a reaction. Check with your doctor on that possibility.

Preventing sunburn is better than treating. Bring along your favorite sunscreen or suntan lotion. If you should be so foolish as to get a burn, bring along a tube of Foille ointment (Carbisulphoil Company, Dallas, TX 75204), which I've been using for nearly 20 years. For other burns, the modern first aid is cold water or ice. Just be careful around fires and hot springs. Burns are painful, not the thing to have with four more days on the river. Be especially careful not to step into the sand where the fire pan stood full of hot coals a few minutes before.

Cuts and scratches, sprains, strains, and bruises can be handled the same way you'd deal with them at home or on any outing. Most are not serious, but all bear watching for any signs of abnormality. Be careful when hiking or clambering up steep slopes to scout rapids, when working your way across slick boulders or through brier patches.

Broken bones suggest careful splinting and getting the victim to a doctor as soon as possible, the pattern you'd follow for any of the more serious mishaps or conditions. In any serious injury or condition or illness, treat for shock by laying the victim down and keeping him warm. Know mouth-to-mouth resuscitation, and use it if necessary. Get help as fast as possible for anyone who is seriously injured or has suffered any kind of serious attack.

Heatstroke and heat exhaustion are serious matters. To avoid them, use plenty of salt on your food and carry salt tablets in the first-aid kit. Drink plenty of water, but be sure it's safe (take along plenty of water if the drinking-water supply is in question). On the chance that someone will need medical attention, you should acquaint yourself with the nearest source and means of help and be ready to respond to the need.

Hypothermia

One further matter that calls for attention here: Temperature loss by the body leads to a condition known as hypothermia, subnormal body temperature. If body temperatures go much below 80 degrees a person may well die if he is not warmed quickly. On river trips this may result from a person's being thrown into the river from a raft or as a result of a boat's upsetting or even from long exposure to cold, wet weather. When water temperatures are below 50 degrees, and especially when they are below 40 degrees, it is vital to get the person out of the water quickly because in a matter of minutes the person may lose enough body heat to cause him to cease functioning. He may no longer be able to help himself.

In Jackson Hole, Wyoming, in the spring of 1974, the Upper Snake reached record levels, with snow-melt delayed until mid-June. Several small boats flipped in the Snake River Canyon where the following episode occurred: Four persons were hanging onto a flipped raft moving down the river in a fast current. A professional guide yelled to the four to let go of the raft and make for shore. Two did and reached safety with no ill effects. At a point of a few hundred feet downstream, a third person let go and swam to shore, but the fourth person stayed with the raft. When number four was finally pulled from the water several miles downstream, he was completely helpless. Hospitalized overnight, he was released the next day, but had there not been a fishing boat on the reservoir, he very well might not have made it.

This is a prime reason that all persons floating during spring snow-melt periods should wear life jackets, not merely PFDs. In fact, cold-weather trips suggest the use of wet suits. Below is a chart from the Stearns Manufacturing Company's booklet on PFDs:

Water Temperature (F.)	Exhaustion or Unconsciousness	Expected Time of Survival
32.5	under 15 minutes	Under 15-45 minutes
32.5 - 40	15 - 30 minutes	30-90 minutes
40 - 50	30 - 60 minutes	1 - 3 hours
50 - 60	1 - 2 hours	1 - 6 hours
60 - 70	2 - 7 hours	2 - 40 hours
70 - 80	3 - 12 hours	3 - indefinite

Somewhat related to hypothermia (too little temperature) is hyperventilation (too much air). A spill into cold water may cause the person to take too many deep, rapid breaths so that his lungs cast off too much carbon dioxide, the compound that triggers our impulse to breathe in air. Fear, tension, emotional stress—all caused by the spill into the water and heightened by the cold water—may bring on the condition that sometimes looks like heart trouble. The victim may be dizzy, numb, faint, suffer muscle spasms and heart palpitation, but the condition can be corrected by having the victim breathe normally for a minute or two or, if a paper bag is handy, have him breathe into it and rebreathe from it.

FIRST-AID KIT

The area will determine the contents of the first-aid kit, to some extent, but certain items are essential: Band-Aids, sterile gauze-pads, triangular bandages, ace bandages, tape and roller gauze; scissors, tweezers, a sharp knife; aspirin, Bufferin, Alka-Seltzer; salt tablets and baking soda; a thermometer; sunburn lotion and various ointments and hand creams (Bag Balm is a must for many river runners); alcohol or some similar antiseptic; perhaps blankets (though sleeping bags that will be along anyway will do); and splints (though improvised materials will usually be readily available). A space blanket makes an ideal first-aid accessory.

Other items worth having along include some sort of sweet oil (olive oil or mineral oil) and petrol-jelly or Vaseline; poison-plant remedies; insect repellent; Q-tips and tongue depressors; sanitary napkins; eye wash and an eye cup; absorbent cotton; campho-phenique; and perhaps a razor.

A snakebite kit may be useful, and on extended trips with or without a doctor (preferably *with*) even antivenom, but the first aider must remember the current treatment for snakebite—cold packs and a constricting bandage, not the old slash and suck technique. The tourniquet has been outmoded for decades as dangerous and should be used only in the most dire emergency when it is the only means of saving a life. I personally don't carry one, preferring to use a triangular bandage should the need arise. A razor may be useful for certain purposes (shaving the hair around a wound, especially on the head, for applying a bandage).

10

Regulating
the River Resource

As I have stressed repeatedly, the rapidly increasing popularity of river running in inflatable craft has put a tremendous strain on the fragile ecology of the river systems used. As overuse began to threaten river systems, regulating agencies responded with rules to control river-running traffic and keep user impact to a minimum. Their struggle continues to be, in many cases, uphill, with increased incidence of success as their experience in river management grows.

THE GRAND CANYON

The Grand Canyon offers a good example of the problems that have been encountered and the solutions that have been attempted. First floated in 1869 by the John Wesley Powell party, the canyon had seen only 44 floaters by 1940, and only

34 people floated it during the 1940s. In the following decade a mere 177 ran the Colorado. Then in the 1960s, river traffic leaped to 14,262, and in the first three seasons of the seventies 37,305 people experienced the thrill of running those dozens of delightful-and-dangerous rapids.

One who did—an experienced river runner who had done Hells Canyon and the Middle Fork of the Salmon—compared the Grand Canyon experience with her trip on the wild Idaho stream: "The Middle Fork was a wilderness experience; the Grand Canyon was a tourist attraction in a wilderness setting." Grand Canyon was being overused in the minds of some.*

The National Park Service realized what was happening before the seventies, however, and made several attempts to put the lid on, to preserve the wilderness character of the Grand Canyon experience (see, "Too Many People on the Colorado" by Peter Cowgill in *National Parks & Conservation Magazine,* November 1971). First they limited the number of commercial outfitters operating in the Grand Canyon (aiming for 20, they wound up with 22), but that didn't work because each outfitter simply geared up for more business.

In 1971 the Park Service instituted a user-day concept. A user day is one day in the canyon for one visitor: a person on a 10-day trip would thus use 10 visitor days. To circumvent this regulation, more of the outfitters turned to motors—or to bigger motors—because by doing so, they could haul more passengers through the canyon during a relatively short season, even though their user-day allotment remained constant. If an outfitter had run 800 people through the canyon on 10-day trips in 1970, he had used 8,000 user days, and that became his allotment for 1971. By using motors instead of oars—or by using a larger motor than he'd used the previous

---

*Sociological and socioeconomic studies prompted by Park Service concern generally found that the ideal size for float-trip parties was the size of the group that the subject happened to be in, a case of selective perception.

year—the outfitter could run 1000 people down the river on 8-day trips. The intent of the Park Service was foiled and the visitor numbers continued to rise:

	People	IOPY*
prior to 1965	1,523	—
1965	547	—
1966	1,067	95%
1967	2,099	96%
1968	3,609	72%
1969	6,019	66%
1970	9,935	65%
1971	10,942	10%+
1972	16,428	50%

The Park Service was trying to insure a quality trip in the Grand Canyon, but many river runners circumvented the regulatory policy. By this time the Park Service was requiring outfitters to carry portable chemical toilets and had phased out certain key areas as campsites in an effort to reduce congestion and the practice of racing for the special features offered by such areas as Redwall Cavern or Elves Chasm. But the impact on the shoreline and on the wilderness character of the Grand Canyon continued.

Still trying to get a handle on the situation, the Park Service issued a new set of regulations (December 6, 1972) aimed at reducing the number of visitor days; phasing out motors; establishing and enforcing strict standards of safety, sanitation, licensing and interpretation; continuing ecological and sociological studies; and ultimately adding the river to the proposed wilderness for Grand Canyon National Park (the Colorado had been omitted from the Wilderness Plan because of the use of motors on float trips).

---

*IOPY=increase over previous year.

+first year user-day concept in effect (note: It took outfitters one season to thwart the Park Service intent).

Several commercial outfitters, by now official con-cessionaires of the park, filed suit, saying the new regu-lations (issued after many of them had oversold their new, reduced allotments) threatened their business. Also, they justified motor use as a safety factor—an argument not many knowledgeable river runners accept, unless it is in their own financial interest. They also launched an effective lobbying campaign both in person, in Washington, D. C., and by letter writing, through their passenger lists. At present, the Park Service, on orders from the Secretary of the Interior, is main-taining a status quo on the cutback and phaseout program.*

The Grand Canyon situation represents the early attempts to prevent overuse and resultant damage to the river resource. It has also been highly publicized, and cer-tainly the Grand Canyon trip is one of the more exciting, one of the more popular.

------

*See National Park Service River Running Policy Statement in Appendix D.

The Grand Canyon of the Snake River (not to be confused with Hells Canyon several hundred miles downstream) is marked by limestone ledges that create some interesting and sometimes dangerous — in high water — rapids. (Verne Huser photo)

THE SNAKE

The *most* popular river, however, is the Snake, floated by well over 100,000 people—three-fourths of them in Grand Teton National Park in Wyoming—the summer of 1973. (Inflation and the energy crisis seem to have reduced the use, slightly, the summer of 1974.)

Not long after Grand Canyon National Park had established a ceiling on the number of commercial outfitters, Grand Teton followed suit, for proliferation on the Snake was rampant. Attempts had been made as early as 1968 to get a better hold on the situation and to upgrade the quality of the trips through Park Service regulations related to passenger safety and comfort, but float-trip traffic continued to increase:

	People	IOPY
1965	14,482	25.5%
1966	18,174	43.8%
1967	26,131	43.7%
1968	29,623	13.4%
1969	40,589	37.0%
1970	51,397	25.5%
1971	68,036	32.4%
1972	71,256	4.7%
1973	75,408	5.8%

(Several things about these statistics are significant: First, the relatively small increase in 1968 reflects both bad weather and initial attempts by the Park Service to control the situation; second, increase was steady and great until 1972 when the Park Service applied the concession concept [18 concessionaires were licensed that season on five-year contracts]; third, the concession concept seems to have slowed the growth rate—and the energy crisis may augment that trend.)

The situation in Grand Teton is different from that in Grand Canyon. While numbers are greater on the Snake than

At the mouth of Pistol Creek, two separate parties stop for lunch after the thrill of running Pistol Creek Rapid. Congestion occurs most frequently at launch and landing areas, at rapids and "special places" on the river that everyone wants to stop and see. (Verne Huser photo)

on the Colorado, the impact is less because there are few overnight trips, and the river banks are closed to camping. It is a much shorter haul: Most Grand Teton Trips run three hours; the others, either one or six hours with only one concessionaire operating extended trips similar to those on the Colorado. Therefore, impact is concentrated at the launch and take-out sites.

THE OBSTACLES

Lack of Research

Despite the apparent differences, however, one similarity exists: no one knows the carrying capacity of the river. Some believe that in both cases the river is presently being overused, but there is little quantitative evidence. A number of studies are currently under way to evaluate carrying capacity and develop reasonable management plans for the agencies who have jurisdiction over various stretches of rivers.

In a letter from the Department of the Interior (November 7, 1972) concerning carrying capacity for rivers, the need for research was stressed: "Determining the carrying capacity of natural areas of any kind is a complex problem, one which has not received the attention it needs. . . . In all of our discussions of the problems, we have found we lack the scientific information necessary for making sound decisions." This was one of the points made in the outfitter suit against the Park Service concerning the proposed phaseout of motors in Grand Canyon and the visitor day cutback. The outfitters stressed that the Park Service regulations were arbitrary and capricious since they were not based on quantitative evidence.

Thus the need for sound research seems evident—and the lack of it is glaring. It is easy enough to set the limits for an opera house or a baseball stadium where seating capacity is determined simply by the number of seats in the facility. But how do you determine the "seating capacity" of a national park or the use level of a river? Four thousand people on the Middle Fork of the Salmon may be enough, while 40,000 on the Upper Snake may not be too many.

Jurisdiction

Another major problem is the question of jurisdiction. Different administrating agencies have different goals, and many times there is mixed jurisdiction (BLM regulating one side of the river; the Bureau of Indian Affairs, the other) or scattered jurisdiction (one jetboat operator in Hells Canyon complained recently, "At the present time there are at least 18 different governmental agencies which exercise control in the Middle Snake"). The agencies who administer the adjacent lands rarely have the budget, personnel, expertise, or legal fiat to regulate the rivers before overuse becomes a problem; consequently they are reluctant to get involved until it's too late.

Today, however, they are being forced into exercising authority by the proliferation of float trips, the increase of river traffic, the problems related to overuse, and even law suits.

The Middle Fork of the Salmon is one of the instant wild rivers set aside for protection under the 1968 Wild and Scenic Rivers Act. Under the jurisdiction of that act, the Forest Service has put into effect some of the most stringent regulations for any stream in America. A special Middle Fork District, carved out of several ranger districts embracing the Middle Fork in several national forests, was established to deal with the problems. Note the traffic on this popular wild river:

A 17-foot Salmon River boat drifts placidly down the Middle Fork of the Salmon. (Verne Huser photo)

Year	Number of Boats	Passengers	Pounds of Garbage*
1967	329	1,299	1,375
1968	398	1,396	1,736
1969	466	1,264	2,633
1970	741	3,028	4,293
1971	793	3,250	2,468
1972	1,135	3,972	926
1973	1,346	4,372	2,775

Forest Service control efforts on the Middle Fork included limiting the number of commercial operators (1972), assigning campsites before launching (1972), and requiring outfitters to haul out trash and garbage. By the end of the 1972 float season (and it is relatively brief on the Middle Fork—only about 10 weeks), the wild river ranger had developed a management plan for 1973. Basically it called for an eight-day turnaround schedule (no outfitter could launch a trip more frequently than once every eight days); a limit of 30 passengers per trip, in no less than two separate parties camping separately; and campgrounds assigned before launch. Private parties were required to have reservations too. Under this plan traffic showed only a moderate increase between 1972 and 1973.

Concerning the matter of garbage, the worst year was 1970, the year of the big burst, and the Forest Service wasn't really ready for it; they played cleanup boy for the river runners. But by 1971 they began to take control, and garbage pickup along the river dropped sharply as the river runners began their own haul-out program, enforced by the Forest Service. In 1972, with strict control—outfitters were assigned numbered bags—the Forest Service garbage pickup dropped remarkably. It rose in 1973 because the service made a concerted effort to clean up all kinds of ancient debris: cables and wrecked boats and litter of long-standing.

*hauled out by Forest Service river patrol

HMS-PNP. What does it mean? This dam-builders' graffiti in Hells Canyon on the Snake River marks the proposed site for the High Mountain Sheep Dam to be built by Pacific Northwest Power. Teen-agers who leave their initials like this are considered vandals. (Verne Huser photo)

Thus the Middle Fork administrators seem to have controlled the situation there as the Park Service has in Grand Teton by assuming the authority and studying the situation, learning from others and from their own mistakes, and through cooperation with Western River Guides Association.

SOLUTIONS

The Western River Guides Association (WRGA), a group of some 200 professional guides and outfitters in the western states, has been working for years to bring some reason into the float-trip regulation picture, trying to educate the agency personnel to the problems and offering responsible solutions. The WRGA began by inviting representatives of the regulating agencies to their semiannual meetings, held in Salt Lake City until the fall meeting of 1973 when the group broke precedent to meet in Boise, Idaho. After several years of attending WRGA meetings, the various agencies finally decided to hold a meeting of their own the spring of 1973—the day before the WRGA meeting—since all of them would be in Salt Lake City for that session. A lot of open minds partici-

I found this mess at Johnson's bar in Hells Canyon. Evidence suggested jet boaters, but people in all kinds of water craft are capable of littering — and of cleaning up after themselves. (Verne Huser photo)

ated in that inter-agency meeting, and a lot of good has come out of it as more agencies in more areas turn to the cooperative approach.

An interagency committee was set up among the Bureau of Land Management, the National Park Service (both under the Department of the Interior), and the U. S. Forest Service (under the Department of Agriculture) to study river problems and recommend action. The initial draft of the Whitewater River Management Guidelines was developed by the Park Service for the February 1973 meeting, but a second draft included comments and cooperation with the other two agencies. A third draft was carefully and thoughtfully discussed at the November WRGA meeting in Boise, and a fourth draft was distributed in early 1974.

Although every agency has had its share of negative reaction from river runners, basically there is a cooperative attitude between administrating agencies and most river runners, and continuing efforts to communicate are made. The WRGA, for instance, sponsored a Hells Canyon Management Plan Workshop for the Forest Service in May 1973 to

help orient some of the agency personnel to the problems of
river running as the commercial operators see them. The participants (including one representative of the Bureau of
Outdoor Recreation and several conservationist writers, as
well as a number of Forest Service personnel) spent three
days floating the river, a day jet boating out of the canyon,
and several days studying background material, visiting
campsites, and discussing the problems around the camp-
fires in the canyon (in just such a session back in 1870 the
idea of a national park first grew to germination in
Yellowstone).

Only three commercial outfitters were running Hells
Canyon in 1971, and one of those ran only one trip. By 1972
there were 7 outfitters, and by 1973 there were 13. As a result
of the workshop, a management plan was developed that
froze the number of commercial operators at 17 and limits
them to 30 people per party, including boatmen. The Forest
Service has adopted the eight-day turnaround schedule for
the 1975 season, based on the Middle Fork Plan, and while
chemical toilets were not required for the 1974 season, a number of outfitters had begun to use them anyway. An arbitrary carrying capacity of 3000 visitors (2500 commercial,
500 private) was established, but, "Capacities will be
adjusted annually, if necessary, based on annual site sur-
veys to correlate site condition and use," according to the
management plan.

Another example of cooperation between the WRGA and
regulating agencies involved the Snake River Canyon a few
dozen miles downstream from Grand Teton National Park in
Wyoming. This stretch of Snake River was virtually uncon-
trolled through the 1972 season. In September 1972 a member of the WRGA invited the Forest Supervisor to a meeting
of Idaho members of the WRGA in Idaho Falls; he sent a representative, who subsequently attended the November and
the February meetings of the WRGA, the interagency meeting in Salt Lake City in February, and the Hells Canyon

Management Plan Workshop in May. By the time the 1973 float season opened in the Snake River Canyon, the Forest Service had set up some guidelines and a major monitoring program.

What they learned was that some 27,364 people floated that stretch of river, probably more than twice as many people as had floated it the previous year—but there were no accurate records. The river itself was rarely congested, but the launch and take-out sites were often crowded. Late in 1973 the Forest Service issued regulations: Active outfitters were restricted to the same number of boats used in 1973; new outfitters were allowed only one boat if they hadn't operated in 1973; new floaters would be assigned launch times and areas not to conflict with established use; no overnight camping would be allowed, and all parties stopping for meals would be required to carry portable chemical toilets. The lid was on, not so tightly as to interfere with established business nor so loosely as to allow further exploitation of the river. (Plans are also under way to establish more permanent launch and landing sites to alleviate congestion.)

River running continues to increase as a means of recreation, both the short day-trips and the extended trips involving camping along the shorelines for days at a time. Do-it-yourselfers at this point are increasing more rapidly than commercial operations, many of which have been limited by agency regulations. But a cooperative spirit seems to pervade the ranks of river runners and administrating agencies more today than ever before, and some real progress is being made in the protection of our river systems, both through the Wild and Scenic Rivers Act of 1968 and through the people involved in the float-trip business, both private and commercial. Research is badly needed to set ultimate guidelines, but the wheels are turning in the right direction. Not all problems related to river running have been solved, but the climate is there for some significant improvement in the total picture.

Passengers participate as paddlers on Jon Dragan's commercial float trips on the New River in West Virginia. Note the precarious position of the guide at the rear of the craft. He has his toe braced to a safety line inside the boat. (Photo courtesy Wildwater Expeditions Unlimited, Inc.)

Rivers to Float
with an Inflatable Craft

In suggesting rivers for inflatable floating, I make
no pretense: I haven't floated a river east of the Mississippi,
nor have I run all the western rivers I'd like to. I call upon the
experts in an area for much of the information I offer here.
Many of them I know personally. Others I know through correspondence. And a few I know only by reputation.

I don't intend to be comprehensive but rather to suggest a
river or two or three within a day's drive of any place in these
United States and some in Canada, so that everyone reading
this book can find at least one runable river fairly close to
home. But I only suggest. It is always best to check out the
situation locally with the various federal and state agencies
I've mentioned elsewhere, with local outing groups or white
water clubs, with outdoor or conservation organizations.
Addresses for many of these are included in the appendixes.
Dig out the sources of information that will help you.

Let me issue a mild admonition: If you call upon a group
or organization with which you are not officially affiliated,
pay your own way. Send along a self-addressed, stamped

envelope if you request information by mail. And make it easy for the information source to reply by sending along a dollar to cover postage, time, and trouble. Most of the groups that may provide the best information don't have professional staffs or budgets to cover the services you may request. Be considerate, and you are more likely to get what you want.

One of the best sources of information is the professional guide or commercial outfitter. Most national parks, monuments, and forests in which commercial float-trips operate; state agencies; and local chambers of commerce will provide you with a list of guides and outfitters in an area. Organizations like the Western River Guides Association, the Eastern River Guides Association, and others (see Appendix A for addresses) can furnish you with a list of members and often with brochures and schedules.

Another good source is a book called *Adventure Trip Guide,* by Pat Dickerman. This book, revised in mid-1974, lists outfitters, guides, services, and associations throughout the nation with a special section on float trips. If you don't find it in your local bookstore, order it from Adventure Guides, Inc., 36 East 57 Street, New York, NY 10022.

One of my most difficult problems in pulling this information together has been to determine what rivers are raftable with inflatable craft. Some waters are better for small boats—inflatable canoes and tiny dinghy-type boats such as the Avon Redcrest or the Zodiak Simplex—while other waters almost require larger craft. I've seen some pretty small boats on some pretty big rivers (like the tiny, yellow Japanese-made two-mans used by one commercial operation on the Snake River in Hells Canyon), but to a certain extent, the size of the river dictates the size of the boat.

Most books about river running in the East deal primarily with canoes and kayaks, and information about rafting *per se* is limited. A few of the books mention that a particular stretch of river is more often rafted than canoed, but it is obvious that rafting hasn't been big in most states east of the Rockies.

Several books have come out in recent years that deal, at least in part, with where to practice the art, which rivers to run, etc. Bill Riviere's *Pole, Paddle & Portage,* obviously written for the canoeist (its sub-title is "A Complete Guide to Canoeing"), has a good section (chapter 17, "Canoe Country") on rivers to run. Many of the streams he mentions might be good for rafting, but if there are too many dams or the water is too shallow or too rocky, inflatable floating may be limited to the Pyrawa-type of craft. A great deal of information developed for canoe- and kayak-floaters may be applicable to inflatable floaters as well.

Michael Jenkinson's *Wild Rivers of North America* includes a major section on "106 Wild Rivers to Run," his chapter 12, which mentions rivers all over North America. He gives specific details on the Rogue, the Salmon (including the Middle Fork), the Green and the Colorado, and Suwannee, the Yukon, the Buffalo (Arkansas), the Rio Grande, as well as the Rio Urique in Mexico, and much of the canoe country around the Canadian border west of the Great Lakes. Much of Jenkinson's information is applicable to inflatable floating, but try to check out the situation locally.

The floatable river—like gold—is where you find it, and rivers worth running dwindle every year as more dams are built, more streams are channelized, more watersheds are timbered; as civilization encroaches upon the untamed parts of the world and as more people run rivers. Some river runners consider wild and scenic river designation a kiss of death for a stream, because such designation almost invariably means heavier use, and without proper management, increased use can destroy a river almost as quickly and as surely as any other abuse.

A good river for inflatable craft is one wide enough for the craft (inflatable canoe to pontoon), with enough water to float the craft and not too many rocks (it's difficult to por-

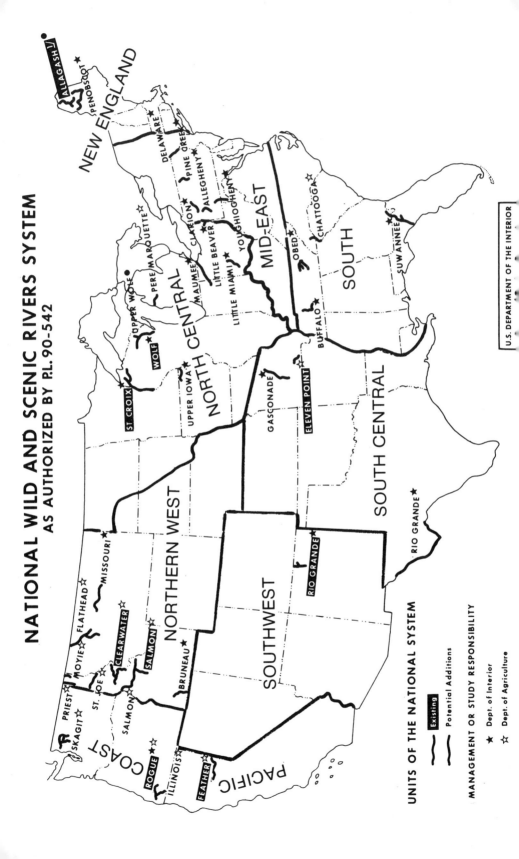

NATIONAL WILD AND SCENIC RIVERS SYSTEM
AS AUTHORIZED BY P.L. 90-542

UNITS OF THE NATIONAL SYSTEM

■ Existing

┃ Potential Additions

MANAGEMENT OR STUDY RESPONSIBILITY

★ Dept. of Interior

☆ Dept. of Agriculture

U.S. DEPARTMENT OF THE INTERIOR

tage most inflatables above canoe size), dams or obstacles—man-made or natural. A scenic shoreline, solitude,
the opportunity to get away and meet nature on her own
terms are fine extras.

For the purpose of suggesting at least one area within a
day's drive of your home where you might run a river with an
inflatable craft, I have divided these United States into eight
areas: New England, the Mid-East, the South, the North Central, the South Central, the Northern West, the Southwest,
and the Pacific Coast, (see map). Also, I have included a
section on Canada.

NEW ENGLAND

There is a lot of good information about rivers in New England—though little of it is directly related to inflatable floating. The Appalachian Mountain Club's (AMC) *New England
Canoeing Guide* has good introductory information on river
running and serves as a guide to streams in sixteen (16) major
watersheds in New England. Headquartered in Boston,
Massachusetts (5 Joy Street 02108), the AMC handles books,
bulletins, journals, maps and guidebooks, one of the best of
which is John T. Urban's *A Whitewater Handbook for Canoe
and Kayak,* mentioned earlier. The AMC is one of several
AWA Affiliates in New England.

In Maine, the Allagash Wilderness Waterway, part of the
National Wild and Scenic Rivers System, is closed to inflatable boats, even inflatable canoes, but it is a fine canoeing
stream.

A unique organization concerned with flood-plain
management, water quality, wetlands, and wildlife is the
Farmington River Watershed Association, Inc. (195 East
Main Street, Avon, CT 06001). Membership includes individuals, communities, businesses; services include providing
public information on the watershed for outdoorsmen and a
60-page guide to the largest and longest tributary of the Connecticut River.

A canoe party on Maine's Allagash River stops to make camp at Long Lake Dam. Note the center-loaded gear, including convenient-to-carry boxes, and the rocky shore line where you can sprain an ankle if you're not careful. (Courtesy Maine Department of Conservation)

New England is the canoeist's, the kayaker's paradise, and much of the water used by these hard-hulled river runners can no doubt be used for inflatables, but there's a lot of flat water in New England, long hours of heavy rowing for rafts. There is plenty of white water too, especially in Maine, but inflatable floating hasn't caught on in New England as rapidly as it has in other parts of the U.S., perhaps due to the long tradition of canoe use and the more recent popularity of kayaks. Rafters need to be aware of dams and water levels (many New England streams run out of water by mid-summer), but much of this information is available from the hard-hulled habituals—check with your local white-water affiliate.

THE MID-EAST

This area is probably the center of inflatable boating activity in the East, especially the three-state area of Pennsylvania, Maryland, and West Virginia. Here run the Cheat and the New, the Shenandoah and the Savage, the Gauley and the Youghiogheny, the Potomac and the Bluestone—fascinating rivers all, and each a unique experience.

Easy weekend trips are possible on any of these rivers from Washington or Baltimore, Cleveland or Columbus, Pittsburgh or Philadelphia. Commercial float-trips are available through several outfitters in Ohiopyle, Pennsylvania and Thurmond, West Virginia: Ralph McCarty's Mountain Streams and Trails Outfitters, P. O. Box 106, Ohiopyle, PA 15470, and Jon Dragan's Wildwater Expeditions Unlimited, P.O. Box 55, Thurmond, WV 25936 are two.

Several good books cover the details of these rivers pretty completely. I especially recommend Bob Burrell and Paul Davidson's *Wild Water: West Virginia* ("They were there and paddled 'em all"). Randy Carter's *Canoeing White Water River Guide* is good, too, for Virginia, eastern West Virginia, and North Carolina, even eastern Tennessee and Georgia, and South Carolina streams. The Pittsburgh Council of the American Youth Hostels, Inc. (6300 Fifth Avenue, Pittsburgh, PA 15232) handles a number of books on river running and lists a number of other publications on the subject and tells you where to get them.

The Penn State Outing Club (Canoe Division, 60 Recreation Building, University Park, PA 16802) publishes a mimeographed booklet, "Select Rivers of Central Pennsyl-

Making the turn at the Dimple during high water on the Youghiogheny.
(Courtesy Mountain Streams and Trails Outfitters)

vania," that deals with Pine Creek, the Yough, and the
Shenandoah Staircase, a series of ledges just above the railroad bridge at Harper's Ferry. Commercial float-trips by raft
are run out of the Kampgrounds of America (KOA) campground at Harper's Ferry — a possible source of information.
The Penn State College of Agriculture publishes an excellent
map of Pennsylvania showing all the waters of the state,
including watershed boundaries, a useful tool for the river
runner.

The Youghiogheny is probably the most popular floating river in the East for inflatable craft, with commercial outfitters alone hauling more than 60,000 people down its raging
rapids in 1974 (there are reports of as many as 200,000 people
a season floating the Yough — rhymes with knock — when
you count private and commercial parties in every kind of
craft; this is roughly twice as many as float the Upper Snake
River in Jackson Hole, Wyoming, the most popular river-
running area in the West). The seven-mile run from Ohiopyle
to Stewarton has a dozen or so class 2 to 4 rapids, good, fun
white water with just enough danger to make it thrilling

(there have been 13 fatalities on the Yough in the past decade, all in inadequate craft, less a reflection of the craft than the judgment of the floaters). An 11-mile stretch below Stewarton has some nice class 2 and 3 rapids — a good intermediate run — but it ends on a reservoir, which means a lot of rowing or paddling at the end of the run.

A 10-mile stretch from Confluence to Ohiopyle is a mild run, not bad for inexperienced boaters as it has only class 1 and 2 rapids, but don't miss the landing at Ohiopyle, or you'll go over the falls. Farther upstream in Maryland (Sang Run to Friendsville) lies a stretch of white water with several class 5 and 6 rapids (class 6, remember, are potential killers). "One of the toughest rivers in the east, even for experts,"* this stretch has gradients of more than 100 feet to the mile, dropping over ledge after ledge through a beautiful gorge — if you have time to see it.

"The Cheat—in the canyon section — is a mean, rough, tough, nasty river with some class 4 and 5 stuff in it," says Ralph McCarty of Mountain Stream and Trail Outfitters, which took more than 3,000 paddling passengers down the

---

AYH Canoeing Guide: Western Pennsylvania/Northern West Virginia.

The Maze Rapids in the Cheat Canyon at low water level, West Virginia. (Courtesy Mountain Streams and Trails Outfitters)

canyon in a six-week season in 1973. The roughly 12-mile
stretch between put-in at Albright and take-out at Jenkins-
burg has "at least 38 rapids of class 3 or greater difficulty,"
say Burrell and Davidson, who call it "an extremely beautiful river tumbling through essentially a wilderness canyon."
Commercial rafting trips run from mid-April through May—
and that's the season for this stretch of the Cheat.

Several stretches of the Casselman River, a tributary of
the Youghiogheny, offer good floating possibilities with
inflatable craft. Mostly class 1, 2, and 3 rapids mark a 25-mile
stretch between Garrett and Harnedsville that should be
good for the inflatable floater.

If I seem to dwell on the three-state area where Pennsylvania, West Virginia, and Maryland merge, it is because no
area in the eastern United States has more rafting activity. It
is also within reach of the majority of the population, and the
waters are infinitely floatable. But in each of the states not far
from this nucleus there are other fine rivers for floating.

The New River in south-central West Virginia has carved
what many people call the Grand Canyon of the East between Thurmond and Fayette Station, a fabulous piece of
white water that boasts of the heaviest flows in the East. Full
of stoppers and souse holes and whirlpools, the New flows
through the canyon in a series of remarkable rapids (class 3 to
5): Surprise, Upper and Lower Railroad, The Keeney Brothers
(triplets—Upper, Middle, and Lower), Sunset or Double Z,
then another trio—Old 99 Hook, Greyhound Bus Stopper, and
Tipple. "Deep yogurt," as a river-running buddy used to say.

As with many of the rivers in this part of the country,
there are adjacent stretches that are runable, but either poor
access or slow water or dams (or both of the latter) discourage floaters from using them with any degree of regu-
larity. If you have the time and want to get away from the
more heavily used areas, and if you don't mind rowing or
paddling or portaging (most rafts in this area are paddled) for
miles, you may want to try such sections.

Jon Dragan (P.O. Box 55, Thurmond, WV 25936) runs commercial float-trips on the New from May through October. His 30-mile trips start at Prince near McCreery. He provides transportation from Thurmond and back and runs to just below Fayette Station—so his passengers can get in one more rapid just below the bridge, a "multi-holed roller coaster with some deceptively vigorous drops in it hidden by the big waves," according to Burrell and Davidson.

(To give you an idea of its location, Thurmond is 612 miles from New York City, 581 miles from Chicago, and 545 miles from Atlanta—fairly centrally located for people living in the eastern part of the country.)

Dragan, by the way, also runs the Bluestone in very early spring and the lower Gauley when the water's right—but only with experienced rafters. Burrell, who has run this section with Dragan, says "The lower Gauley is for *expert* rafters and not just anyone who can afford a raft," and he means it; there have been fatalities here even with rafters who knew what they were doing—it's dangerous.

Pine Creek in north-central Pennsylvania has carved a fabulous canyon known as "the Grand Canyon of Pennsylvania," which offers a fine, fairly mild ride (compared to some of the rivers just mentioned). Put in at the town of Ansonia on U.S. 6—or for a longer run spoiled slightly by the presence of a main highway—at Galeton (also on U.S. 6). From Galeton to Blackwell (a logical take-out because civilization begins to crowd in at this point), you can run roughly 30 miles; if you don't mind a secondary road alongside, you can run all the way to Waterville (just west of Williamsport) for another 40 miles. The lower stretch is slow and less wild than the upper reaches, but most of this run is good training water for bigger stuff. The 9-mile run from Ansonia to Tiadaghton is the Grand Canyon proper, a deep, green canyon with only one real rapid (Owasee, a good 2 or light 3). There are commercial raft-trips on this section (Ed McCarthy, The Antlers, R.D. 4, Wellsboro, PA 16901).

In Maryland there's the Savage, which drops 163 feet in less than six miles, but like the Yough, 100 of those feet are in the first mile. It is one almost continuous piece of raging white water, more frequently used by kayakers than by rafters. At 800 cubic feet per second (cfs) it is mostly class 3, but at 1200 cfs it goes up to a solid class 4; above that level it reaches a nasty, even dangerous class 5. Alas, the Savage is controlled by a dam, and floaters must depend upon reservoir releases, usually four a year: late March; sometime in May (perhaps Memorial Day); Labor Day weekend; and sometime in November (check with local authorities or with local white-water clubs for more specific information).

The Yough, the Cheat, the New—take your pick; the Gauley, the Savage, the Grand Canyon of Pennsylvania. All are within a day's travel of major metropolitan areas in the East—or at least are possibilities for a weekend trip with an overnight or two. Much of the country through which these rivers flow is full of historic sites and scenic beauty, national forests and state parks with plenty of campsites. Inflatable floating lies within your reach.

THE SOUTH

The South has not been a major rafting area. Canoes have been popular in many areas, and a wide variety of john boats have been the traditional means of floating southern rivers. In recent years, as rafts have become more readily available, some inflatables have come into use, but by and large the South has not seen much inflatable boat use except in a few local areas.

There is perhaps too much flat water in the South—both sluggish streams and reservoirs—for rafting ever to become as common as it is in some quarters. As a recreation I & E officer for the Forest Service in Alabama wrote me, "None (of the rivers in Alabama) are suitable for rafting, as I visualize that sport, because of rock shoals, narrows, beaver dams and other obstructions." But in the hill country and mountains there are some fine streams, and with a little imagination and perhaps a lot of rowing or paddling, many of the popular canoeing streams might be run with inflatable craft.

Probably the most popular stream in the South for inflatable raft trips at present is the Chattooga, which flows out of North Carolina to form part of the Georgia-South Carolina state line. Flowing between the Chattahooche National Forest (Georgia) and the Sumter National Forest (South Carolina), the Chattooga is experiencing an average of about 1500 people per week in some type of craft (certainly by no means all inflatables). Forest Service officials who administer the popular stretch of river attribute its popularity to two things: 1) the Chattooga's nomination as a possible wild and scenic river, and 2) the release of the movie *Deliverance,* which was filmed largely on the Chattooga.

Ervin Jackson, Jr., in an excellent article in the March/April 1974 issue of *Wilderness Camping,* has described the Chattooga. He also suggests—as I have elsewhere in this book, in relation to all rivers—that you should make your first trip with someone who knows the river. The Chattooga has been especially hard on boaters. In the past three seasons (1972-1974) no fewer than 18 people have drowned on this rocky river. Forest Service officials attribute these drownings to the following causes:

1. lack of experience—little previous river experience or none at all;
2. lack of river knowledge—no realization of the power of running water, inability to recognize a dangerous rapid, or to avoid one,
3. failure to use safety procedures and equipment (most drowned individuals either were not wearing a PFD or were wearing it improperly, and it came off);
4. high water—the majority of drownings occurred during flood conditions in the steep drainage system of the Chattooga where flash floods are common.

I'm not trying to frighten anyone but just present the facts to let people know that river running is a serious—and can be a dangerous—activity, that it pays to use common sense and standard precaution, that experience is probably the most important single factor in safe river running. Get some experience before you try it on your own (even selecting proper equipment requires experience).

The Forest Service breaks the Chattooga run into four sections: I—from Burrell's Ford to S.C. Highway 28; II—from S.C. 28 to Earle's Ford (Whetstone Road); III—from Earle's Ford to U.S. Highway 76; and IV—from U.S. 76 to Tugaloo Lake. *Section I* is extremely steep and shallow and not recommended for floating; it has a narrow range of runable water and is dangerous to run at any level. *Section II* is an easier float-trip over small shoals and rapids with nothing above a class 3; it is recommended for family trips, beginners, even inner tubes. *Section III* includes a number of class 3 or higher rapids, including Bull Sluice, where a number of the drownings have occurred; it is recommended for intermediate boaters, and no inner tubes are allowed. *Section IV* is as challenging a stretch as can be found east of the Mississippi River, according to Jim Barrett, district ranger. The seven-mile stretch has eight class 5 or 6 rapids, and the last half-mile, called the Five Falls, consists of five class 5 and 6 rapids back to back. This section is recommended for only the very experienced boaters.

Be sure to check with Forest Service officials before you try the Chattooga. Regulations governing river use include the following: 1) All floating traffic must have approval of the U.S. Forest Service through written registration. 2) Inner tubes are allowed only on Section II. 3) Rafts which do not have a minimum of two air chambers; air mattresses; motored craft; or any other float craft deemed by the Forest Service to be unsafe or otherwise unsuitable are not allowed. 4) Coast Guard approved PFDs are required for all persons and *must be worn.* 5) There is a minimum of at least two persons and two float craft per float party (violations are subject to fines of up to $500 and/or imprisonment for up to six months). For specific information on this area write to the U.S. Forest Service, Andrew Pickens Ranger District, Star Route, Walhalla, SC 29691.

Commercial outfitters on the Chattooga River include the following: Whitewater Ltd. (summer: Long Creek, SC 29678; winter: 154 Marshall Terrace, Danville, Va.); Nantahala Outdoors, Inc. (c/o John Kennedy, UU 19 at Wesser, NC, Bryson City, NC 28713); Southeastern Expeditions, Inc. (c/o Claude Terry, 1317 University Drive, NE, Atlanta, GA 30306).

Two rivers in Tennessee are worth mentioning here: the Obed and the Buffalo. The Obed is currently under consideration for inclusion in the National Wild and Scenic Rivers System; the Buffalo is already a part of that system, though its preservation predates the federal Wild and Scenic

Bowman can fish while the sternman paddles the canoe along a slow-moving Tennessee stream that has cut a gorge through layers of sedimentary rock. (Courtesy of the Tennessee Game and Fish Commission by David Murrian)

Rivers Act by six months: The State of Tennessee had the foresight to pass a state scenic-rivers act even before Congress got around to it.

The Obed flows through a deep, relatively inaccessible gorge in the Catoosa Wildlife Management Area. Barely 12 miles in length, this scenic white-water canyon provides a pleasant float. The put-in point is on Big Daddy Creek, which flows into the Obed a couple of miles downstream. Some three miles below that confluence is a class 4 rapid; several class 3 rapids keep things lively. The take-out is on the Emory River a short distance below the Obed's confluence with that stream; in effect, you can float three streams for the price of one, but you'd better plan to float it before July unless you hit a rainy summer—it runs too low for floating most years.

The Buffalo is floatable for more than 100 miles. It is a slow river, certainly too slow for those looking for exciting white water, but it makes an excellent training river and an ideal get-away-from-it-all experience. This is a year-round trip that offers good fishing and interesting tributary streams.

Black Creek, which flows through DeSoto National Forest in the southeastern part of Alabama, offers another good training float run. With a current of barely a mile an hour, you'll have to work, but you can run a 42-mile stretch or various short segments thereof. It trains the muscles and gives the beginner a feel for the river, but don't expect to train for the Chattooga on Black Creek—it's an entirely different situation when you get into white water.

The Mississippi River itself has great potential for inflatable boats. A delightful article in the St. Louis *Post-Dispatch,* by Jim Creighton, documents a Boy Scout cruise down the mighty river. To white-water enthusiasts, the Mississippi may seem like dullsville, but you can make a river trip what you want it—within limits, of course—and an inflatable boat trip down the Father of Waters may be just the ticket to an entirely new vacation concept. Huck Finn, of course, initiated the idea more than a century ago, but the spirit seems to have been lost somewhere along the way. With a little imagination and a little information, a big pontoon with sweeps—why, you could have a ball, and think of the energy saving.

SOUTH CENTRAL

Major rivers in this six-state area include the mighty Mississippi (already discussed briefly in the section on the South); the lower Missouri (a big slow, mostly muddy river in this area); the Rio Grande (forming the border between Texas and Mexico and offering some delightful floating experiences); numerous fast-flowing, clear-water streams that head in the Ozarks; and a scattering of smaller local streams, some of which I'll mention in passing.

Certainly the Ozarks—mostly Missouri and Arkansas—offer floating. Leonard Hall, author of *Stars Upstream* (a book about floating the Current River) and a man who has been floating Ozark rivers for decades, says, "The rubber raft doesn't seem necessary (for safety) or otherwise especially adaptable to our rather mild streams." But Dr. Neil Compton, like Hall a conservationist and floater by canoe and john boat, says, speaking of inflatable canoes, "I believe that such craft would be the answer to boating on many of our headwaters in the Ozark uplands."

Hall writes: "Our float streams are, from east to west, the St. Francis (rough in high water), the Black, Current, Jacks Fork (tops), Eleven Point, Bryant Creek; then we run into impoundments on White River, James, and North Fork. Near St. Louis, the Meramec is an easy, picturesque stream." Those are all in Missouri. Down in Arkansas there are the Buffalo, the Eleven Point (again—same river), the Kings River, the Mulberry River, and Big Piney Creek.

Maps of the Current and Jacks Fork are available from The Map Shop, 10th and Olive, St. Louis, MO. A 1973 book written by Oz Hawksley, a river runner of wide experience, and published and distributed by the Missouri Conservation Commission is available for only a dollar: *Missouri Ozark Waterways,* which covers 37 streams (2200 miles of clear, fast water). Hawksley, a professor of zoology at Central Missouri State College, is a member of the American Rivers Conservation Council Steering Committee and stays close to the problems of river running. His book is a good one with excellent introductory remarks and sound coverage of the streams he describes, mile by mile.

The National Park Service (Superintendent, Ozark National Scenic Waterways, Van Buren, MO 63965) is of course a good source of information about the Current and Jacks Fork.

Arkansas has its share of fine floatable rivers including a few, such as the Eleven Point, that flow through both Arkansas and Missouri. The Buffalo can be run for more than 100 miles in the spring when flowering shrubs are at their best and streams are high. The upper Buffalo may be too low for floating by May, but the lower stretches, except in exceptionally dry years, can be floated year-round. The Arkansas Game and Fish Commission provides maps of a number of streams in the state—including the Buffalo, of which it says rather magnanimously, "Don't float just for fish—the Buffalo has much more to offer."

The Eleven Point originates in Missouri, flows for more than 100 miles, and takes its name from the 11 major tributaries originating from large springs. It is clear, cold, and unpolluted; it has a constant, swift flow. It has wildlife, but it is close enough to such population centers as Memphis and St. Louis and Kansas City to enable the city folk to float its miraculous waters over a weekend. The Missouri segment has been protected under the Wild and Scenic Rivers Act.

The Kings River is also pure and unpolluted, issuing forth from the Boston Mountains and flowing 57 miles to the impounded White River in Missouri. It drops an average of 24 feet to the mile throughout its course, much of which is narrow and rocky. Famed as a smallmouth bass stream and as an attractive canoeist mecca, it is the only major free-flowing stream running into the White River in the northwest Arkansas-Missouri-Kansas triangle (the White has been heavily harnessed by man and is largely reservoir downstream from the Missouri state line).

The Mulberry River, like the Kings and the Buffalo, has its beginning on the south slopes of the Boston Mountains, flowing 55 miles to the Arkansas River with an average fall of 20 feet per mile. Largely controlled by the Forest Service, this stream offers exciting white-water possibilities for inflatable floaters in a semiwild setting. Big Piney Creek, similar to the Mulberry in many ways, flows some 67 miles to provide the white-water enthusiast with many opportunities to test his skill in a relatively unspoiled land of forest and river-cut gorge.

Oklahoma also has a couple of floatable rivers worth mention: the Glover and the Illinois. For up-to-date information on the Glover, write to Jim Jones, 501 East Craig, Broken Bow, OK 74728, or phone him: 405-584-2650. Jones, speaking of the Glover, says it "often flows over solid bedrock, with many boulders along the bank and in and under water. It has many natural dams—up-tiled hardrock ledges across the river—with the water spilling down in noisy falls and cascades." The Glover runs for some 45 miles, mostly in the southern Ouachitas.

The Illinois is covered mile by mile in a brochure published by the Department of Wildlife Conservation (1801 North Lincoln, Oklahoma City, Oklahoma 73105). The brochure describes the Illinois, one of Oklahoma's state scenic rivers which flows through the northeastern part of the state, as "an easy-flowing river with delightful scenery and several stretches of mild rapids. Floating the Illinois is not dangerous." Sounds like a good river to start on with an inflatable craft.

Bob Burleson, a lawyer in Temple and a former executive director of the American Whitewater Affiliation, is probably the best authority on Texas rivers. Write to Bob Burleson, President, Texas Explorers Club, P.O. Box 844, Temple, TX 76501, but give him the courtesy of enclosing a stamped self-addressed envelope.

Burleson has written a guide to the Rio Grande in Big Bend National Park that is recommended by the National Park Service. It is an informal document with lots of information about the various canyons of the Rio Grande. Jenkinson covers the Rio Grande—several sections of it including the canyons of the Big Bend—pretty well (pages 278 to 293) in his *Wild Rivers of North America*. A neat thing about this part of the world is that floating is best from October through March, the summer being hot beyond words and the winter months quite pleasant for the most part—just at the time of year when most other rivers are shut down by cold weather. The Rio Grande in the Big Bend country is probably the most active area for inflatable boats in the state, though the canyons are also run by canoe and kayak (see, "Rapids Round the Bend," by Edwin Shrake, *Sports Illustrated*, May 1974).

NORTH CENTRAL

This area is bordered on the south by the Ohio and Missouri rivers for the most part, and it includes most of the Great Lakes. It is canoeing country historically and traditionally—but not necessarily. Most of the literature on the rivers of the area is written from the point of view of the canoeist. Here again, the inflatable boat is an oddity, perhaps more rare than the kayak, which has come into more common use in recent years.

Two of the original wild and scenic rivers flow through this area—the Upper Wolf in Wisconsin and the St. Croix in Wisconsin and on the Wisconsin-Minnesota state line. A

Poling upstream on the St. Croix in Wisconsin. (Courtesy of the Wisconsin
Natural Resources Department, Madison)

third river—The Little Miami in Ohio—has been added to the
system, and several others are currently being studied for
possible inclusion. Each of these rivers offers fine floating
opportunities, as do many others. Several states in the area
publish canoeing guides or water-trail guides, and a number
of national forests provide information on river trips.

Wisconsin's Department of Natural Resources publishes
an adequate guide, *Wisconsin Water Trails,* which covers
nearly 50 rivers in not quite 60 pages, but *Wisconsin Trails*
(P.O. Box 5650, Madison, WI 53705) sells a trio of much more
detailed guides: *Canoe Trails of Northeastern Wisconsin*
($4.75); *Canoe Trails of North-Central Wisconsin* ($4.00);
and *Canoe Trails of Southern Wisconsin* ($4.95). The state
publication has the advantages of being free, of covering the
whole state, and of keeping it all together. The book on the
northwest part of the state is available from Wisconsin
Indian Head Country, 1316 Fairfax Street, Eau Claire, WI
54701.

Within reach of such metropolitan centers as Chicago
and Milwaukee, Minneapolis and St. Paul, even Detroit and

Cleveland, the streams of Wisconsin offer some fine floating waters. In the northwest corner of the state, the Bois Brule flows north into Lake Superior. In the roughly 50-mile run from its head of navigation to the lake, this famous trout stream has nearly 100 rapids, including the Lenroot Ledges and May's Ledges, which make rafting exciting. It has been run in open canoes (except for the ledges, which are normally portaged) by expert paddlers, and while it has not been frequently rafted, it has potential for inflatables. Superb scenery—its entire length lies within the Brule River State Park—and fine fishing add to the thrill of white water. You'll find details in *Northwestern Canoe Trails*.

Shooting Cedar Rapids on the Flambeau River. (Courtesy of the Wisconsin Natural Resources Department, Madison)

The Flambeau River, especially the stretch from Nine
Mile Creek to Ladysmith, is one of the finest white-water
stretches in the area. It has wilderness scenery and wildlife,
good fishing and roaring rapids, but there are also dams that
may have to be portaged—depending on how long a run you
want. However, *Wisconsin Trails* editorial assistant Maggie
Dewey says, "I would suggest that parts of it are useable for
inflatables, but I would not suggest that novices try to run the
rapids on the river. The Beaver Dam Rapid, in particular, is
dangerous unless one knows the situation." ARTA, a
commercial float-trip operator using inflatable boats, says,
"The Flambeau holds excitement with its many rapids," and
lists the rapids they run, which include Beaver Dam.

Flowing through the central part of the state in a south-
erly direction, the Wisconsin River is a delightful stream for
canoe parties but may be a bit slow for rafting; the Wolf River
farther east—and a tributary of the Wisconsin—offers some
fine floating possibilities, with dense forests and long, rocky
stretches. Considered "the state's most scenic, exciting,
rugged, and dangerous canoe water trail," the Wolf is also one
of the state's most important trout streams. George Steed, at
Wolf River Lodge in Langlade, rents rafts for float trips;
Drayna considers the 20 miles below Langlade as "first-class
rafting water." (See, *Canoe Trails of Northeastern Wisconsin* for details).

Still farther east, the Menominee River marks the Wis-
consin-Michigan state line. Considered dangerous by many
canoeists—and it has its annual fatalities—it is a good can-
didate for inflatable floating, though it has a few dams and
some potentially dangerous rapids (see *Canoe Trails of
Northeastern Wisconsin* for details). There is an awful lot of
runable water in Wisconsin.

The same is true for sister states Michigan and Minnesota. Michigan's *Guide to Easy Canoeing* (Department of
Natural Resources, Steven T. Mason Building, Lansing, MI
48926) is a very brief guide to some 54 streams in the state,

but it ignores such "white-water" rivers as the Black and Presque Isle in the Upper Peninsula and other streams like the Sturgeon in northern Lower Michigan. They are challenging for the expert paddler, too tough for family canoeing, and therefore, possibly good streams for inflatable craft. Always check them out locally, however. Several of the more popular streams—the Au Sable, Pere Marquette, Pine and Manistee—are too congested most summer weekends to be enjoyable for those who like a little solitude. Dave Sumner, who edits *Colorado Magazine,* says, "The Au Sable and Manistee Rivers in Michigan (old Hemingway haunts) are the two finest float-fishing streams I've ever been on."

Minnesota, land of lakes, has some runable rivers too. *Minnesota Voyageur Trails,* a publication of the Department of Conservation (Division of Parks and Recreation, 320 Centennial Building, St. Paul, MN 55101), covers nearly 20 canoe routes including the Upper Mississippi, the Big Fork, the St. Croix, and the Root. The latter two streams were run commercially in 1974 by ARTA, which also ran the Flambeau in Wisconsin. A number of national forests in the state—Huron, Chippewa, Manistee—also boast canoe routes, many of which may be good inflatable waters.

Ohio, Indiana, Illinois, Iowa—all have floatable rivers and all have agencies that provide some kind of canoeing guide. They vary greatly in kind and quality. Portions of the great rivers of the area may be floated, but pollution becomes a factor on some, commercial river traffic on others, dams and too much civilization on still others. Northern Wisconsin and adjacent wilder areas offer better opportunities for the kind of floating that enables you to get away, to relax and enjoy the peace and quiet of a river trip.

THE SOUTHWEST

Now we're into the big-water rivers. This is Grand Canyon country. Everyone has heard of the roaring rapids of the Colo-

Canoeing is the only way to go on many of the more placid streams. (Courtesy Michigan Department of Natural Resources)

rado in that mile-deep gorge, but have you heard of Cataract Canyon on the same river? Roughly half of its rapids have now been drowned out by the rising waters of Lake Powell (which has also inundated much of Rainbow Bridge National Monument), but in the spring there are few places on earth with bigger rapids.

In this whole vast area of great rivers, only the upper Rio Grande in northcentral New Mexico has been protected under the Wild and Scenic Rivers Act. Half a dozen others, at least, are worthy of the designation: the Yampa and the Green, several stretches of the Colorado, parts of the Dolores, perhaps the Chama, parts of the Gunnison, the Arkansas, the San Juan. The BLM in Utah has suggested no less than 11 rivers for possible study in that dry state, half of which is part of the Great Basin.

Major river-running activity in this area is centered around the Colorado and the Green and their various tributaries and around the upper Rio Grande and its tributary, the Chama. An extremely short season—no more than three weeks in late March, early April—is possible on the Gila, in southwestern New Mexico, which runs through wilderness for nearly 40 miles from a put-in point where N.M. 527 crosses the river to take-out points at Turkey Creek or Sapello Creek (check with local authorities and river runners for more detail and specific runable periods).

The best authority on the Chama and the Upper Rio Grande is "Stretch" Fretwell in Los Alamos, New Mexico, who has probably trained more white-water river runners than any other man alive. Commercial trips are run by Dave Murphy (Taos Expeditions, South Plaza, Taos, NM 87571). Fretwell's chapter on river running in H. E. Ungnade's *Guide to the New Mexico Mountains* (University of New Mexico Press) is a good starter.

Several stretches of the Rio Grande—many with poor access unless you run the whole works—offer a wide variety of water from easy class 1 (Manassa Bridge on Colorado 142 to Lobatos Bridge) to wild class 4 and 5 expert runs (Arroyo

Hondo to Taos Junction Bridge or Pilar to Tinconada). The most popular stretch in the whole state—according to Fretwell—is White Rock Canyon (from Otowi Bridge on New Mexico 4 to construction sites for the building of a dam that will drown most of the canyon—better get this run in soon.)

The Chama, already dammed, flows into the Rio Grande several miles above White Rock Canyon. It offers a couple of class 2 and 3 stretches, but water level is controlled by reservoir release. Check out local conditions before you try it.

In his chapter in *Wild Rivers of North America* on the Colorado River (chapter 5—"River of Shining Mountains: The Colorado"), Jenkinson includes the Green as well as tributaries of both.

An excellent series of books is available that covers the whole runable Colorado River system: Westwater River Guides (P.O. Box 365, Boulder City, NV 89005).

Virtually all of these waters are under the control of a variety of governmental agencies, primarily the National Park Service (Dinosaur, Canyonlands, Grand Canyon, even Glen Canyon, Flaming Gorge and Lake Mead) and the BLM (Desolation, Westwater). Some of it—the Upper Green below Flaming Gorge Dam—is under Forest Service jurisdiction, and much of it may also be under the jurisdiction of the State of Utah. All of them require registration with the agency in charge, and for some you may have to wait a year to get a permit to float due to the masses of people who want to float western rivers which, in the eyes of the agencies, are overcrowded.

The muddy Yampa, in Dinosaur, has only three major rapids—Tepee, Big Joe, and Warm Springs—in a 46-mile run, but Warm Springs rates with the worst in Grand Canyon. The canyon walls may be the most impressive of any river I've floated—straight up, not moving back in a series of steps like the Grand Canyon.

The Green River, cold and clear from the dam releases at Flaming Gorge, has numerous rapids through the Canyon of Lodore—though its flow is mild enough for family floating

Above a triple rig takes a beating in Cataract Canyon (photo by Eric Grohe, courtesy of Holiday River Expeditions). Below a Green River raft takes the Big Kahuna on the upper Snake River near Jackson Hole, Wyoming.

Side canyon in Cataract Canyon (Ray Varley photo)

above the Gates of Lodore, and the fishing is good, the bird life abundant. Several miles below its confluence with the Yampa, the river has carved Split Mountain Gorge, a one-day run through four major rapids: Moonshine, SOB, Schoolboy and Inglesby Rock. Either trip through Dinosaur—Lodore to Split Mountain or Deerlodge Park to Split Moun-

A river runner with a guitar sings to the placid river and canyon walls at Box Elder Campsite on the Yampa River in Dinosaur National Monument. (Verne Huser photo)

tain—makes a nice three-day run, and much of the way is slow, easy water. Floaters often run miles of the trip floating beside the boat in their life jackets, which must be worn at all times under NPS regulations.

Westwater Canyon has an even dozen rapids in about 10 miles of canyon, though the whole trip runs closer to 20 miles. In Cataract Canyon, which topped 60,000 cubic feet per second in 1973 and 1974, the big rapids get bigger with higher water levels: Mile-Long, Big Drop, Satan's Gut. Gypsum is already under the waters of Lake Powell in violation of the Colorado River Storage Project Act of 1956, and Glen Canyon, the place no one knew, lies buried under that lovely reservoir.

Below the reservoir known as Lake Powell, the Colorado River runs again, cold and clear, dependent upon power demands in Los Angeles. Three-day weekends frustrate the river runners because with low-power demands, there is often mighty thin water in the canyon. I can recall having to move a ton of pontoon 50 feet to water when the river dropped overnight. There are fantastic rapids and fabulous places. Float the river if you have half a chance.

Before I leave the Southwest, I must mention one more river, the Dolores, a tributary of the Colorado. It flows for the most part through southwestern Colorado, and not many people run it—yet. No less than two major dams are planned for it. One way or the other, it probably won't last long, but

Long stretches of calm current let you relax and enjoy the scenery in the Grand Canyon of the Colorado. (Courtesy American River Touring Association)

Dave Sumner, editor of *Colorado Magazine* and a good friend with whom I've floated a river or two, says of a trip he took on the Dolores, "Best river experience I ever had."

NORTHERN WEST

The center of floating activity of this area without a doubt is the Upper Snake in Jackson Hole Country just south of Yellowstone National Park where more than 100,000 people float every summer, most of them with commercial outfitters, but increasingly on their own in canoes, kayaks, and rafts. Two minor areas of floating activity center around the Lower Snake in Hells Canyon and the central part of Idaho where the Middle Fork of the Salmon, the Selway, and the Main Salmon River offer floating opportunities for perhaps a tenth as many river runners a season. Montana rivers have begun to see more action by river runners during the past few years, especially the Yellowstone, the Missouri, and the various forks of the Flathead.

The Snake's value as a floating stream was discovered some 20 years ago when the Grand Teton Lodge Company began running big black pontoons down the Snake's braided channels with tourists watching wildlife and enjoying the scenery—no white water here except a short stretch above Jackson Lake (just south of the Yellowstone boundary) and the torrid canyon 50 miles downstream. Now nearly every stretch of the Upper Snake is run by some kind of commercial-float-trip operator, almost exclusively in inflatable boats. Several hundred Boy Scouts run a 60-mile stretch in canoes every summer, and kayakers have been more common than big trout in the Snake River Canyon just above Alpine Junction.

The National Park Service and the Forest Service share jurisdiction of controlled portions of the Upper Snake. No floating is allowed in Yellowstone National Park, but a

Two deer pause to watch a raft drift by on the Snake River in Jackson Hole country (Wyoming). As many as 70 rafts a day may float this stretch on scenic trips run by 18 commercial outfitters operating in the park. (Verne Huser photo)

narrow canyon immediately below the boundary offers 6- to 8-foot standing waves during June when the water is high. A milder stretch often canoed starts at Flagg Ranch and ends on Jackson Lake (commercial trips on this stretch take along a small motor to run out with).

But the most popular stretch begins below the dam that has raised Jackson Lake's level by nearly 40 feet. The 20-mile stretch from Pacific Creek Landing to Moose, location of park headquarters, experiences an almost constant flow of rubber rafts throughout the day all summer. About halfway down that stretch is another put-in point known as Deadman's Bar where even more floats launch, adding to the crowded conditions that may mean 70 boats per day (more than 75,000 people floated in Grand Teton National Park during 1973).

My own *Snake River Guide,* one of the Westwater river guides, covers more than 100 miles of Snake River from the south entrance of Yellowstone National Park to the Palisades Reservoir, including the popular white-water stretch in the canyon and the scenic stretches in Grand Teton National Park.

A 27-foot bridge pontoon rigged for two sets of 12-foot oars drifts along in one of the quieter stretches of the Snake River in Hells Canyon. Note that everyone has on a life jacket (Type I PFD) even in this calm stretch. (Verne Huser photo)

Two Snake River tributaries have begun to be floated in recent years, the Hoback with inflatables and the Gray's, mostly with kayaks. Several sections of the Lower Snake are floated between reservoirs, but with more than 20 dams in just over 1000 miles of river, there isn't a great deal of free-flowing water.

Even in Hells Canyon, under Forest Service jurisdiction the flow is regulated by reservoir releases—up to 80,000 cfs in recent years. Launch for the Hells Canyon trip normally is just below the Hells Canyon Dam, third and last, and farthest downstream, of Idaho Power and Light Company's power-generating dams. An 85-mile run to the mouth of the Grand Ronde River in Washington State is possible, usually in five or six days, though it can be done easily in four at high water levels in the spring. There is some natural flow from tributary streams as well as release from the reservoir to make room for snow-melt waters from upstream.

The Salmon River joins the Snake in Hells Canyon, and I've seen the Snake running 120,000 cfs below the confluence (I once ran 20 miles in two and a half hours on such a head of water.)

The Salmon is a free-flowing river with no impoundments; it rises naturally every spring, picking up lots of driftwood and silt. As it drops when the snow-melt season is past, it clears, leaving behind it the most beautiful camping beaches I've ever known. It also leaves great piles of driftwood for fires at the campsites. Camping is so much better below the confluence that many float parties spend their first couple of days running hard to relax at the sandy campsites at the end of the trip.

The Salmon River, both the main stream and its tributary, the Middle Fork, and the Selway are under the jurisdiction of the Forest Service and require registration. The Selway is one of the few rivers in the nation that came under control early enough to really prevent its being spoiled by overuse; only 5 commercial outfitters have permits to run it

It's a rainy day on the Main Salmon River as a 25-foot pontoon slips through the rocks of Devils Teeth Rapid. Note the quiet water in the foreground produced by the back eddy below the rapid, a typical situation when guard rocks such as those on the right swing the current to the opposite side of the river. (Verne Huser photo)

(as compared to 18 in Grand Teton National Park, 22 in Grand Canyon, and 40 on Oregon's Rogue—one of the original wild rivers).

The Middle Fork, another of the original eight wild rivers, is considered by many as the most highly regulated river in the country, with strict control of use (an outfitter can launch only one trip every eight days and is limited to the size of party and assigned to the campsites he may use). The Middle Fork flows north out of the Idaho wilderness, dropping something like 27 feet per mile. This ferocious stream is floated by about 4,000 people a season, which is only about 10 weeks long (late June through August) for all practical purposes. The U.S. Forest Service provides good

A Salmon River boat on the Middle Fork of the Salmon. (Verne Huser photo)

river maps to both the Middle Fork and the main Salmon, showing rapids and campsites and giving a bit of the history and background of the area. Scott and Margaret Arighi, in their *Wildwater Touring,* cover the Salmon from Dagger Falls on the Middle Fork all the way to the Snake in Hells Canyon. The Upper Salmon has seen more floating activity in the past few years—including two drownings in 1974—and the South Fork of the Salmon has become a favorite kayak stream along with Big Creek, a major tributary of the Middle Fork.

The Selway River, just across the ridge from the Salmon River drainage, is a rocky, roaring white-water torrent that flows out of the Idaho-Montana high country along the Continental Divide. It joins the Lochsa River to form the Clearwater, which in turn flows into the Snake at Lewiston. The

Lochsa is bordered by U. S. 12, but the Selway is roadless and wild.

It is one of the major rivers of the West that has not yet been overused—only because the Forest Service got a handle on it early enough and began restricting its commercial use before it became overrun with floaters. During 1973, fewer than 500 people floated the Selway, and in 1974, due to high water during the scheduled season, even fewer ran it. Capacity for the Selway is one launch per day with no more than 15 persons per party, including boatmen. Commercial outfitters include ARTA, Hatch, Western River Expeditions, White Water Adventures, and Idaho Wilderness School. All private parties must schedule launch dates. The Selway may be even more intensively managed than the Middle Fork of the Salmon.

The Clearwater itself has become more popular among river runners in recent years. In 1972 it was the scene of one of the last log runs in the West. Part of the Lewis and Clark route, the Clearwater country is full of history (Chief Joseph of the Nez Percés came this way, too, during the 1877 war forced on him by military justice). Several historic routes can be followed, largely by boat, in this vast land of river sources.

In Montana, the various forks of the Missouri and the Missouri itself offer fine floating opportunities. The Montana Fish and Game Department (Helena, MT 59601) publishes a pair of information bulletins: "Montana's Popular Float Streams" and "Ride the Wild Missouri Recreation Waterway." The May-June 1973 issue of the department's official publication, *Montana Outdoors,* carried a good background article, "The Wild Missouri," complete with a map and a list of tips for boaters.

The Madison and the Jefferson, two of the three main forks of the Missouri, and the Yellowstone have become popular float streams in recent years, and if you want to follow the Lewis and Clark route, you'll want to try the Beaverhead Fork of the Jefferson as they did. In the northern part of the state, in the neighborhood of Glacier National Park, the various forks of the Flathead offer white-water action in some of the most beautiful country in the West.

This Northern West region is in a sense the apex of the nation: three of its most important river systems originate here, and inflatable floating has had its heyday here. The Middle Fork of both the Salmon and the Clearwater are among the original eight wild rivers. Several others may well join them during the next few years. Much of it is mountainous country: The nation's first, second, and third deepest river gorges are here—the Hells Canyon of the Snake, the Salmon River canyon and the Middle Fork of the Salmon (the Colorado's Grand Canyon ranks way back, in fourth). Much of it is forested, and wildlife abounds. It may be too far from home for many as a weekend float, but it may also be worth planning for as a vacation—be sure to get your reservation early.

PACIFIC COAST

The Rogue River in Oregon and the Stanislaus in California are the primary inflatable-floating rivers in the Pacific Coast states. Both are under federal regulation, the Rogue as one of the original wild rivers. Numerous other streams in both areas plus several in Washington and literally dozens in Alaska offer floating possibilities and are rapidly being discovered by river runners.

Ann Dwyer's *Canoeing Waters of California* (P.O. Box 61, Kentfield, CA 94904) published in 1973 provides river-running details on more than 30 of the California rivers. The Arighis' book, *Wildwater Touring,* covers in some detail the Rogue, the Grande Rounde, the John Day (two sections), and the Owyhee (two sections)—all in Oregon—as well as the Salmon River system. For Washington State, two publications, *Kayak and Canoe Trips in Washington* and *Water Trails of Washington,* from Signpost (16812 36th Avenue West, Lynnwood, WA 98036) are good.

Dave Helfrich, Oregon chairman for the WRGA, has run a number of coastal rivers in Washington State—the Sole- duck (60 miles), the Calawash (20 miles), the Bogachiel (20 miles), the Hoh (30 miles), and the Queets (25 miles). "The Soleduck and the Calawash have the best white water," he says, "like the Upper Middle Fork and Selway rivers" (in Idaho).

As I've mentioned elsewhere, the BLM (P. O. Box 2511, Juneau, AL 99801) has probably the best available infor- mation on Alaskan rivers. Bill Kenyon, a BLM employee in Glennallen, has initiated an information service called the Alaska Whitewater Association. And Mary Kaye Hession (3304 Iowa, No. 5, Anchorage, AL 99503) has produced an edited write-up on a dozen or so rivers in our largest and wildest state.

Alaska may be too far away for practical floating for most people, and there may be rivers much closer to home that already have the reputation of good floating streams. But if you really want to get away, if you really want to explore, if you really want to experience the wilds—try an Alaskan river.

There is much fine floating in the upper reaches of the tributary watersheds of the John Day, the Deschutes and the Willamette. The driftboat is king here, but inflatables may be used on practically any river run by driftboaters. Contact the Oregon Guides and Packers and the Oregon Marine Board for detailed information, and check with local or regional BLM and Forest Service offices through whose area streams flow.

Oregon coastal rivers include the Rogue, the Smith (named for Jedediah Smith, the mountainman who explored the area 150 years ago), the McKenzie, the Clackamas, the Klamath, and others. The Rogue, portions of which have been preserved under the Wild and Scenic Rivers Act, is without doubt the most popular floating river in Oregon. Adminis- tered jointly by the Bureau of Land Management and the Forest Service, it almost got out of hand when the number of commercial outfitters rose from 20 in 1972, to 29 in 1973, to 40 in 1974, when the administering agencies put a ceiling on the number of commercial operations—as had been done earlier on several other rivers (Colorado, Snake, Middle Fork of the Salmon, Selway).

The Rogue is a good learning river with several white-water schools currently conducted on its cool, clear waters: Jerry Bentley's Orange Torpedo Trips, ARTA's American White-Water School, and Vladimir Kovalik's Wilderness World, one of the best in the business. Kovalik, whom I know personally, says, "We've found that the best location is the Rogue in southern Oregon, because of the variety of rapids, conditions, wildlife, geology, history, etc., and the fact that it is protected under the Wild and Scenic Rivers Act, offering a wilderness situation for most of the run, with some good practice runs by the roadside at the beginning."

The Forest Service and the BLM, in a cooperative effort, provide floaters with a map of the Wild and Scenic Rogue covering the area from Grants Pass to the Coast, roughly 100 miles.

The Stanislaus, in the western foothills of the Sierra Nevada in California, gold country in the middle of the last century, is without doubt the most popular river on the West Coast. Run only by kayak before 1962, the Stanislaus blossomed for float-trip traffic during the next decade, and by 1973 more than 30,000 people had floated its raging waters. Some 45 percent of them were on commercial trips, but 17,954 people floated it on private trips.

There are two basic runs on the Stanislaus: One begins at Camp Nine and runs to Parrotts Ferry Take-out, a run of 10 miles of heavy white water that requires expert river-running ability; the other begins at Parrotts Ferry and runs 7 miles to the town of Melones (Robinson's Ferry). The upper stretch is run by everything from inner tubes and air mattresses to kayaks and 15-man rafts, but there were four drownings on the Stanislaus in 1973 and no less than 13 serious injuries. The lower stretch is milder, a good training ground for kayakers and rafters, a good playground for expert canoeists.

There's a lot of white-water floating activity in California. Try Ann Dwyer's book and check in with the nearest white-water club or take a trip with the Sierra Club or with one of the many California-based outfitters who run coastal streams. Inner tubes and air mattresses and toy rubber rafts are used aplenty on the Merced and the Mokelumne. The Tuolumne, an unbelievable river that drops 45 feet per mile and 100 feet to the mile for the first 3 miles, has become the most recent in a long line of "ultimate" rivers to run.

Certainly there are other rivers to run—in the West, in the East, in the South, in every quarter of the continent, but I would remind the reader that I have not attempted to be comprehensive. I have tried to present pertinent information to help you find a river or two or three near enough your own home to enable you to try it on your own, once you have the proper equipment and have picked up a little experience. Gauge your own ability wisely. Be cautious and careful. See you on the river.

CANADA

Many of the white-water publications cover floatable streams and lakes in Canada, and both Jenkinson's *Wild Rivers of North America* and Bill Riviere's *Pole, Paddle and Portage* mention Canadian waters. And you might find information in *The Beaver* (Hudson's Bay House, Winnipeg 1, Canada), the official publication of Hudson's Bay Company. I thought the Snake was a big river below the mouth of the Salmon the spring of 1972 when it topped 120,000 cfs, but the Fraser, in British Columbia, may run four times that volume. Friends of mine disappear into eastern Canada for a month every spring and fall, canoeing a different route every season. The Boundary Waters Canoe Area, embracing the International Border between the Untied States and Canada, is certainly one of the continent's greatest canoeing centers—though it offers less excitement for rafters and kayakers.

Starting in the east and working westward, we find a great deal of wild country in Newfoundland and even more in Labrador, which is under the jurisdiction of Newfoundland. Because of the wild nature of much of the country, all non-residents are required to have licensed guides in Labrador (check with the Department of Mines, Agriculture and Resources, St. Johns, Newfoundland, for information).

In Newfoundland itself, while the main highway (Route 1) provides access to many of its streams, the headwaters are inaccessible by road. Therefore, many of the best trips begin by heading upstream which is fundamentally impossible for rafters and often wearing for canoeists and even kayakers. Consequently, floating hasn't been big in Newfoundland.

In Nova Scotia and New Brunswick, a licensed guide is required for trips through forest lands (write the New Brunswick Travel Bureau, Box 1030, Fredericton for information). The St. John and Miramichi rivers are among the most popular: The former ends at the Bay of Fundy, famed for its tremendous tides, and the latter consists of a wide, fast-flowing current from Boiestown to the sea. An upper branch of the Miramichi, the Southwest, provides nearly a 50-mile wilderness run. The St. Croix River, which separates New Brunswick from Maine, also offers floating possibilities. Most of the Nova Scotia routes involve lakes and portage problems for rafts and little excitement for the kayaker. This is primarily canoe country.

Quebec, a massive province in which 82 percent of the people speak French, offers massive canoeing opportunities, but here again the routes offer hard work for the rafter—unless he uses a small motor—and tame water for the kayaker, for the most part (contact the Department of Tourism, Fish and Game, Parliament Building, Quebec City;

and the Boy Scouts of Canada, 2085 Bishop Street, Montreal, for information).

Jenkinson recommends a trip in northeastern Quebec: "down the Swampy Bay River past the ruins of the Old Hudson's Bay Post of Fort McKenzie, into the Kaniapiskau River and down it to Koksoak" to Fort Chimo near Ungava Bay. The Mattawin, also in eastern Quebec, offers a real challenge to white-water enthusiasts, but it is controlled by reservoir release.

Ontario embraces the canoe country of Minnesota and Wisconsin and Michigan and offers the Quetico, but once again this is largely lake country. However, extensive river trips are possible on many of the streams flowing northward: the Albany, the Missinaibi, the Mattagami and the Abitibi all flow into James Bay, the lower (southern) extension of Hudson Bay. Many of the Canadian rivers are best reached by railroad, but if you float to James or Hudson bays, you may very well have to fly back to your starting point or home. A real wilderness experience with plenty of wildlife is available on the Winisk River, which flows into Hudson Bay proper, and both the Flint and the Wanapitei offer shorter white-water trips. (Check with the Department of Tourism and Information, 185 Bloor Street, East, Toronto 5).

In Manitoba, the Nelson, the Hayes, and Gods rivers, in the northeast part of the province, the Red (flowing north out of the United States—between Minnesota and North Dakota), and the Assiniboine offer floating opportunities. While some of these streams have fine rapids, some of the routes involve lakes and relatively flat water plus some real transportation problems getting to the river and back home again. (Tourist Development Branch, Department of Industry and Commerce, Winnipeg 1).

Saskatchewan waters, according to Bill Riviere's *Pole, Paddle & Portage,* have the best-developed canoe routes in Canada, but most of the routes include lake or flat-water stretches that make it tough on rafters. Still, there is plenty of wilderness, especially in the far north where the Churchill River runs to the sea, Hudson Bay where the snow geese nest and other wildlife observations add to the thrill of floating those far-north waters. (Information Branch, Department of Natural Resources, Government Administration Building, Regina).

Alberta is full of fantastic rivers as is British Columbia, right next door. Several years ago I had a couple on one of my float trips who—at ages 73 and 68, respectively—had canoed the McKenzie 1,000 miles to the Arctic Ocean, but as Jenkinson points out in his *Wild Rivers of North America,* it is probably the tributaries of this great river of the north that offer the most interesting floating possibilities: the Athabasca, which runs along the edge of Wood Buffalo National Park; the Peace, which runs through it; the Hay. There are also the Smokey and the Wapiti, whose waters join the Peace, in the northwestern part of the province, the Red Deer, the North and South Saskatchewan, which join in Saskatchewan and ultimately end up in Hudson Bay after a long and circuitous route. (Government Travel Bureau, 331 Highways Building, Edmonton).

British Columbia, with fantastic mountains, some of them bordering on Alberta, offers some really great river trips: the Fraser, the Thompson, the upper Columbia, the Bowron (a tributary of the Frazier or Fraser), the Canoe River, the Stikine. Scenery is spectacular, fishing quite good, and wildlife seasonally abundant, but there are such hazards as logjams and bears. Railroads and highways are infrequent but provide necessary access. Riverboats and airplanes may also be used to get you where you want to start or where you end your trip, but check out the details with appropriate agencies (British Columbia Travel Bureau, Department of Recreation and Conservation, Victoria).

In the north country—Yukon Territory, which shares a common border with Alaska and offers access to several rivers that flow into Alaska, and the Northwest Territories—you'll be largely in wilderness, especially in the latter. Here routes are long with great distances between put-in and take-out points with little help of any kind between. It pays to go in groups of two or three crafts, and you need to go fully provisioned, fully prepared for almost anything. You may need to fly in, and certainly you'll want to get all necessary details from the authorities (Northwest Territories, 400 Laurier Avenue, West, Ottawa 5, Ontario; Department of Travel and Publicity, Box 2703, Whitehorse, Yukon Territory).

The MacKenzie is the great river of the area, the big one flowing northwest. And the Yukon flows westward, the big, broad, relatively slow stream that breaches the international border below Dawson, famous during the gold-rush days. The Teslin and the Pelly, the Peel and the Porcupine all offer fine floating possibilities. See both Jenkinson and Riviere for greater detail, and be sure to contact local authorities and guides whenever possible.

There's always one more rapid to float such as Dubendorf Rapid in Grand Canyon. (Ray Varley photo)

Appendix A

Sources of Information

FEDERAL AGENCIES
ASSOCIATED WITH RIVER RUNNING

Department of the Interior:

Bureau of Outdoor Recreation,
Interior Building, Washington DC 20240

Regional Offices:

Pacific Northwest, 1000 Second Avenue, Seattle, WA 98104

Midcontinent, P.O. Box 25387, Denver Federal Center, Denver, CO 80225

South Central, 5000 Marble Avenue N.E., Albuquerque, NM 87110

Lake Central, 3853 Research Park Drive, Ann Arbor, MI 48104

Pacific Southwest, Box 3602, 450 Golden Gate Avenue, San Francisco, CA 94102

Southeast, 810 New Walton Bldg., Atlanta, GA 30303

Northeast, 600 Arch Street, Philadelphia, PA 19106

Bureau of Reclamation, Interior Building, Washington, DC 20240

Regional Offices:

Region 1, 550 West Fort Street, Boise, ID 83707

Mid-Pacific Region, 2800 Cottage Way, Sacramento, CA 95825

Lower Colorado Region, P.O. Box 427, Boulder City, NV 89005

Region 4, P.O. Box 11568, Salt Lake City, UT 84111

Region 5, Herring Plaza, Box H-4377, Amarillo, TX 79101

Region 6, P.O. Box 2553, Billings, MT 59103

Lower Missouri Region, Building 20, Denver Federal Center, Denver, CO 80225

Bureau of Sport Fisheries and Wildlife, Interior Building, Washington, DC 20240

Regional Offices:

Northwest Region, P.O. Box 3737, Portland, OR 97208

Midwest Region, Federal Building, Fort Snelling, Twin Cities, MN 55111

Southeast Region, 17 Executive Park Drive, NE, Atlanta, GA 30329

Northeast Region (5), Room 821, U.S. Post Office and Courthouse, Boston, MA 02109

Southwest Region, P.O. Box 1306, Albuquerque, NM 87103

National Park Service, Interior Building, Washington, DC 20240

Regional Offices:

Southeast Region, 3401 Whipple Avenue, Atlanta, GA 30344

Midwest Region, 1709 Jackson Street, Omaha, NB 68102

Southwest Region, P.O. Box 728, Santa Fe, NM 87501

Western Region, 450 Golden Gate Avenue, Box 36036, San Francisco, CA 94102

Northeast Region, 143 South Third Street, Philadelphia, PA 19106

National Capitol Parks, 1100 Ohio Drive, SW, Washington, DC 20242

Department of Agriculture, U.S. Forest Service, Dept. of Agriculture, Washington, DC 20250

Regional Offices:

Northern (1), Federal Building, Missoula, MT 59801

Rocky Mountain (2), Federal Center, Bldg. 85, Denver, CO 80225

Southwestern (3), 517 Gold Street, SW, Albuquerque, NM 87102

Intermountain (4), Federal Bldg., Ogden, UT 84401

California (5), 630 Sansome Street, San Francisco, CA 94111

Pacific Northwest (6), Box 3623, Portland, OR 97208

Eastern (9), 633 West Wisconsin Ave., Milwaukee, WI 53203

Alaska (10), Box 1628, Juneau, AK 99801

also: U.S. Forest Service, Division of Recreation & Watershed Management, 1720 Peachtree Road, NW, Atlanta, GA 30309

Department of the Army, U.S. Army Corps of Engineers, Recreation-Resource Management Branch, DAEN-CWO-R, Washington, DC 20314

Division Offices:

Lower Mississippi Valley Division, P.O. Box 80, Vicksburg, MS 39180

Missouri River Division, P.O. Box 103, Omaha, NB 68101

North Atlantic Division, 90 Church Street, New York, NY 10007

North Central Division, 536 South Clark Street, Chicago, IL 60605

New England Division, 434 Trapelo Road, Waltham, MA 02154

North Pacific Division, 210 Custom House, Portland, OR 97209

Ohio River Division, P.O. Box 1159, Cincinnati, OH 45201

South Atlantic Division, 510 Title Bldg., 30 Pryor Street, SW, Atlanta, GA 30303

South Pacific Division, 630 Sansome Street, San Francisco, CA 94111

Southwestern Division, 1114 Commerce Street, Dallas, TX 75202

Environmental Protection Agency, Washington, DC 20460

Tennessee Valley Authority, Division of Reservoir Properties, 109 West Cumberland, Knoxville, TN 37902

U.S. Coast Guard Offices

U.S. Coast Guard, 400 Seventh Street, SW, Washington, DC 20590

1st Coast Guard District, 150 Causeway Street, Boston, MA 02114

2nd Coast Guard District, 1520 Market Street, St. Louis, MO 63103

3rd Coast Guard District, Governors Island, New York, NY 10004

5th Coast Guard District, 431 Crawford Street, Portsmouth, VA 23705

7th Coast Guard District, 51 SW First Avenue, Miami, FL 33130

8th Coast Guard District, Custom House, New Orleans, LA 70130

9th Coast Guard District, New Federal Bldg., 1240 E. 9th Street, Room 2021, Cleveland, OH 44199

11th Coast Guard District, 19 Pine Avenue, Long Beach, CA 90802

12th Coast Guard District, 630 Sansome Street, San Francisco, CA 94126

13th Coast Guard District, 618 Second Avenue, Seattle, WA 98104

17th Coast Guard District, FPO, Seattle, WA 98711

Other Coast Guard Offices (primarily marine inspection stations)

427 Commercial Street, Boston, MA 02109

P.O. Box 108, Portland, ME 04112

104 Customhouse, Providence, RI 02903

P.O. Box 1400, Paducah, KY 42001

Box 695, Dubuque, IA 52001

550 Main Street, Cincinnati, OH 45202

600 Federal Place, Louisville, KY 40202

167 North Main Street, Memphis, TN 38103

801 Broadway, Nashville, TN 37203

312 Stanwix Street, Pittsburgh, PA 15219

P.O. Box 2412, Huntington, WV 25725

SOURCES OF STATE RECREATION INFORMATION

ALABAMA Bureau of Publicity & Information, Room 403, State Highway Building, Montgomery, AL 36104

ALASKA Division of Parks, Department of Natural Resources, 323 East 4th Avenue, Anchorage, AK 99501

ARIZONA State Office of Economic Planning and Development, 1645 West Jefferson, 4th Floor, Phoenix, AZ 85007

ARKANSAS Department of Parks and Tourism, 149 Capitol Building, Little Rock, AR 72201

CALIFORNIA Department of Parks & Recreation, P.O. Box 2390, Sacramento, CA 95811

COLORADO Division of Parks and Outdoor Recreation, 1845 Sherman, Denver, CO 80203

CONNECTICUT Department of Commerce, 210 Washington Street, Hartford, CT 06106

DELAWARE Bureau of Travel Development, 45 The Green, Dover, DE 19901

DISTRICT OF COLUMBIA, Washington Area Convention & Visitors Bureau, 1129 - 20th Street, N.W., Washington, DC 20036

FLORIDA Department of Commerce, 107 West Gaines Street, Tallahassee, FL 32304

GEORGIA Department of Natural Resources, Parks and Historic Sites Division, 270 Washington Street, S.W., Atlanta, GA 30334

HAWAII Visitors Bureau, 2270 Kalakaua Avenue, Honolulu, HI 96815

IDAHO Department of Commerce & Development, Capitol Building, Boise, ID 83720

ILLINOIS Department of Conservation, State Office Building, Springfield, IL 62706

INDIANA Department of Commerce, Tourist Division, 336 State House, Indianapolis, IN 46204

IOWA Development Commission, Tourism and Recreational Development Division, 250 Jewett Building, Des Moines, IA 50309

KANSAS Department of Economic Development, Tourist Division, State Office Building, Topeka, KS 66612

KENTUCKY Department of Public Information, Advertising and Travel Promotion, Capitol Annex Building, Frankfort, KY 40601

LOUISIANA Tourist Development Commission, P.O. Box 44291, Baton Rouge, LA 70804

MAINE Department of Commerce and Industry, Promotion Division, State House, Augusta, ME 04330

MARYLAND Park Service, Tawes State Office Building, 580 Taylor Avenue, Annapolis, MD 21401

MASSACHUSETTS Department of Commerce & Development, Division of Tourism, State Office Building, 100 Cambridge Street, Boston, MA 02202

MICHIGAN Department of Commerce, Tourist Council, Suite 102 Commerce Center, 300 South Capitol Avenue, Lansing, MI 48933

MINNESOTA Department of Natural Resources, Centennial Office Building, 658 Cedar Street, St. Paul, MN 55155

MISSISSIPPI Agricultural & Industrial Board, Travel and Tourism Department, 1504 Walter Litters Street Office Building, Jackson, MS 39201

MISSOURI Tourism Commission, P.O. Box 1055, Jefferson City, MO 65101

MONTANA State Department of Highways, Advertising Unit, Helena, MT 59601

NEBRASKA Game and Parks Commission, 2200 North 33rd Street, P.O. Box 30370, Lincoln, NB 68503

NEVADA Department of Economic Development, Carson City, NV 89701

NEW HAMPSHIRE Department of Economic Development, Box 856, Concord, NH 03301

NEW JERSEY Department of Environmental Protection, Bureau of Parks, P.O. Box 1420, Trenton, NJ 08625

NEW MEXICO Department of Development, 113 Washington Avenue, Santa Fe, NM 87501

NEW YORK State Department of Commerce, 99 Washington Avenue, Albany, NY 12210

NORTH CAROLINA Department of Natural and Economic Resources, Travel and Promotion Division, P.O. Box 27687, Raleigh, NC 27611

NORTH DAKOTA Travel Division, State Highway Department, Bismark, ND 58501

OHIO Development Department, 65 South Front Street, Columbus, OH 43216

OKLAHOMA Department of Tourism and Recreation, 504 Will Rogers Building, Oklahoma City, OK 73105

OREGON Highway Department, Travel Information Division, Salem, OR 97310

PENNSYLVANIA Department of Environmental Resources, P.O. Box 1467, Harrisburg, PA 17120

RHODE ISLAND Development Council, Tourist Promotion Division, Roger Williams Building, Hayes Street, Providence, RI 02908

SOUTH CAROLINA Department of Parks, Recreation and Tourism, P.O. Box 1358, Columbia, SC 29202

SOUTH DAKOTA Department of Economic and Tourism Development, Division of Tourism, Office Building No. 2, Pierre, SD 57501

TENNESSEE Department of Economic Development, Tourism Development, Suite 1004 Andrew Jackson Building, Nashville, TN 37219

TEXAS Highway Department, Travel and Information Division, P.O. Box 5064, Austin, TX 78763

UTAH Travel Council, Council Hall - Capitol Hill, Salt Lake City, UT 84114

VERMONT Agency of Development & Community Affairs, Information Travel Division, Montpelier, VT 05602

VIRGINIA Travel Council, 2309 East Broad Street, Richmond, VA 23219

WASHINGTON Department of Commerce & Economic Development, Travel Development Division, General Administration Building, Olympia, WA 98504

WEST VIRGINIA Travel Department, Department of Commerce, 1900 Washington Street East, Building B, Charleston, WV 25305

WISCONSIN Department of Natural Resources, P.O. Box 450, Madison, WI 53701

WYOMING Travel Commission, 2320 Capitol Avenue, Cheyenne, WY 82002

STATE BOAT REGISTRATION AND SAFETY LAWS

List of State and Territorial Agencies Responsible for Boat Numbering and Safety Laws. Compiled by Ron Stone. Write to Government Relations Department, Boating Industry Association, 401 North Michigan Avenue, Chicago, IL 60611.

RIVER-RUNNING ORGANIZATIONS

Alaska Whitewater Association, Glenallen, AK 99588 (formed "to obtain and disburse river information, to encourage a simple exchange of information among persons with similar interests").

American Canoe Association, 4260 East Evans Avenue, Denver, CO 80222 (a nonprofit, tax-exempt organization that provides "educational, informational, and training services to increase the enjoyment, safety, and skills" for those who use canoes, kayaks, and rafts). *Canoe* is its official publication.

American River Touring Association, 1016 Jackson Street, Oakland, CA 94607 (a nonprofit organization that proposes "to teach the basic skills necessary to safely enjoy our wilderness waterways . . . , to teach people to protect adjacent shores, to publish information, describe routes, access areas, campsites, points of interest, and facilities along the way"). Publication: *Looking Downstream*

American Whitewater Affiliation, P.O. Box 1584, San Bruno, CA 94066 (a national organization of kayakers and canoeists, perhaps even a few rafters, with dozens of local affiliations). Publication: *American Whitewater Journal*

Eastern River Guides Association, P.O. Box 33, Ohiopyle, PA 15470 (an organization of professional river guides in the eastern states).

Western River Guides Association, Inc., 994 Denver Street, Salt Lake City, UT 84111 (an organization of professional river guides in the western states).

Pacific River Outfitters Association, c/o George Wendt, OARS Incorporated, Box 67, Angels Camp, CA 95222.

Rogue River Guides Association (address changes with each year's election of officers; write to Oregon state agencies for up-to-date addresses).

CONSERVATION ORGANIZATIONS (Devoted Fully or in Part to River Conservation)

American Rivers Conservation Council, 324 C Street SE, Washington, DC 20005 (publishes an excellent newsletter, actively lobbying for wild and scenic rivers, a good source of information).

Appalachian Mountain Club, 5 Joy Street, Boston, MA 02108 (valuable source of information about river running, especially in the Northeast).

Friends of the Earth, 529 Commercial Street, San Francisco, CA 94111 (publishes *Not Man Apart,* excellent source of environmental information including much on river protection).

National Audubon Society, 950 Third Avenue, New York, NY 10022 (strong active organization deeply involved in river conservation, publishes excellent magazine, *Audubon,* has numerous local chapters throughout the Continent).

National Wildlife Federation, 1412 Sixteenth Street, NW, Washington, DC 20036 (publishes both *National* and *International Wildlife* magazines, failed to oppose Grand Canyon dams in early 1960s but generally oriented to river conservation).

Sierra Club, 1050 Mills Tower, San Francisco, CA 94104 (very effective national conservation organization with numerous local chapters, publishes monthly *Sierra Club Bulletin,* sponsors non-motorized commercial float trips, lost tax-exempt status by opposing Grand Canyon dams in 1960s).

River Touring Section, 3962 Fordham Way, Livermore, CA 94550 (the river-running arm of the Sierra Club, publishes a fine informational newsletter).

The Wilderness Society, 1901 Pennsylvania Avenue, NW, Washington, DC 20006 (devoted to wilderness preservation, including wild and scenic rivers, publishes quarterly *The Living Wilderness,* sponsors commercial float trips).

also: American Forestry Association, 1319 Eighteenth Street, NW, Washington, DC 20036 (sponsors river trips, sometimes more exploitive than conservation-oriented due to a dominance by timber interests).

Sample of State Conservation Groups (for Idaho)

Hells Canyon Preservation Council, Inc., Box 2317, Idaho Falls, ID 83401

Idaho Environmental Council, Box 3371, University Station, Moscow, ID 83843

River of No Return Wilderness Council, Box 844, Boise, ID 83701

(Most states have local issue-oriented conservation groups: write state agencies and national conservation organizations for information on your area).

Appendix B

Sample Gear List

Sleeping bag and ground cloth
Rubber sleeping pad or air mattress
Waterproof bags for clothes and sleeping gear
Waterproof ammo cans for camera, food, etc.
Tents (personal, toilet, cook shelter)
Eating utensils (personal, kitchen)
Cooking utensils

>   Dutch ovens
>   Fire pans
>   Grill
>   Griddle
>   Nesting pots
>   Pressure cooker
>   Potato peeler
>   Can opener
>   Pancake turners
>   Ladles
>   Big spoons
>>   cooking
>>   serving

Long-handled forks

Fuel stoves and fuel
    charcoal
    propane
    sterno
    butane
    Coleman

Aluminum foil

Dishwash gear
    detergent
    scrubbers
    disinfectant
    buckets or pans
    towels, rags, brushes

Variety of knives—not belt or pocket knives (for health reasons, some states have laws relating to this policy)

Baggies, garbage bags

Paper towels

Ice pick

Hand soap

Portable sanitary facilities (required by regulations on many rivers)

Life jackets

Bail buckets

Water jugs and canteens

Pump for boat, perhaps a vacuum cleaner (for pumping boats, if you have an electrical hookup or generator at launch area)

Coolers for perishables; ice chests (required by regulations on many rivers)

Food

Shovel and broom

Oars or paddles or motor (if a motor is used, a special repair kit, extra parts, and fuel are required), sweeps

Spare oarlocks, eyelets, etc. for repair
Spare ropes, tie-down material
Motor mount (if motor is used or if one is taken along
    for emergency use)
More personal:
    Jeans and/or shorts (one pair of long pants for
        hiking off the river)
    Shirts (some long-sleeved recommended to prevent
        sunburn)
    Underwear and socks
    Bathing suit
    Sweater or sweatshirt
    Jacket
    Two pairs of tennis shoes (or wet boots)
    Rainsuit or poncho
    Hat with string or tie-on
    Towel and washcloth
    Biodegradable soap
    Flashlight and extra batteries
    Sun glasses
    Suntan lotion
    Insect repellent
    Chap stick, hand cream, bag balm
    Small packs of Kleenex
    Shaving kit (optional)
    Toothbrush, toothpaste
    Binoculars, optional (carefully carried in water-
        proof bag or box)
    Gloves, pliers, belt knife
Camera equipment
    Basic camera outfit, waterproof case
    Extension tubes, close-up attachments
    Sturdy compact tripod, film case
    Filters, light meter, electronic flash
    Plastic bags

Waterproof cases (ammo cans) for everything

Day pack, hiking boots

Plenty of film (what you normally use but don't underestimate your need, have plenty)

"Possibles bag" for tobacco, matches, gum, sunglasses, chap stick

First-aid kit

Standard tape and gauze, gauze pads and Band Aids

Aspirin and Bufferin and Alka-Seltzer, etc., milk of magnesia or similar laxative, Kaopectate, Pepto-Bismol, (don't try to be a doctor, but be prepared; try to take a doctor along)

Triangular bandages (several)

Splints (can usually be made on the spot, but it's a good idea to have some along)

Scissors, tweezers, sharp knife

Blankets, space blanket

Salt tablets, baking soda

Sterile "sweet oil" (mineral or olive); petroleum jelly

Absorbent cotton

Ace bandages (stretch)

Thermometer, safety pins

Alcohol, antiseptics

Poison-plant remedy

Sunburn lotion

Eye wash and eye cup

Ammonia capsules

Campho-phenique

Hand cream, Bag Balm

Sanitary napkins

Q-tips, tongue depressors

Ointments (zinc oxide, etc.)

Perhaps a razor

Snakebite kit (learn new technique for first aid)

Repair kit

Soft wire, pliers

Nails, hammer

Screws, eyelets

Bolts, nuts, washers

Tough cord, needle (big, for sewing rips in boat)

Spare parts for anything that might be broken or wear out, including spare frame material

Ax, collapsible saw

Wire cutters

Appropriate wrenches

Screwdrivers

Extra fabric for patching

Patching cement

Solvent

Spare D-rings

Extra rope

Appendix C

International Scale of River Difficulty*

If rapids on a river generally fit into one of the following classifications but the water temperature is below 50 degrees F. or if the trip is an extended trip in a wilderness area, the river should be considered one class more difficult than normal.

CLASS I

Moving water with a few riffles and small waves. Few or no obstructions.

CLASS II

Easy rapids with waves up to 3 feet, and wide, clear channels that are obvious without scouting. Some maneuvering is required.

CLASS III

Rapids with high, irregular waves often capable of swamp-

---

*According to the American Whitewater Affiliation's Safety Code, revised in 1974.

ing an open canoe. Narrow passages that often require complex maneuvering. May require scouting from shore.

CLASS IV

Long difficult rapids with constricted passages that often require precise maneuvering in very turbulent waters. Scouting from shore is often necessary, and conditions make rescue difficult. Generally not possible for open canoes. Boaters in covered canoes and kayaks should be able to Eskimo roll.

CLASS V

Extremely difficult, long, and very violent rapids with highly congested routes which nearly always must be scouted from shore. Rescue conditions are difficult and there is significant hazard to life in event of a mishap. Ability to Eskimo roll is essential for kayaks and canoes.

CLASS VI

Difficulties of Class V carried to the extreme of navigability. Nearly impossible and very dangerous. For teams of experts only, after close study and with all precautions taken.

Appendix D

National Park Service River Running Policy Statement

RATIONALE

The enclosed policy statement clarifies our position on the major current issues over white-water boating at Grand Canyon and Canyonlands National Parks. We believe it is also compatible with boating activity at Big Bend, Dinosaur, and Grand Teton. Essentially, the policy will stabilize existing ceilings, allotments, ratios, concession permits and motorized use until such time as there are defensible reasons for change. It shall not be changed except for just cause or through benefit of fresh scientific knowledge.

The National Park Service is managing white water and other rivers where the public enjoyment of float trips has expanded at an unparalleled rate. Had this trend in use been permitted to continue unchecked, it would have caused severe and possibly irreparable ecological damage in the river environs. The rate of accelerated use was so great that there was no time to prepare management plans on a controlled, scientific basis.

Within 3 to 5 years, scientific research should help in the refinement of the carrying capacity of each river ecosystem, analyze the social and economic ramifications of river running, and provide management parameters for future decisions. All carrying capacity research on rivers where use now occurs shall be completed by December 31, 1977. It cannot resolve socioeconomic arguments about the decision of available time and space or evaluation of the relative merits of different user groups. To a certain degree, some management decisions must always be subjective.

The National Park Service recognized the basic conflicts between river use groups and appreciates the underlying causes. We also understand the differences in character and use between the different river systems and the impossibility of satisfying all present and potential users. However, since there is significant apprehension, misunderstanding and uncertainty about the future control of float-trip boating, it is desirable to establish a national policy. It is not a complete policy, but it states the service's position on current major issues.

We urge the affected superintendents to make wide distribution of the interim policy and the contents of this memorandum so that all concerned river runners will be informed.

POLICY STATEMENT

In order to enhance visitor enjoyment and safety and in order to preserve environmental quality, the following policy is adopted to regulate float-trip activities on segments of the Colorado, Snake, Rio Grande, and Alaskan river drainages within existing and proposed units of the National Park System.

Carrying Capacity. Establish through scientific research the level of use that each river system can sustain. Complete necessary research by December 31, 1977. Temporarily establish as a safe interim capacity a level of use which will prevent unacceptable resource deterioration.

Management Plans. A river-running management plan will be developed for each appropriate unit of the National Park System. During the plan preparation, alternatives and their environmental impacts will be discussed in appropriate environmental impact documents. The plans for all affected areas are scheduled to be completed by December 31, 1974, with final approval no later than April 30, 1976.

Volume of Use. Established use ceilings will not be changed unless such a change is supported by sufficient scientific evidence. Changes in overall ceilings shall be prorated equitably.

The size and ratio of established use allotments among users will not change unless supported by adequate justification. Individual allotments may be reduced or vacated by mutual agreement, and the allotment may be reassigned at the discretion of the government. No penalty will accrue due to nonuse of an allotment or a portion thereof. Unused portions of allotments shall be disposed of in the best interest of the government.

Commercial Permits. There is an adequate number of concessionaires to serve the needs of the public in each park with well-established commercial use. If new services are required, they may be provided as a condition of one or more of the existing permits. There shall be no new permits issued in any park where significant commercial boating presently occurs. The number may be reduced through attrition or through issuance of a concession prospectus specifying a lower number.

Rationing Use. Where the demand exceeds a ceiling level, use may be rationed. The no-repeat rule is an acceptable tool to assure that any group or groups of private boaters does not monopolize the private allotments; provided, however, qualified party leadership shall not be jeopardized. Commercial outfitters shall be strongly encouraged to enforce a similar rule with their clientele.

Motorized Use For the present, where motorized craft are presently used, there will not be a mandatory elimination of motors; nor shall there be an increase in motorized use, and those people using motors shall be encouraged to voluntarily reduce that use.

There shall be no permanent decision made about motorized boating until additional data on safety and pollution has been obtained.

Where motors are used, daily mileage limitations may be imposed to prevent fast, substandard trips for commercial passengers.

Public Notification. All river users shall be notified of proposed management decisions and have an opportunity to participate in the decision-making process. When decisions will have a major effect on any group or sector of boaters, the implementation time will be commensurate with the degree of operational or economic impact.

If during this period there is evidence through research or other factors that a change in the policy can be made, such changes will be implemented only after the above conditions of public notification are met.

Appendix E

Selected Bibliography

BOOKS ON RIVER RUNNING

American River Touring Association (ARTA). *River Guides' Manual*. ARTA, 1016 Jackson Street, Oakland, CA 94607, 1973. This small paperback is not for sale but is available to ARTA members; write for information.

Angier, Bradford, and Taylor, Zack. *Introduction to Canoeing*. Harrisburg, PA: Stackpole Books, 1973. $2.95. This paperback contains useful chapters on river running, favorite floating areas, canoe camping, and one especially good chapter, "The Happy Canoe Trip."

Appalachian Mountain Club (AMC). *New England Canoeing Guide*. AMC, 5 Joy Street, Boston, MA 02108, 1971. $6. A guide to the canoeable waters of New England.

Arighi, Scott and Margaret S. *Wildwater Touring*. New York: MacMillan, Inc., 1974. $8.95. This book contains an especially good appendix on flow and gradient data; otherwise, it is primarily for the northwest—Idaho and Oregon.

Automobile Club of Southern California. *Riverboat Trips*. 1973. This publication is for members only, but is useful, if you can obtain a copy, for float-trip coverage on most western rivers serviced by commercial outfitters.

Burrell, Bob, and Davidson, Paul. *Wild Water: West Virginia*. McClain Printing Company, Parsons, WV 26287, 1972. $3. A most valuable guide to the rivers of West Virginia and a few in surrounding states.

Canoe Trails of Southern Wisconsin ($4.95), *Canoe Trails of Northeastern Wisconsin* ($4.75), *Canoe Trails of North-Central Wisconsin* ($4). All available from Wisconsin Trails, P.O. Box 5650, Madison, WI 53705.

Canoe Trails of Northwestern Wisconsin. Wisconsin Indian Head Country, 1316 Fairfax Street, Eau Claire, WI 54701.

Carter, Randy. *Canoeing White Water*. Appalachian Books, Oakton, VA 22124, 1967, 1974. $4.75. Covers rivers in Virginia and eastern West Virginia, North Carolina, and eastern Tennessee, even Georgia and South Carolina.

Colwell, Robert. *Introduction to Water Trails in America*. Harrisburg, Pa. Stackpole Books, 1973. $2.95. This paperback lists dozens of water trails near most major cities, plus a brief description of river-trip possibilities throughout the nation.

Dickerman, Pat. *Adventure Trip Guide*. Adventure Trip Guide, 36 East 57th Street, New York, NY 10022, 1974. A guide to river trips thoughout the nation—a good source of data on guides.

Dwyer, Ann. *Canoeing Waters of California*. GBH Press, 125 Upland Press, Kentfield, CA 94904, 1973. The best book on floatable waters in California.

Furrer, Werner. *Kayak & Canoe Trips in Washington*. Signpost Publications, 16812 6th Avenue West, Lynnwood, WA 98036, 1971. Covers a dozen Washington rivers and a couple of lakes.

Geological Survey Professional Paper 669: The Colorado River Region and John Wesley Powell. U.S. Government Printing Office, Washington, DC 20402, 1969. $4.25. Includes Luna B. Leopold's, "The Rapids and the Pools—Grand Canyon."

Hall, Leonard. *Stars Upstream.* Columbia: University of Missouri Press, 1969. $2.50. This paperback deals with numerous river trips on the Current and the Jacks Fork.

Jenkinson, Michael. *Wild Rivers of North America.* New York: E.P. Dutton & Company, Inc., 1973. $12.95. This book deals specifically with several rivers and more generally with another "106 Wild Rivers to Run."

Leydet, Francois. *Time and the River Flowing: Grand Canyon.* A Sierra Club-Ballantine Book, 1050 Mills Tower, San Francisco, CA 94104, 1964, 1968. $3.95.

Malo, John. *Malo's Complete Guide to Canoeing and Canoe-Camping.* Chicago: Quadrangle Books, 1969. $6.95.

Malo, John. *Wilderness Canoeing.* Available from the American Canoe Association Book Service, 4260 East Evans Avenue, Denver, CO 80222.

McNair, Robert E. *Basic River Canoeing.* American Camping Association, Inc., Bradford Woods, Martinsville, IN 46151, 1972. $2.

Nash, Roderick, ed. *Grand Canyon of the Living Colorado.* A Sierra Club-Ballantine Book, 1970. $8.50. Includes contributions by David Brower, Colin Fletcher, Allen J. Malmquist, Roderick Nash, and Stewart L. Udall.

Penn State Outing Club. *Select Rivers of Central Pennsylvania.* Canoe Division, Penn State Outing Club, 60 Recreation Building, University Park, PA 16802, 1973. A guide, continually being updated, that covers many Pennsylvania streams.

Pittsburgh Council. *Canoeing Guide: Western Pennsylvania/Northern West Virginia.* Pittsburgh Council, American Youth Hostels, Inc., 6300 Fifth Avenue, Pittsburgh, PA 15232, 1973. This book contains excellent material and has an excellent appendix with good local and general information.

Powell, John Wesley. *The Exploration of the Colorado River and Its Canyons.* New York: Dover Publications, Inc., 1961. $3. This is a paperback edition of Powell's journal on his exploration of the previously unknown canyons of the Green and Colorado rivers. The American Museum of Natural History has also sponsored an edition, published by Doubleday.

Riviere, Bill. *Pole, Paddle & Portage: A Complete Guide to Canoeing.* New York: Van Nostrand Reinhold Company, 1973. $6.95. This is one of the best books on the subject I've seen, with comprehensive appendix material and good data on what rivers to run in both the United States and Canada.

Staveley, Gaylord. *Broken Waters Sing.* A Sports Illustrated Book published by Little, Brown and Company, Boston, 1971. $6.95. A retracing of the Powell expedition route a hundred years later by an experienced river runner, a personal friend.

Texas Rivers and Rapids. Texas Rivers and Rapids, P.O. Box 673, Humble, TX 77338. $5.95 plus 60¢ for postage, tax, and handling. This book contains 128 pages of adventures and discovery on 24 Texas rivers, streams, and bayous, plus maps and summaries of several rivers in nearby states.

Urban, John T. *A White Water Handbook for Canoe and Kayak.* AMC, 1973. $1.50. Excellent background material.

Whitney, Peter Dwight. *White-Water Sport: Running Rapids in Kayak and Canoe.* Ronald Press Company, 15 East 26th Street, New York, NY 10010, 1960. $4.

BOOKS ON RELATED SUBJECTS

History

Abbey, Edward. *Desert Solitare.* New York: McGraw-Hill. $6.45. This book is a classic among conservationists, especially in the southwest.

Bonney, Orrin H. and Lorraine. *Battle Drums and Geysers.* Chicago: The Swallow Press, 1970, $15. This book includes an account of the first attempted exploration of the Snake River and the first scientific exploration of the Yellowstone country and a biography of the man who did both.

Irving, Washington. *Astoria.* Norman: University of Oklahoma Press, 1964. $7.95. An account of early exploration in the Rocky Mountain West with some accounts of early river-running experiences.

Krutch, Joseph Wood. *Grand Canyon.* An American Museum of Natural History (N-20) book by Doubleday, 1958, 1962. $1.25. Krutch on Grand Canyon, inside and out.

Leopold, Aldo. *Sand County Almanac.* New York: Oxford University Press, 1948, 1969. $1.95 ($2.15 in Canada). This classic commentary by the father of popular ecology is must reading for anyone who would explore the outdoor world.

Murphy, Robert. *The Stream.* New York: Pyramid Books, 1971. $1.25. This book has nothing to do with river running but a lot to do with ecological relationships and the need to do battle on the conservation front.

Norton, Boyd. *Snake Wilderness.* San Francisco: Sierra Club, 1972. $7.95. An account of the conservation battles in the Snake River drainage.

Stegner, Wallace. *Beyond the Hundredth Meridian.* Boston: Houghton Mifflin Company, 1962. $2.45. A paperback account of the Powell expeditions.

Natural History

The Peterson Field Guide Series. All of these books are very good.

Robbins, Bruun, and Zim. *Birds of North America.* New York: Golden Press, Western Publishing Company, Inc., 1966. $5.95. This is a good bird book to have along on river trips, with adequate maps and good color plates.

Geology

Hayes, Philip T., and Simmons, George C. *River Runners' Guide to Dinosaur National Monument and Vicinity.* Volume 1. River Runners' Guide Series. Powell Society, Ltd., 750 Vine Street, Denver CO 80206, 1973. $3. This book covers the Yampa and Green rivers with an emphasis on geologic features.

Love, J.D., and Reed, John C. *Creation of the Teton Landscape.* U.S. Geologic Survey, 1968. $2. An account of the geologic forces at work in northwest Wyoming where the Upper Snake River has carved its path through the glacial gravels of Jackson Hole; although it deals specifically with the Teton area, it has implications for many other river trips.

Mutschler, Felix E. *River Runners' Guide to the Canyons of the Green and Colorado Rivers.* Volume 2. River Runners' Guide Series. Powell Society, Ltd. Covers Labyrinth, Stillwater and Cataract Canyons.

Simmons, George C., and Gaskill, David L. *River Runners' Guide to Marble Gorge and Grand Canyon.* Volume 3. River Runners' Guide Series. Powell Society, Ltd.

RIVER GUIDES

All the guides listed are published by Westwater Books, Box 365, Boulder City, NV 89005. They are all available in a standard edition ($3.95), and all but the

Snake River Guide are also available in a waterproof edition ($5.95).

Belknap, Buzz. *Canyonlands River Guide.* On parts of Green and Colorado rivers.

Belknap, Buzz. *Grand Canyon River Guide.* On Lee's Ferry, Arizona to Lake Mead.

Evans, Laura, and Belknap, Buzz. *Desolation River Guide.* On the Green River.

Evans, Laura, and Belknap, Buzz. *Dinosaur River Guide.* On the Yampa and Green rivers.

Huser, Verne, and Belknap, Buzz. *Snake River Guide.* On the Upper Snake River in Wyoming.

FEDERAL AND STATE AGENCY PUBLICATIONS

Mostly paperbacks and pamphlets.

Agriculture Stabilization and Conservation Service. *Public Access Fact Book.* U.S. Department of Agriculture, Washington, DC 20250, 1974.

Black Creek Float Trip. Supervisor, De Soto National Forest, Box 1291, Jackson, MS 39505.

Boster, Mark A. *Colorado River Trips within Grand Canyon National Park and Monument: A Socio-Economic Analysis.* Technical Report No. 10 (June 1972), University of Arizona, Tucson, AZ 85721.

Bureau of Land Management. *Alaska Canoe Trails.* Bureau of Land Management, Box 2511, Juneau, AK 99801. Several other pamphlets on specific areas are also available.

Bureau of Outdoor Recreation. *Buffalo River, Tennessee: Wild and Scenic River Study.* Bureau of Outdoor Recreation, Southeast Region, Atlanta, GA, August 1974.

Bureau of Outdoor Recreation. *A Catalog of Guides to Outdoor Recreation Areas and Facilities.* Bureau of

Outdoor Recreation. U.S. Department of the Interior, Washington, DC 20240.

Bureau of Outdoor Recreation. *Proposed Obed National Wild and Scenic River Study.* Draft Environmental Statement, Bureau of Outdoor Recreation, U.S. Department of the Interior, Southeast Regional Office, Atlanta, GA, August 1974.

Clowes, John. *Canoeing in Kentucky.* Department of Public Information, Capitol Annex, Frankfort, KY 40601.

DeHart, Don and Vangie. *A Guide of the Yukon River.* Don and Vangie Hart, Hart D Ranch, Gakona, AK 99586 (Winter: Box 3073, Cheyenne, WY 82001), 1971.

Department of Conservation. *Canoeing Trails in Indiana.* Department of Conservation, 612 State Office Building, Indianapolis, IN 46209.

Department of Conservation. *Minnesota Voyageur Trails.* Division of Parks and Recreation, Department of Conservation, 320 Centennial Building, St. Paul, MN 55101.

Department of Economic Development. *Canoeing in Maine.* Department of Economic Development, Tourism Division, Augusta, ME 04330.

Department of Environmental Conservation. *Adirondack Canoe Routes.* Department of Environmental Conservation, Albany, NY 12226.

Department of Natural Resources. *Florida Canoe Trail Guide, 1972-73.* Department of Natural Resources, Tallahassee, FL 32304.

Department of Natural Resources. *Michigan Guide to Easy Canoeing.* Department of Natural Resources, Steven T. Mason Building, Lansing, MI 48926.

Department of Natural Resources. *Ohio Canoe Adventures.* Department of Natural Resources, Division of Watercraft, 1350 Holly Avenue, Columbus, OH 43212.

Department of Natural Resources. *Wisconsin Water Trails.*

Department of Natural Resources, Madison, WI 53701.

Department of Wildlife Conservation. *Scenic Rivers.* Department of Wildlife Conservation, 1801 North Lincoln, Oklahoma City, OK 73105.

Fish and Game Department. *Montana's Popular Float Streams.* Fish and Game Department, Helena, MT 59601.

Game and Fish Commission. *Buffalo River Float Map.* Game and Fish Commission, Box 40747, Nashville, TN 37220.

Hawksley, Oz. *Missouri Ozark Waterways.* Conservation, North Ten Mile Drive, Jefferson City, MO 65101, revised in 1972.

Illinois Department of Conservation. *Illinois Canoeing Guide.* Illinois Department of Conservation, Boating Section, 200 South Spring Street, Springfield, IL.

Iowa Conservation Commission. *Iowa Canoe Trips.* Iowa Conservation Commission, 300 Fourth Street, Des Moines, IA 50319.

Nebraska Game and Fish Commission. *Canoeing Nebraska.* Nebraska Game and Fish Commission, 2200 North 33rd Street, Lincoln, NB 68503.

Pennsylvania Fish Commission. *Canoeing in Delaware and Susquehanna Watersheds.* Pennsylvania Fish Commission, Box 1673, Harrisburg, PA 17120.

State Parks and Recreation Commission. *Allagash Wilderness Waterway.* State Parks and Recreation Commission, Augusta, ME 04330.

Stream Preservation in Arkansas. Printed by Midwest Research Institute, Kansas City, MO, but distributed by Arkansas Fish and Game Commission, February 1969.

Tourism Development Division. *Canoeing in Tennessee.* Tourism Development Division, Andrew Jackson Building, Nashville, TN 37219.

A Joint Report of the U.S. Department of Agriculture and U.S. Department of the Interior. *Wild Rivers.* Available through the Bureau of Outdoor Recreation, 1965.

U.S. Department of the Interior. *Scenic River Study of the Lower St. Croix River.* U.S. Department of the Interior, February 1973.

U.S. Forest Service. *Canoeing the Chattooga.* U.S. Forest Service, Box 1437, Gainesville, GA 30501.

U.S. Forest Service. *Eleven Point National Scenic River Unit Plan.* Mark Twain National Forest, Eastern Region, U.S. Forest Service, Department of Agriculture, Milwaukee, WI.

U.S. Geological Survey. *John Wesley Powell's Exploration of the Colorado River* (INF-74-19). U.S. Geological Survey, U.S. Department of the Interior, Washington, DC 20240.

University of Oregon. *Public Input Workbook for River Adventurers & Environmentalists.* Outdoor Program, Erb Memorial Union, University of Oregon, Eugene, OR 97403.

Vermont State Division of Recreation and Department of Water Resources. *Canoeing on the Connecticut River.* Vermont State Division of Recreation and Department of Water Resources, Agency of Environmental Conservation, Montpelier, VT 05602.

MAGAZINES

American Whitewater. Journal of the American Whitewater Affiliation, Box 1584, San Bruno, CA 94066.

Canoe. Magazine of the American Canoe Association, 1999 Shepard Road, St. Paul, MN 55116.

Down River. Box 366, Mountain View, CA 94040.

Oar & Paddle. Box 83401, Idaho Falls, ID 83401.

Rio Grande Gurgle. Ms. Helen F. Redman, editor; Route 1,

Box 177, Santa Fe, NM 87501.

MAPS

U.S. Geological Survey offices

Les Jones, Star Route, Box 13A, Heber City, UT 84032. Maps of many western rivers including a number in Canada and at least one in Mexico.

Westwater Books, Box 365, Boulder City, NV 89005.

Other federal and state agencies, especially the U.S. Forest Service.

MAGAZINE ARTICLES

Almost anything you find in such publications as *Canoe, Down River, Oar & Paddle, American Whitewater,* ARTA's *Looking Downstream,* the American Rivers Conservation Council *Newsletter,* and other similar publications will be worth your reading. This list is representative rather than comprehensive.

"Beating the New River." *Time,* Modern Living section, 16 July 1973.

Burris, Fred and Dora. "How to Make Bears Bearable." *Field and Stream,* June 1974.

Craighead, John and Frank. "Whitewater Adventure on Wild Rivers of Idaho." *National Geographic,* February 1970.

Czura, Pete. "Running the River: Conflict on the Colorado," *True,* May 1974. I find this a biased article.

Featherstone, Vaughn J. "Adventure of White-Water River Running," *The New Era,* an LDS Church publication, June 1974.

Frome, Michael. "Must This Be Lost To the Sight of Man?" *Field and Stream,* July 1969.

Hanna, Jon. "River of Rapid Streams," *Pennsylvania Angler,* July 1974.

Jackson, Ervin, Jr. "Exploring the Chattooga River." *Wilderness Camping,* March-April 1974.

Jones, Robert F. "The Old Man and the River." *Sports Illustrated,* August 1970.

Joy, Elizabeth. "Guiding Vacation Adventurers Down Utah's Green River." *National Geographic School Bulletin,* 18 February 1974.

Kline, Doyle, "The Rio Grande: First To Go Wild." *New Mexico Magazine,* Spring 1971.

Netherby, Steve. Camping Column entitled, "Opening the Survival Kits." *Field and Stream,* August 1974.

Norton, Boyd. "The Last Great Dam." *Audubon,* January 1970.

Pettingill, Olin Sewall, Jr. "Birding Down the River." *Audubon,* October 1968.

Pratt-Johnson, Betty. "Canoeing Canada's Bowron Lake Wilderness." *Trail Camping,* June 1973. There is also a column on Fiberfill II in the same issue.

Rossbach, George B. "By Canoe Down Thelon River." *The Beaver,* Autumn 1966.

Rutstrum, Calvin. "Wilderness Canoe Travel." *The Beaver,* Summer 1966.

Sands, Tom. "Suwanee River." *Southern Telephone News,* September 1960.

Shrake, Edwin. "Rapids Round the Bend." *Sports Illustrated,* May 1974.

Wallace, Robert. "Wooden Boats Plus Colorado Rapids Equal Adventure." *Smithsonian,* May 1974. This should be read to balance the Czura article listed above.

NEWSPAPER ARTICLES

Representative rather than comprehensive:

Anderson, Mike. "Area Rivers Whet White Water Appetite." *The Pittsburgh Press,* 25 June 1974, page 32.

Brokaw, Tom. "That River Swallows People. Some It Gives Up; Some It Don't." *West,* the Sunday magazine in the *Los Angeles Times,* 1 November 1970, pages 12-19. This is one of the best pieces ever done on river running, a real classic.

Creighton, Jim. "Riding the River." *St. Louis Post-Dispatch,* 26 June 1974.

Grass, Ray. "Westwater: Wild Rapids and History!" *Desert News* of Salt Lake City, 20 June 1974.

Hunter, David. "Canoes Reach Wilderness of the Little Miami." Summer Travel section in *The Cincinnati Enquirer,* 9 June 1974, page 1-L.

Levy, Harris, and Newman, Felice. "Wild West Virginia: Almost Heaven," *The Pitt News,* 10 July 1974, page 7.

Montgomery, Jerry. "Wild Rivers." *The Seattle Times,* 28 November 1971.

"Park Preparing Plan to Control River Traffic." *Jackson Hole News,* 8 August 1974, page 11.

Satterfield, Archie. "The River Act: Its Aims and Provisions." *The Seattle Times,* 28 November 1971.

Index

A

Adventure Guides, Inc., 208
Adventure Trip Guide, 96
Air mattresses, 46
Air pressure, 87-90, 104, 113, 176
Alabama, 15, 218-19, 259
Alaska, 12, 15, 230, 231, 246, 259
Alaska White Water Association, 15, 246, 263
Allegash River, 68, 211
American Canoe Association, 263
American Forestry Association, 265
American River, 12
American Rivers Conservation Council, 264
American River Touring Association (ARTA), 178, 263; *River Guides Manual,* 178, 181, 185, 277; White-Water school, 96, 230, 247, *illus.* 97, 102
American Safety Equipment Corp. 62
American Whitewater, 67, 94, 286
American Whitewater Affiliation (AWA 66, 96, 263
Ammo cans, 23-24, *illus.* 24, 79, 106
Appalachian Mountain Club, 211, 264
Arizona, 15, 259
Arkansas, 223, 224, 259
Armstrong Products Co., 36
ARTA. See American River Touring Association
Atlantic-Pacific Mfg. Corp., 32

Au Sable River, 12, 230
Avon Rubber Company, 59-60, 208, *illus.* 22, 61

B

Bailing systems, 83, 112, *illus.* 82
Barker, Dick, 5, 7, 58, 90
Bauer (Eddie) tent equipment, 45
Beacon Chemical Co., 36
Beaver, The, 248
Belknap's (Bill) Fastwater Expeditions, 59, 96
Bentley's (Jerry) Orange Torpedo Trips, 96, 247
Big Piney Creek, 225
Bird watching, 157, 158, 164-68
Black Creek River, 12, 222
Boats, 55-67. See also names of crafts
Boat Safety Act, Federal, 9, 14, 29
Bois Brule River, 228
Bruneau River, 12, 17
Buffalo River, 12, 18, 221-22, 224
Burleson, Bob, 226
Buoyant devices, 29

C

Calawash River, 231
California, 230, 248, 259
Camera equipment, 27, 47, 48, 268-69
Campbell, Jim, 48
Camping, 116-24, *illus.* 117, 118, 121; equipment, 42-48, *illus.* 43, 44, 45

Canada, 248-52
Canoe, 67, 94, 263, 286
Canoes, *illus.* 65; inflatable, 63-64; hard-hulled, 65-67
Canoe Trips West, Inc., 67
Capsizing, 179-82
Casselman River, 216
Cataract Canyon, 232, 236, *illus.* 3
C-Craft CD 9, 60
Chama River, 234
Chattooga River, 4, 12, 18, 68, 219-21
Cheat River, 215-16
Children, safety of, 107-8, *illus.* 31
Clackamas River, 232
Clearwater River, 12, 71, 244
Clothing, 27, 49-50, 268
Coleman Company, Inc., 34; coolers, 40; lanterns, 33-34; pumps, 88, 104; sleeping bags, 46; stoves, 39; tents, 45
Colorado, 15-16, 259
Colorado River, 7, 11, 12, 13, 193-96, 234, 235, 237, *illus.* 3, 20, 237; exploration, 1, 2
Commercial float trips, 7, 8, 37, 95-98, 194, 196-99. *See also* Eastern River Guides Assn., Western River Guides Assn., *and names of outfitters*
Connecticut, 16, 259
Connecticut River, 211
Containers, waterproof, 23-27, *illus.* 117
Cooking, 119-20; equipment, 37-42; menu planning, 98-100
Coolers, 40, 267
Cosumnes River, 12
Craighead, John and Frank, 59-60, 158
Curlers, 129
Current River, 11, 223-24
Currey, Jack, 85

D
Dacor Company, 32
Dacron Fiberfill II, 46
Deliverance (movie), 4, 219
Delousing bags, 25
Deschutes River, 231
Dickerson, Pat, 96, 208
Dolores River, 237-38
Down (filling), 46, 50
Down River, 67, 286
Downstream, 94

Dragan, Jon, 58, 70, 96, 213, 217, *illus.* 206
Dwyer, Ann, 26-27, 96, 230, *illus.* 26

E
Eagle River, 12
Eastern River Guides Assn., 208, 263
Easy Rider, 67
Eddies, 112, 128, 129, 145, 146, 184-85 *illus.* 131, 132
Eleven Point River, 4, 12, 224
Emergencies, 32, 107, 178-86. *See also* First aid
Equipment, 23-53; checklists, 266-70. *See also names of types of equipment*
Ewing, Frank, 57, 58, 90, 138

F
Farmington River Watershed Assn., Inc., 211
Fatalities from river running, 4, 28, 108-9, 175, 215, 219
Feather Craft, Inc., 67
Federal Boat Safety Act, 9, 14, 29
Ferguson, Mike, 36
First aid, 186-91
First aid kit, 52, 107, 191-92, 269-70
Flambeau River, 229, 230
Flexpaint Manufacturing Co., 38
Floating techniques, 109-12, 115, 139-49, *illus.* 110, 116, 140, 141
Floors, 81-83, *illus.* 82, 89, 106
Folbot Corporation, 27, 66
Folding boats, 66
Frames, 74-81, *illus.* 77, 78, 80, 82, 106
Fraser River, 248
Fretwall, "Stretch," 234
Friends of the Earth, 264

G
Gaco Western, Inc., 36
Gauley River, 217
Gear. *See* Equipment
Georgia, 10, 219, 259
Glover River, 225
Goodrich (B.F.) Co., 58
Grand Canyon, 15, 37, 193-96, 235, *illus.* 20, 237
Grande Ronde River, 12, 231, 241
Green River, 11, 12, 234, 235
Green River model, 57, 58, 59, *illus.* 90

Greys River, 12, 241
G-rig, 83, *illus.* 84,
Grumman Allied Industries, 66, 67

H

Haystacks, 129, *illus.* 131
Health and safety. *See* Emergencies;
    First aid; Safety
Helfrich, Dave, 231, 246
Hells Canyon, 203-4, 241, *illus.* 156
High Performance Products, Inc., 66
Hoback River, 241
Hoh River, 231
Holliday, Dee, 119-20, *illus.* 119
Hypothermia, 190-91

I

Ice chests, 40, 267
Idaho, 11-12, 16, 259, 265
Iliad Inc., paddles, 71
Illinois River, 225
Imperial Manufacturers, 31-32
Imtra Corp., 60
Inflatable boats, 58-64; canoes and
    kayaks, 63-64; licensing, 14;
    standards, 16-17; storage, 125
Inflatable Boats Co., 36
Inland Marine Co., 60
Interagency Whitewater Committee (IWC),
    10-11, 13
Iowa, 17, 260

J

Jacks Fork River, 11, 223-24
Jarbridge River, 12
Jefferson River, 244
John Day River, 231
Jones, Jim, 225
J-rig, 85

K

Kayaks, 63-64, 65-67, *illus.* 63, 174
Keith, Elmer, 138-39
Kentucky, 17, 260
Kings River, 12, 224-25
Klamath bag, 26-27, *illus.* 26
Klepper Corp., 27, 66
Kovalik, Vladimir, 62-63, 96, 247

L

Landing procedures, 112-13, *illus.* 114
Lantern, Coleman, 33-34, *illus.* 33
Leisure Imports, 64
Life jackets, 29, 30, 62, *illus.* 28,
    30, 51. *See also* Personal
    Flotation Devices

Lightning, 153
Lights, 33-34
Lines and ropes, 91, 105-9, 177
Little Miami River, 227
Lochsa River, 12, 243-44

M

M-16 raft, *illus.* 47, 57
McCarthy, Ed, 217
McCarty, Ralph, 96, 213, 215-16
Mackenzie River (Canada), 252
McKenzie River (Oregon), 232
Maine, 211, 212, 260
Manistee River, 230
Man overboard, 182-83
Mansfield Sanitary, Inc., 34
Maryland, 215, 218, 260
Mattawin River, 250
Meal Planning, 98-100
Menominee River, 229
Merced River, 12
Michigan, 17, 229-30, 260
Middle Fork. *See* Salmon River
Minnesota, 17, 230, 260
Miramichi River, 249
Mississippi River, 222, 230
Missouri, 223, 260
Missouri River, 223, 244
Mokelumne River, 12
Monogram Industries, Inc., 34
Montana, 244, 260
Motorboats, 13, 37, 67-68, 143-44,
    195, 196, 276
Mountain Streams and Trails Outfitters,
    96, 213
Mulberry River, 225
Murphy, Dave, 234

N

Nantahala Outdoors, Inc., 221
Nash, Dr. Roderick, 64, 94, *illus.*
    174
National Audubon Society, 264
National Park Service, 10, 11-12,
    194-95, 235, 238, 255-56, 273-76
National Water Resources Data
    Network, 13
National Wildlife Federation, 264
Natural Progression Kayaks, 66
Newcos rafts, 62
New River, 216-17, *illus.* 19, 201
North Carolina, 219, 261
North Face, The, 45

O
Oar and Paddle, 67, 94
Oarlocks, 73-74, *illus.* 75
Oars, 71-74, 81, 139, 140, 142, *illus.*
    69; spares, 31, 107
Obed River, 221, 222
Oklahoma, 225, 261
Old Town Canoe Company, 66
Oregon, 18, 230-31, 231-32, 246, 261
Outdoor Adventures, 62
Outfitters. *See* Commercial float
    trips, *and names of outfitters*
Owyhee River, 12

P
Pacific River Outfitters Assn., 264
Paddles, 68, 70-71, 139, 140, *illus.*
    69; spares, 107
Penn State Outing Club, 213-14
Pennsylvania, 214, 217, 261
Personal Flotation Devices (PFDs),
    9-10, 28-31, 62, 109, 190-91, *illus.*
    28, 30, 31, 51; type I, 10, 29, 30,
    31; type II, 10, 29, 180; type III,
    10, 29; type IV, 10, 29; type V, 29
Personal gear, 48-50
Phillips Hardware Company, 32
Phoenix Products, Inc., 66
Pine Creek River, 217
Pittsburgh Council of the American
    Youth Hostels, Inc., 213
Pollution and abuse of river
    resources, 8, 42, 118, 119-20, 155,
    193, 198-99, 201, *illus.* 202, 203
Pontoons, 57-58, 59, 83, *illus.* 54,
    59
Powell, John Wesley, v, 1, 2, 13, 94,
    135-36, 193
Powell, Lake, 232, 237
Pumps, 87-91, 104, *illus.* 87, 89, 124

Q
Queets River, 231

R
Rafts, 55-58, 61, *illus.* 56, 57
Rapids, classification of, 129-35,
    271-72; techniques for, 113-15,
    128, 129-35, 135-39, 145, *illus.*
    126, 132, 133, 134, 137, 147
Redstart, Redcrest, Redseal, Redshank
    (dinghys), 60
Repair kit, 35-37, 107, 270
Rice River, 12

Rigging, 103-9, *illus.* 104, 106, 108
Rigs, 74-87, *illus.* 76; floors,
    81-83; frames, 74-81
Rio Grande, 11, 223, 226, 232, 234
River management, 8-9, 9-21, 199-200,
    202-6. *See also names of agencies
    as* National Park Service
Rock, types of, 170-72
Rocky Mountain River Expeditions, 36
Rogue River, 12, 230, 231, 232, 242,
    245, 246-47
Rogue River Guides Assn., 264
Ropes and lines, 91, 105-9, 177
Rubatex Corporation, 32
Rubber Fabricators, 57

S
Safety, 175-78, 42, 263; equipment,
    28-37, 176, *illus.* 12. *See also*
    Emergencies; First aid
St. Croix River, 226, 230
St. John River, 249
Salmon River, 7, 12, 17, 37, 68, 139,
    200-201, 241, 242-43, *illus.* 11,
    141, 149
Salmon River models, 57, 58, *illus.*
    59, 80, 82, 106, 200
San Juan River, 11, 12
Sanke River, 241, 248
Savage River, 218
Sawyer Canoe Company, 67, 71
Sea Eagle models, 64
Seagull Marine Sales, 60
Seda Products, 27, 62
Selway River, 12, 17, 241-242, 243-44
Sevylor U.S.A., Inc., 64
Shigellosis outbreak, 8, 42
Sierra Club, 265
Signaling devices, 32-33, 107
Sleeping bags, 46
Smith-rig, 86, *illus.* 20, 86
Smith River, 231-32, 246
Smith, Ron, 36, 58, 59, 86
Smoker Lumber Company, 67
Snake bite, 188-89, 192
Snake River, 7, 11, 12, 17, 37, 67,
    197-98, 204-5, 238-41, *illus.* 239
Soleduck River, 231
South Carolina, 18, 261
Southeastern Expeditions, Inc., 221
Sportyak model, 59
Stanislaus River, 7, 12, 230, 245,
    247-48, *illus.* 144

State regulations, 14, 259-63
Staveley (Gay) Canyoneers ROWorkshop
    and Follow-Me Floats, 96
Stearns Manufacturing Co., 29, 30-31
Stoves, 38-39, *illus.* 38, 49
Suck-holes, 142, 148-49
Sunburn, 49, 154, 189
Surf-Kayak Company, 66
Suspended floors, 81-83, *illus.* 82,
    89, 106
Swanson Boat Oar Company, 71
Sweeps, 68-70, 81, 139, 142-43, *illus.*
    69, 143; spares, 107

T
Tahiti (model), 64
Tailwaves, 129, 130
Taos Expeditions, 234
Tennessee, 18, 221-22, 261
Tents, 43-46, *illus.* 43, 44, 45
Texas, 18, 226, 261
Toilets, chemical, 34-35, 45, 118-19,
    187-88, 195; *illus.* 35, 119, 187
Tool kit, 35-37, 107, 270
Trail Camping, 46
Triple-rig, 85, *illus.* 84, 126
Tuolumne River, 12, 248
Turtle River, 12

U
U.S. Army Corps of Engineers, 10,
    256-57
U.S. Bureau of Land Management (BLM),
    10, 12, 231, 235, 254
U.S. Bureau of Outdoor Recreation,
    254
U.S. Bureau of Reclamation, 10, 255
U.S. Bureau of Sport Fisheries and
    Wildlife, 255
U.S. Coast Guard, 9-10, 29, 30, 257-58
U.S. Dept. of the Interior, 254-56
U.S. Forest Service, 4-5, 10, 12,
    200-201, 203-204, 205, 220-21, 238
U.S. Geologic Survey, 9, 13
Utah, 19, 234, 262

V
"V" pattern, 136, *illus.* 134
Volpert, Bob, 62
Voyageur Enterprises, 25-26, 39

W
Warm Springs River, 235
Washington, 231, 262
Water Meister Sports, 67

Waterproof storage of equipment, 23-27,
    illus. 117
Western River Guides Assn., 11, 202-3,
    208, 264
Western States Boating Administrator's
    Assn, 13-14
West Virginia, 216, 262
Westwater Canyon, 236
Wet-weather gear, 31-32, 49, 50, 190,
    illus. 51
White, Georgie, 83
Whitewater Ltd., 221
White Water River Runner, 60
White-Water Sports, Ltd., 66
Wild and Scenic River Act (1968),
    vii, 200, 205, 209
Wilderness Encounters, 48
Wilderness Society, 265
Wilderness World, 62, 96, 247
Wildlife, 158-69
Wildwater Expeditions, 96, 213
Willamette River, 231
Wind factors, 151-52
Wisconsin, 226-29, 232, 262
Wisconsin River, 229
Wolf River, 226, 229

Y
Yampa River, 11, 232, 235, 236
Yampa River model, 57, 58
Youghiogheny River, 5, 212, 214-15
Yukon River, 252

Z
Zodiac Simplex, 60, 61, 208
Zurn Industries, Inc., 34